Georgia Education Law

A State Law Companion to John Dayton's
Education Law: Principles, Policies, and Practice

Second Edition

John Dayton, J.D., Ed. D.

Adam L. Kurtz, Ph. D.

Wisdom Builders Press ™

www.wisdombuilderspress.com

Second Edition © 2016
Wisdom Builders Press
Bangor, Maine, USA

© **John Dayton**. All rights reserved. No part of these materials or any derivative works protected under the U.S. Copyright Act or applicable international laws may be reproduced by any means without the written permission of both the author and the publisher. To acquire permission to use copyrighted material please contact the author and the publisher through Wisdom Builders Press via the publisher's website: www.wisdombuilderspress.com

Please also visit the Wisdom Builders Press website for related titles and other outstanding works, current and forthcoming: www.wisdombuilderspress.com

Nota bene: These materials and any derivative works contain academic information and opinions and are intended for educational purposes only. These materials are not intended as legal advice and should in no way be interpreted as legal advice. Legal advice can only be obtained from an attorney licensed to practice law in your jurisdiction and with specific knowledge concerning the facts in your case. The author and the publisher have made good faith efforts in the preparation of these materials, but neither the author nor the publisher make any warranties of comprehensiveness, accurateness, or fitness for a particular purpose. Further, any opinions or strategies suggested in these materials may not be appropriate for your circumstances. Always consult with an appropriate professional concerning your specific circumstances. This notice serves as an express disclaimer of all liability and warranties by the author or the publisher.

ISBN-13: 978-1522992837
ISBN-10: 1522992839

Dedication

To our wives, children, families, and colleagues who supported us in writing this book. And to the Great State of Georgia and its People, especially to our colleagues in law and education: May this book be a useful tool as we work together to build a better future for our children and our communities.

John Dayton

Adam L. Kurtz

About the Authors

John Dayton, J.D., Ed. D.

John Dayton is a Professor of Education Law and Policy; Adjunct Professor of Higher Education; Editor-in-Chief of the *Education Law & Policy Review*; and the Director of the Education Law Consortium. Professor Dayton is an internationally recognized expert, author, and speaker on law and policy. He is a lawyer with experience in public and private legal practice. He has also served as a judicial clerk, and as a public school teacher and program director. In recognition of his academic achievements he was offered academic scholarships from many outstanding law schools including the Indiana University-Bloomington School of Law in his home State. Professor Dayton holds both a law degree and a doctoral degree in educational administration and policy from Indiana University. Dr. Dayton has taught law and policy courses for over two decades including education law; higher education law; special education law; medical law; school safety and security; and professional ethics. Dr. Dayton is currently a professor at the University of Georgia where he was the first recipient of the Glickman Award for excellence in research and teaching and is a member of the University Teaching Academy. Dr. Dayton is the author of over a 100 law review articles, books, and other publications on law and policy.

Adam L. Kurtz, Ph. D.

Adam L. Kurtz is currently the Principal of Chase Street School in Athens, Georgia, and is an adjunct professor in Educational Administration and Policy at the University of Georgia. Dr. Kurtz brings extensive experience to his work in education and law, having served as a law enforcement professional, and having nearly two decades experience in public education as a vocational director, curriculum specialist, teacher, and administrator. During his tenure as Principal of Chase Street School, the school improved from being classified as a school that failed to make Adequately Yearly Progress to being recognized as a National Blue Ribbon School. Under his leadership, the school was also named one of only 47 National Title I Distinguished Schools in 2013. In recognition of his achievements as a school leader Dr. Kurtz received nominations for the Terrell H. Bell and Kathy H. Hug Leadership Awards. He was also a finalist for the United States Department of Education Principal Ambassador Fellowship in 2015. In addition to his success in practice, Dr. Kurtz has achieved notable success in academia as well. Dr. Kurtz was a recipient of the prestigious David J. Mullan Sr. Scholarship at the University of Georgia. His research focuses on using theory to inform practice in schools. Dr. Kurtz's research has been presented at state and national research conferences and his research has been published in the esteemed *Peabody Journal of Education*.

Summary of Contents

	Page
Chapter 1: Introduction to Law and Governance	1
Chapter 2: Children, Families, and the State	32
Chapter 3: First Amendment Freedoms and Religion	54
Chapter 4: First Amendment Freedoms and Speech	62
Chapter 5: Search and Seizure	71
Chapter 6: Due Process of Law	84
Chapter 7: Equal Protection of the Laws	123
Chapter 8: Disability Law	134
Chapter 9: Contracts and Employment Law	160
Chapter 10: Tort Law and other Liability Issues	206

Table of Contents

	Page
Preface	ix
Chapter 1: Introduction to Law and Governance	1
State Powers, Limitations, and Sources of State Law	2
Local School Boards	4
Essential Practice Skills: Conducting Effective Meetings	5
Interpreting Constitutions, Statutes, Regulations, and Case Decisions	10
State Constitutional Law	10
Interpreting Legislation	12
Interpreting Case Law	14
Selected Georgia Laws	16

Chapter 2: Children, Families, and the State 32

    Levels of Evidence of Abuse or Neglect 32
    Continuum of Parental Care 33
    Indicators of Abuse or Neglect 34
        General Indicators of Child Abuse or Neglect 34
        Indicators of Child Neglect 34
        Indicators of Verbal or Emotional Abuse 35
        Indicators of Physical Abuse 35
        Indicators of Sexual Abuse... 35
    Appropriate responses 36
    Questioning children concerning suspicious circumstances 36
    Selected Georgia Laws 38

Chapter 3: First Amendment Freedoms and Religion 54

    Establishment Clause "Lemon Test"... 55
    Free Exercise Test 56
    Selected Georgia Laws 57

Chapter 4: First Amendment Freedoms and Speech 62

    Potential Universe of Protected Speech 63
    Student Speech Rights 64
    Tinker & Fraser/Hazelwood Tests 65
    Employee Speech Rights 66
    Pickering Test 67
    Lawful Limitations on Speech: TPM Restrictions 68
    Selected Georgia Laws 69

Chapter 5: Search and Seizure 71

    Associated Fourth Amendment Rights 71
    Elements of Proof Leading to Probable Cause 72
    Elements of Proof Leading to Reasonable Suspicion 73
    Strip Searches of Students 74
    School Locker Searches 75
    Metal Detectors and Administrative Searches 75
    Security Cameras 77
    Electronic Privacy 77
    Dog Searches 78
    Searches of School Employees 78
    Seizure and Bailment 79
    Student Search Flowchart 80
    Selected Georgia Laws 81

Chapter 6: Due Process of Law 84

Weighing Admissibility: Probative Value v. Prejudicial Effect 85
Conducting Investigations and Interviewing Witnesses 85
Preparing for a Successful Hearing 87
Questioning and Evidence 89
Summary of the Essential Rules of Evidence 92
Basic Guide to Questioning 95
Basic Guide to Objections 95
Student Discipline: Hearing and Appeals Process 96
Selected Georgia Laws 97

Chapter 7: Equal Protection of the Laws 123

Judicial Review of Equal Protection Challenges 124
Judicial Standards of Review 125
Sexual Harassment under Title IX 126
Proving Peer Sexual Harassment 127
Title IX Litigation 128
Selected Georgia Laws 129

Chapter 8: Disability Law 134

A Brief Overview of the IDEA, § 504, and the ADA 135
A Summary of Discipline Options under the IDEA 136
Manifestation Determinations in Disciplinary Proceedings 138
Dealing with a Dangerous IDEA Eligible Student 139
Developing Positive Parental Relationships and Cooperation 140
Promoting a Culture of Respect and Inclusion 141
Helping Children Receive Needed Services 142
Selected Georgia Laws 144

Chapter 9: Contracts and Employment Law 160

Equal Opportunity Employment 161
Job Announcements and Recruitment 161
Pre-employment Screening of Applicants 162
Pre-employment Interviews 162
Reference and Background Checks 164
Employee Supervision 165
Performance Evaluations 165
Dismissals 167
Tenure and Due Process 168
Common Defenses in Dismissal Proceedings 169
Selected Georgia Laws 170

Chapter 10: Tort Law and other Liability Issues 206

School Safety and Security 206
Personnel Safety and Security 207
Adequate Child Supervision 207
Harassment, Assaults, and Abductions 208
Safety Intervention and Self-Defense 211
Safe Facilities 213
Safe Grounds, Parking Areas, and Transportation 214
Safe Play Areas 217
Accident and Injury Prevention 218
Gang Violence Prevention 220
Environmental Safety 221
Emergency Planning and Response 223
Selected Georgia Laws 226

General Index 236

Index of State Laws 238

Preface

Welcome to the second edition of *Georgia Education Law*. This book was written as a state law companion for the textbook *Education Law: Principles, Policies, and Practice*. The core textbook provides you with a comprehensive review of legal principles and federal level education law. It is essential, however, that professionals working with schools also know and understand state laws governing their work, and be able to translate legal principles and policies to the level of daily practice. This book expands on key issues of law and practice presented in the core textbook and provides educators with the essential state laws governing their work.

In studying this book and the core textbook together, please note that the most important fundamental principles of law were purposely restated in summary in the state law book to promote a more thorough mastery of these essential legal principles. Mastery of any subject or skill requires a mastery of its fundamental principles. As the musician must practice scales throughout his or her career to improve performance, and the athlete must regularly drill the fundamentals of the sport to realize his or her full athletic potential, so too the student of law must persistently study the application of fundamental principles of law to his or her daily work.

Only by mastering the fundamental principles of law can you acquire the ability to quickly and accurately apply the law as a useful guide to wise and lawful conduct under the ever-changing circumstances of your daily work. After studying law and its application for decades, I can tell you with absolute certainty that every time you study these fundamental principles of law you will see new facets of the law and its applications, and increase your ability to use the law as a useful guide in your professional practice.

As a professional you must know the laws governing your profession for these essential reasons:

1) *Self Preservation*: Ignorance of the law can have dire personal and professional consequences. Career ending legal landmines can only be avoided if you know where they are and how to safely navigate around them;
2) *Professional Confidence*: Professionals who know the law are far more confident and successful. They effectively utilize the law and need never fear it;
3) *Protecting Your Institution and Colleagues*: Employees who do not understand and comply with the law may cause devastating financial liability and serious damage to the reputation of the institution, often with ruinous consequences for their colleagues as well;
4) *Professional Responsibility and Leadership*: Professionals are leaders in their communities. They must know and respect the law, and strengthen and improve their communities by modeling lawful and ethical conduct in practice.

Acquiring a strong working knowledge of the law will give you the skills and professional confidence necessary to become an invaluable asset to your institution and community. The materials in this book, in conjunction with the core textbook, will provide you with guidance in mastering fundamental principles of law and translating these legal principles into effective practice. Further, each chapter provides you with essential state laws governing education.

Chapter 1 of this book reviews fundamental principles of law and governance with an emphasis on state constitutions and governance systems. This chapter also includes a guide to essential legal interpretation skills, recognizing that these skills are necessary to successful practice in a profession governed by law. By mastering essential legal interpretation skills you will be able to more effectively read, interpret, and apply the law in practice. This chapter also provides a useful guide for conducting effective meetings, and essential skill for all leaders.

Chapter 2 further explores the legal relationships among children, families, and the state, with an emphasis on state laws mandating reports of suspected abuse or neglect of children to state officials. This chapter includes a review of general indicators of child abuse or neglect; verbal or emotional abuse; physical abuse; sexual abuse; a guide to questioning children about these issues; and direction in making reasoned decisions on an appropriate course of action in individual cases of suspected abuse or neglect.

Chapters 3 and 4 provide readers with a concise review of First Amendment issues (i.e., religious freedoms and freedom of speech), in the U.S. Constitution and similar provisions in the state constitution. First Amendment jurisprudence is among the most complex and conceptually difficult areas of law. Nonetheless, professionals working with schools commonly encounter First Amendment issues, and they must regularly make decisions with First Amendment implications. To aid in legal compliance and support respect for individual rights, chapters 3 and 4 provide readers with useful flow-charts to help bring these complex legal theories to the level of effective daily practice.

Chapter 5 addresses search and seizure law in public schools, clarifying the elements of proof necessary to establish lawful probable cause or reasonable suspicion. This chapter further explains the application of the law to student strip searches; locker searches; the operational details for administrative searches using metal detectors; the use of security cameras; electronic privacy; dog searches; searches of employees; and seizure and bailment in schools. A flow-chart for navigating student searches is provided.

Chapter 6 presents a summary of the fundamental principles of due process with an emphasis on due process in practice. This chapter addresses the most important aspects of managing lawful investigations and hearings including planning investigations; interviewing witnesses; preparing for a successful hearing; questioning and evidence; a summary of the essential rules of evidence; an overview of the appeals process; and essential state law rules for due process proceedings in schools. Quick use guides to questioning and objections in hearings are also included, as is a flow-chart describing the hearing and appeals process.

Chapter 7 provides a review of equal protection principles under both the federal and state constitutions, with a focus on the complex area of gender discrimination. Gender discrimination remains among the most challenging areas of equity concerns in schools. Discrimination based on race, color, ethnicity, or national origin are recognized as *per se* irrational and strictly prohibited by law. But there are sometimes relevant physical differences based on gender that may justify differential treatment in limited cases. These limited gender differences cannot, however, be allowed to become a pretext for irrational discrimination based on gender. This chapter reviews legal principles governing gender based discrimination and harassment under Title IX, and provides a helpful flow-chart explaining Title IX litigation in cases of alleged sexual harassment of students.

Chapter 8 provides a brief overview of the IDEA, § 504, and the ADA, comparing and contrasting these three principal statutes governing disability law in schools. Recognizing that discipline procedures under the IDEA may be among the most significant and confusing provisions for many educators and lawyers, this chapter provides a summary of incrementally severe disciplinary options under the IDEA. This chapter further addresses manifestation determinations; dealing with a dangerous IDEA eligible student; developing positive parental relationships and cooperation; promoting a culture of respect and inclusion for children with disabilities; and helping children to receive needed services, with a chart of example indicators that a child may need IDEA or other disability services.

Chapter 9 addresses contracts and employment law. This chapter reviews relevant laws and employment practices related to equal opportunity employment; job announcements and recruitment; pre-employment screening of applicants; pre-employment interviews; reference and background checks; employee supervision; performance evaluations; dismissals; tenure and due process; and common defenses in dismissal proceedings.

Chapter 10 takes an innovative and proactive approach to tort law, focusing on school safety and security as the areas of potential tort liability that are both the most important to address to protect safety, and among the most preventable areas of potential loss. The primary goal of this chapter is to raise awareness of potential and known dangers, and to encourage proactive preventive efforts in schools and communities. If even one child avoids an injury, assault, abduction, or death, this effort will have been far more than worthwhile. It is hoped, however, that with the collective efforts of readers working with their communities, that many children can be spared unnecessary harms. Some of the issues addressed may seem obvious, and many of the suggestions common sense. But if everyone already knew about these dangers, and how to prevent or respond to them, we would not keep having so many unnecessary and easily avoidable incidents of harm to children. Raising awareness can help to reduce incidents of harm. And knowing what to do if an incident occurs can help keep incidents from becoming tragedies.

In this book every effort was made to present you with an accurate academic presentation of the law and related practice issues. Perfect objectivity is impossible. This book has no agenda, however, other than to explain principles of law, current policies, and their useful application in practice. The included state laws were current as of the time of writing. Remember though that the law is constantly changing and evolving. This book will be periodically updated with the latest statutes and regulations. In the interim between editions, however, be certain to check online and/or consult legal counsel for the most current case law, statutes, and regulations.

It is important to note that no book can give you legal advice. Legal advice can only be obtained from an attorney licensed to practice law in your jurisdiction and familiar with the unique facts in your case. If you need to seek legal counsel or other professional guidance, however, having a solid working knowledge of current law can help you to work more effectively and efficiently with your lawyer and other professionals.

Although this book was reviewed by many highly qualified reviewers and a very capable editor, any errors are ultimately my responsibility and my fault alone. My apologies for any errors, and any discovered errors will be corrected in the next addition. I hope you will enjoy your journey through the unique and fascinating realm of the law. By studying the law it is guaranteed that you will become a more capable professional and a wiser person. I want to give you my very best personal wishes for an enjoyable adventure in learning. It is my great hope that you will find your studies engaging, enlightening, and highly useful in your future.

John Dayton   **January 1, 2016**

Chapter 1: Introduction to Law and Governance

All professionals must know the laws governing their profession. Further, it is critically important that educators working in public institutions understand the mandates of their federal and state constitutions and the lawful systems of governance established under the Rule of Law. Public school educators are government officials legally bound by applicable federal and state constitutional provisions, statutes, regulations, and case law. Public officials who violate their oaths of office may be subject to dismissal and monetary damages under 42 U.S.C. § 1983 or other applicable laws.

As a matter of both professional competence and self-protection it is essential that educators understand the laws and governance systems applicable to their profession. This is necessary so that they may perform their professional duties in accordance with the law; protect their own rights; and help protect the legal rights of their students, colleagues, and community. Further, compliance with professional ethics requires not only that educators obey the law, but that they must never be a party to violations of the law or condone unlawful conduct by others.

The U.S. Constitution divides governance powers between the federal and state governments in a governance system known as federalism. American federalism is a system of governance in which the federal government holds only those powers that are deemed most effectively exercised by a central government, such as the powers to declare war and to regulate inter-state commerce. All powers not delegated to the federal government are reserved to the state governments or the People themselves, as counter-balances guarding against the accumulation and abuse of power by the federal government. Federal and state constitutions create further protections against abuse of government power through a system of internal governmental checks and balances called separation of powers. Governance powers of each governance system, federal and state, are separated into three separate and co-equal branches of government:

Separation of Governance Powers

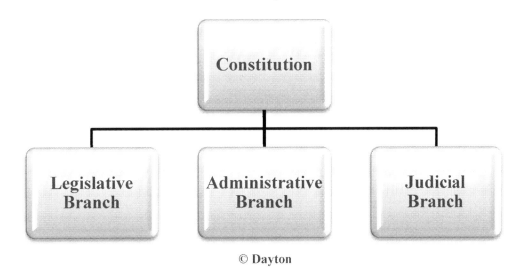

© Dayton

Under the Tenth Amendment to the U.S. Constitution the federal government may exercise only those powers expressly delegated to the federal government in the text of the U.S. Constitution. The Tenth Amendment declares: "The powers not delegated to the United States by the Constitution, nor prohibited by it to the States, are reserved to the States respectively, or to the people." All powers not expressly delegated to the federal government remain with the states (with their own internal systems of separation of powers and other checks and balances), or ultimately to the People.

Division of Powers under the U.S. System of Law and Governance

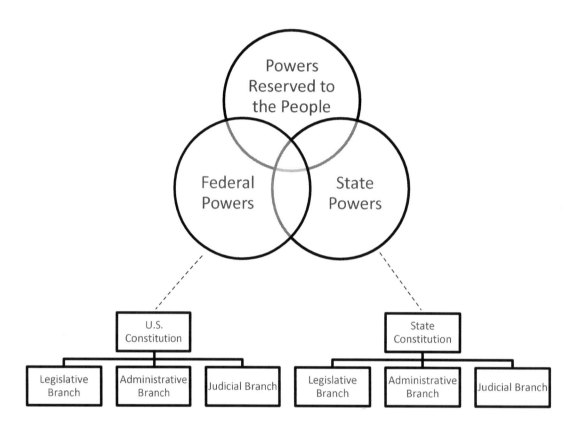

© Dayton

State Powers, Limitations, and Sources of State Law

In part, the U.S. Civil War was fought over the constitutional limitations of state powers and the scope of sovereignty retained by the states. The U.S. Constitution primarily imposes limits on federal powers. But following the Civil War and the adoption of the Fourteenth Amendment in 1868 it could no longer be credibly argued that the U.S. Constitution imposed no limitations on the powers of states. The Fourteenth Amendment declared: "No State shall make or enforce any law which shall abridge the privileges or immunities of citizens of the United States."

Under the Fourteenth Amendment, rights of federal citizenship superseded any state limitations on these rights. This was indicated by the Supremacy Clause of Article VI of the

U.S. Constitution prior to 1868, but expressly stated in the Fourteenth Amendment. The Supremacy Clause states:

> This Constitution, and the Laws of the United States which shall be made in pursuance thereof; and all treaties made, or which shall be made, under the authority of the United States, shall be the supreme law of the land; and the judges in every state shall be bound thereby, anything in the constitution or laws of any state to the contrary notwithstanding.

States can protect fundamental rights such as religious freedoms, free speech, due process, equality under the law, etc., at a higher level than is guaranteed by the U.S. Constitution. But states cannot fall below the floor of protection for fundamental rights guaranteed under the U.S. Constitution. As a practical matter, if guarantees of individual rights are to be meaningful those rights must be protected from unlawful intrusions by all agencies of government. It makes little difference to the individual whether their rights are denied by federal, state, or local agents. The infringement on those rights is equally as harmful to the individual regardless of which government agency is responsible.

Although the U.S. Constitution imposes some limits on state power, states still exercise broad and plenary powers in those areas outside of the scope of the U.S. Constitution and legitimately within the realm of state authority. Education is a power generally reserved to the state through public systems of education, or the People themselves through private schools and home study programs. There are variations among the 50 U.S. states, but generally concerning public education plenary authority is vested in the legislative branch, the state general assembly.

The general assembly has broad authority over education in the state, subject only to the limits of the U.S. Constitution, the state constitution, and the expressed will of the People through their daily free speech and periodic votes in elections. Because education is the largest single item in most state's budgets, however, and the administration of a state-wide system of public education is an enormous, complex, and politically sensitive undertaking, Governors and state departments of education are generally very actively involved in the administration of public schools at the state level. Disputes under state laws or the state constitution are resolved by state courts.

The constitutions of all 50 states make it the responsibility of the state's general assembly to create and support a public system of education. The general assembly then enacts appropriate legislation necessary to create a system of public schools, including, for example, statutes governing school finance; attendance; curriculum; student discipline; and teacher employment, tenure and dismissals. The administrative branch of state government, including the governor, the state board of education, the state superintendent, and the state department of education establish policies and regulations for the state-level administration of education statutes.

Sources of State Laws

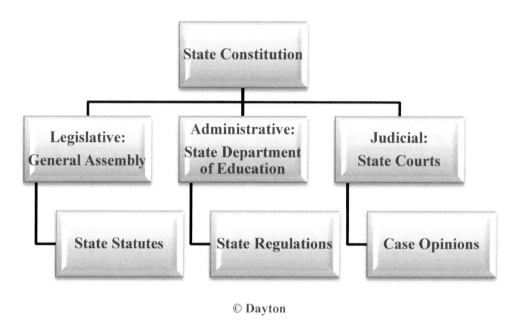

© Dayton

Local School Boards

Local school boards are responsible for local compliance with state and federal education laws. Having local schools governed by community members allows for a stronger community voice in local school decisions to accommodate unique community needs and preferences in local school operations. Generally, school board members are elected by local voters and are therefore politically accountable to community members. In a few states and cities, however, school board members are appointed by elected officials.

School district level oversight and policy establishment are the primary functions of the local school board. The school board is granted broad powers to achieve these important missions, and courts generally recognize broad judicial deference to boards in making decisions about local matters. It should be noted, however, that there are clear limits to these powers. School board members must comply with all applicable federal and state laws. And school board members should respect the functional limits of their official roles. School board members are not school administrators or teachers. The school board hires professional administrators and teachers for the daily administration of local schools and to deliver the board approved instructional program. Further, school board members have no individual legal authority and may only exercise legitimate legal authority by collectively acting as the school board.

In the performance of official duties the local school board exercises powers from all three branches of government: Quasi-legislative authority in enacting local policies; quasi-administrative authority in school district oversight and legal compliance, and quasi-judicial authority in hearing and ruling on disciplinary actions involving school employees and students. The specific powers and duties of school boards are further defined in the state constitution, statutes, and regulations. Generally, however, the school board is charged with overseeing district level school operations including the review and approval of local school revenue sources, budgets, contracts, employment, and district policies on facilities, curriculum, extracurricular programs, personnel, student discipline, etc. The school board has the authority to enter into legally binding contracts for all services and goods necessary for the efficient operation of the schools.

Local governance of education is highly valued in most states. Nonetheless, the state retains plenary authority over public education. Local school board members and all school employees are state officials ultimately governed by and accountable to the state. Further, all local public school property and funds belong to the state. Official school board business is conducted in meetings subject to state open meetings laws and other applicable state laws. To operate effectively and efficiently, school leaders must be prepared to conduct effective and efficient meetings, whether these are meetings of the board, faculty, or other formal meetings.

Essential Practice Skills: Conducting Effective Meetings

For as long as there have been meetings and debates, it has been recognized that common sense rules of procedure were needed to maintain order and to assure a full and fair discussion of issues. American colonists brought parliamentary procedures with them from England. Thomas Jefferson applied these procedures to Congressional debates in *A Manual of Parliamentary Practice for the Use of the Senate of the United States* (1801). Luther Cushing created *Cushing's Manual* (1845) as a guide to procedural rules for civic societies. And Henry M. Robert published *Robert's Rules of Order* (1876), a procedural guide still commonly used in the governance of formal meetings.

Although *Robert's Rules of Order* remains the most commonly used procedural guide, democratic organizations may adopt any procedural rules deemed best by the majority. *Robert's Rules of Order* may be useful in managing organizational business and debates, especially in larger meetings. But an organization may adopt *Robert's Rules*, or any other procedural rules, in whole or in part, adding, deleting, or amending procedures to best suit unique organizational cultures and needs. In establishing procedural rules, generally, procedural simplicity is superior to procedural complexity. Procedural rules should facilitate and not complicate meetings.

Specific procedural rules become binding on members only if the organization has lawfully adopted these rules in advance and served reasonable notice of the rules to members. Organizational procedural rules derive their lawful authority from the collective power of organizational members as expressed through a majority vote. Members who wish to remain in good standing must abide by the procedural rules lawfully adopted by the organization.

Despite its institutional ubiquity, *Robert's Rules* are not automatically and universally binding. An individual member of an organization cannot, for example, unilateral insist on enforcing any of *Robert's Rules* if the organization has not already adopted the rule as binding on members in its organizational meetings. The authority to adopt procedural rules resides with the majority, not individuals, and it is up to the Chair of the meeting (or another designated official) to interpret and enforce procedural rules during the meeting.

Procedural rules for meetings should be interpreted and applied so as to facilitate civil debate and promote efficiency in completing the necessary business. The Chair should not allow procedural rules to be used as strategic weapons to silence substantive debate on the merits of an issue, or to impede organizational business. There is no organizational benefit to allowing members with disproportionate expertise in the rules of procedure to strategically stifle good faith debate by other members with less procedural expertise, or to manipulate procedural rules to block institutional progress. The purposes of procedural rules are to maintain order, assure full and fair debate on important questions, and to facilitate the efficient conduct of business. Procedural rules should be adopted, interpreted, and applied with these purposes in mind.

Different types of meetings require different leadership styles by the Chair. Larger formal meetings require more formal procedural rules and styles of leadership, while less formal procedures and leadership styles work better in smaller and less formal meetings. A large formal public meeting of the school board, for example, with hundreds of participants, could quickly devolve into chaos without a consistent adherence to appropriate procedural rules, while an overly rigid adherence to *Robert's Rules* in a small informal meeting will seem absurd and likely only get in the way of completing the necessary business. In chairing meetings, follow a leadership style that is appropriate for the context and consistent with the institutional culture and purposes. All but the most informal meetings, however, generally follow this basic format:

1) Call to Order
2) Approval of the Minutes
3) Committee Reports
4) Unfinished Business
5) New Business
6) Adjournment

Preparing a guiding script in advance of the meeting can be very useful, especially for less experienced meeting Chairs.

Example Script for Chairing a Formal Business Meeting:

"The [DATE] meeting of the [ORGANIZATION] is now called to order."

"We will begin business with the approval of the minutes. Are there any necessary corrections or amendments to the minutes?" [PAUSE TO ADDRESS ANY CORRECTIONS]. "If there are no (additional) corrections the minutes are approved."

"We will now hear any committee reports. The Chair recognizes [NAME OF COMMITTEE CHAIR] reporting on behalf of the [NAME OF COMMITTEE]" (and when the speaker's time has expired announce: "Thank you [NAME OF SPEAKER]").

ADDRESS ANY MOTIONS/DEBATES/CALL QUESTION/VOTE/REPORT RESULT

"We will now address any unfinished business. The Chair recognizes [NAME OF MEMBER WISHING TO SPEAK] concerning [ISSUE OF BUSINESS].

ADDRESS ANY MOTIONS/DEBATES/CALL QUESTION/VOTE/REPORT RESULT

"We will now address any new business. The Chair recognizes [NAME OF MEMBER WISHING TO SPEAK].

ADDRESS ANY MOTIONS/DEBATES/CALL QUESTION/VOTE/REPORT RESULT

"The Chair finding that there is no further business for this meeting, this meeting is adjourned."

Addressing Motions: To be recognized a member rises and addresses the Chair. "The Chair recognizes [NAME]." The member states the motion. Another member seconds the motion (or the motion fails for lack of a second). "It is moved and seconded that [STATE MOTION]. Shall we call the question?"

Managing Debates: After the Chair states the motion any member may stand and be recognized by the Chair for purposes of debating the motion. The Chair only recognizes one speaker at a time for the time allowed by the Chair. Interruptions of speakers are ruled out of order by the Chair. The Chair assures that there is a fair opportunity for a full and fair debate by members, and that the debate is focused on issues relevant to the motion. No member should be recognized to speak for a second time until all members wishing to speak have been recognized once. The Chair is responsible for efficiently moving through the agenda while maintaining order and civility. Any *ad hominem* attacks, irrelevant issues, unrecognized speakers, etc., are ruled out of order by the Chair.

Calling the Question: If there is no debate, or after sufficient time for debate has been allowed, the Chair calls the question: "The question is on the adoption of the motion to [STATE MOTION]."

Voting and Reporting the Result: A quorum must be present (as defined in organizational bylaws) to cast legally binding votes. "Those in favor of the motion shall signify by [saying "aye" [PAUSE FOR COUNT] those opposed say "no" [COUNT] [OR CHAIR RULES ON VOICE VOTE; *e.g.*, "In the opinion of the Chair the "ayes" have it"]; *or* raising the right hand; [PAUSE FOR COUNT] those opposed [COUNT]; *or* voting by roll call, ballot, etc. [FINAL COUNT IS CERTIFIED BY A NEUTRAL PARTY]. "The motion is adopted/has failed."

General Guidelines for Managing Effective Meetings

1) *Promote a Local Culture that Values and Supports Highly Capable and Responsible Local Governance*: The quality of the meeting and the quality of the decisions and actions resulting from the meeting are always a function of the quality of the participants. Be proactive in recruiting the best people for governing boards. Of course, all highly capable, responsible, and productive people are busy, and it is human nature that busy people tend to avoid additional responsibilities. But these are commonly the persons you most need for your local governing boards. Because local governance plays such a vital role in educational institutions and the welfare of the local community, work to promote a local culture in which local governance is highly valued, and highly capable and responsible participation is encouraged and supported. Understand that incompetent or self-interested board members gone rogue can do enormous damage to the schools and the community. Therefore it is essential to encourage the most capable and responsible persons to serve on governing boards, and not just default to the status quo; those with little else to do; a personal axe to grind; the desire to exercise petty authority; etc.

In the absence of the best local persons serving on the governing board, you open the door to the worst persons, and personnel related governance problems are far easier to prevent than to fix. Good local governance is a necessary prerequisite to good local schools. The local school board oversees the local school system and has a strong voice in critically important decisions concerning school mission, policy, personnel oversight, and student discipline. These decisions affect the educations, careers, lives, and future of the entire community. Capable and responsible board members and school leaders carefully consider the likely consequences of their decisions, both intended and unintended, and act wisely to advance the common good. You want only the most capable and responsible governing board members, so be proactive in recruiting the best persons, because no matter how well you run your meetings, bad people make bad decisions, and bad decisions result in bad consequences for the schools and community.

2) *Respect Everyone's Time with Fewer and More Efficient Meetings*: Meetings consume time and energy. If a meeting isn't necessary, don't meet, or find a more efficient alternative. Formal school board meetings must comply with state meetings laws which may somewhat limit creativity and flexibility. But for faculty meetings and other less formal meetings always seek the most efficient means of completing the necessary work. Communicate information though memos instead of meetings; meet with individuals or small groups when the full group isn't needed; excuse persons from parts of meetings that are unnecessary for them; have informal, brief, stand up meetings when formal sit down meetings are not required; etc. Regrettably, education institutions have a long and wasteful tradition of scheduling regular, long, faculty meetings whether they are necessary or not. If you must schedule meetings far in advance in order to get them on everyone's calendar, cancel any unnecessary meetings to free up time and energy for more pressing needs. Always start meetings on time and end on time or sooner (as soon as all necessary business is completed), building a reputation for running efficient, effective meetings that respect participants' time. If you commonly start meetings late, persons are likely to begin showing up even later, further delaying the start of the meeting and making those who arrived on time wait even longer for the start of the meeting and less likely to arrive on time in the future.

3) *Thoughtfully Plan and Execute the Agenda*: Well planned and executed agendas are the keys to efficient, effective meetings. Plan the agenda to maximize the use of participants' time and efforts. Make meeting agendas concise and clearly focused on outcome-based objectives. Remember that the way the agenda item is phrased influences participants responses to the agenda, so phrase action items to stimulate active involvement and effective outcome-based actions (e.g., instead of "Vote on ad" try "Identify strategies for the most effective implementation of our marketing plan"). Phrase discussion items to stimulate productive brainstorming and problem solving (e.g., instead of "Review of student data" try "How can we maximize student learning and outcomes using student data?"). Keep to the agenda. Persistently refocus the discussion on agenda items. As soon as the agenda has been satisfactorily completed, adjourn the meeting. Meetings scheduled for two hours do not have to last for two hours, and the realistic possibility of completing necessary work and early adjournment encourages cooperation and more efficient use of time by meeting participants.

4) *Understand that the Physical Environment Shapes Behavior*: Given available facilities and resources, what can you do to create the most welcoming, professional, and functional

environment for the meeting? With the purposes of the meeting in mind, set up the room in advance to facilitate and support meeting participants in efficiently achieving those purposes. Have any necessary media materials loaded, tested, and ready to go. If supplies or break-out areas are needed, have these ready in advance. Take advantage of strategic seating and furniture placements to improve communications or prevent potential social interaction problems (e.g., mix up seating options to avoid persistent groupings that reinforce factions; if someone persistently opposes you as Chair in meetings, provide no chair opposite you at the table, thereby eliminating the symbolic position of opposition and requiring that person to be seated among the other participants; if some participants tend to sit at the back and be unengaged, remove all seats from the back so they will join the group; etc.).

5) *Assure that Everyone Has a Fair Opportunity to Contribute*: Meetings are for group interaction. Allowing anyone to dominate the meeting will defeat that purpose. Make sure everyone who wants to speak has a reasonable opportunity, but discourage or cut short unnecessary monologues and lectures. When you must cut someone short, do so as kindly and respectfully as possible. Be careful not to engage in viewpoint bias as the Chair. Everyone understands that the person serving as the Chair also has perspectives and opinions on important issues. But participants will respect a meeting Chair who assures that all persons and all viewpoints are treated fairly and without bias in the meeting.

6) *Keep the Meeting Focused, Efficient, Civil, and Productive*: It is the responsibility of the Chair to keep meetings focused, efficient, civil, and productive. If anyone introduces a distraction, politely but firmly refocus the meeting on agenda items. Be sure that all faculty time is being used as efficiently as possible. Discussions and votes may require the participation of the larger group, but delegate more time consuming and complex tasks to smaller committees or individuals who can report back to the full group as necessary. Do not allow uncivil or disrespectfully treatment of anyone in the meeting. When meetings are focused and efficient, there is less room for incivility, and productive outcomes are more likely.

7) *Maintain Control of the Meeting*: Be prepared to respectfully but firmly set reasonable limits on anyone that is disruptive, obstructionist, or otherwise out of order during the meeting. As the meeting Chair, always remain professional and take the moral high road, even when others do not. It is up to the meeting Chair to set and maintain the professional tone of the meeting and to assure that all meetings are respectful and productive events.

8) *End the Meeting with a Clear Plan for Action*: Before the meeting is adjourned clearly restate in summary what was decided. This helps to promote goal oriented meetings and solidify group consensus. End the meeting with a concise statement of the plan for necessary next actions, and clearly assign responsibility for all necessary tasks to appropriate individuals or committees. Be certain the action plan is accurately recorded in the minutes, and provide regular status reports to members to encourage and recognize progress.

Like all other state officials, local school officials are bound by applicable federal and state constitutions, statutes, regulations, and case decisions. To responsibly and effectively perform their duties all school officials must know the laws that define and govern their duties. School officials must be able to reasonably interpret applicable laws in the context of practice, making essential legal interpretation skills invaluable for all professionals.

Interpreting Constitutions, Statutes, Regulations, and Case Decisions

Because education is governed by constitutions, statutes, regulations, and case decisions, the sections below provide useful guidance in interpreting these sources of law. Special emphasis is given to state law sources as education is primarily governed by state law.

State Constitutional Law

State constitutions play a vital role in the U.S. system of governance, empowering state residents to establish their own state-level system of governance; provide greater protections for individual rights if they choose to; enact additional guards against abuses of governance powers; and establish and fund state-level public priorities such as a state system of education.

Historically the development of constitutional text has always been a derivative process, with newer constitutions drawing on the principles and language in prior constitutions. When the U.S. Constitution was drafted it incorporated legal concepts and provisions found in earlier colonial charters and constitutions. In turn, provisions in newer or amended state constitutions were modeled on provisions found in the federal constitution. As the number of U.S. states expanded, newer states commonly modeled their constitutions on the constitutions of the established states.

But despite the historical interchange of constitutional ideas and language between federal and state charters, there are significant differences between the federal and state constitutions. State constitutions are clearly not just miniature federal constitutions. To the contrary, consistent with the wide-ranging powers of the states, state constitutions address a broader range of issues. State constitutions are generally significantly longer and more detailed than the federal constitution and address issues not within the scope of legitimate federal powers.

While state powers are broad, they are not unlimited. Article IV of the U.S. Constitution established some limitations on state governments including a requirement that "Full Faith and Credit shall be given in each State to the public Acts, Records, and judicial Proceedings of every other State"; "The Citizens of each State be entitled to all Privileges and Immunities of Citizens of the several States"; and a "guarantee to every State in this Union a Republican Form of government." The Supremacy Clause of Article VI also established limits on state power, making the U.S. Constitution and federal laws the supreme law of the land concerning powers granted to the federal government by the Constitution, and declaring that "the Judges in every State shall be bound thereby, any Thing in the Constitution or Laws of any State to the contrary notwithstanding." On legitimate issues of state law, however, state law is supreme.

The most direct limitation on state power, however, is the expressed will of the citizens of the state. Most state constitutions can be amended by a simple majority of the citizens of the state. Through their votes citizens can change their state constitution with relative ease compared to the more burdensome process for amendment of the federal constitution. They can also vote to assure that their state government protects individual liberties, privacy, etc., at higher levels than they are protected under the federal constitution.

The federal constitution recognized limited enumerated powers to form a limited government. In contrast state constitutions recognize only enumerated limits on the otherwise broad general governance powers of the state. States may exercise all powers not delegated to the federal government or prohibited to states by the U.S. Constitution. Beyond these limits it is up to the citizens of the state to decide what powers are allowed to the state or reserved to the People.

Another significant difference between state and federal constitutions is that in contrast to the federal constitution, state constitutions grant citizens positive rights. Concerning individual rights, the federal constitution recognizes negative rights. Negative rights are rights to not have the government do something (*e.g.*, not intrude on religious liberties; make no law abridging freedom of speech; etc.). In contrast, state constitutions also recognize positive rights, for example, a right to a free public education for eligible citizens.

State constitutions, statutes, and regulations form a comprehensive system of governance. The most significant long-term state issues are addressed in the text of the state constitution. Laws necessary to realize constitutional goals and mandates are enacted through state statutes. And state regulations are promulgated to administer state programs established through the constitution and statutes. Concerning state law, the state constitution, as interpreted by the state's highest court, is supreme. Statutes must not contravene the constitution and are subordinate to the constitution. State regulations are promulgated to comply with state constitutional and statutory mandates, and are subordinate to the state constitution and statutes.

Hierarchy of State Laws

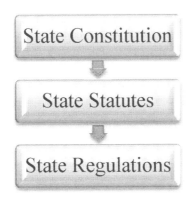

© Dayton

State constitutions typically begin with a preamble explaining the broad purposes and goals of the state constitution. State constitutions also generally contain a state bill of rights, recognizing additional rights and protections equal to or beyond those protected under the federal constitution. State constitutions define the structure of government including the establishment of the legislative, administrative, and judicial branches and require appropriate separation of powers. A process for amendment is included. And state constitutions address a broad range of issues not within the scope of federal powers, including a system of public education.

The constitutions of all 50 states have articles specifically addressing state level mandates for public education and recognizing that the primary responsibility and authority over education is vested in the state General Assembly. But because education is the largest single item in the state budget, and it ultimately touches the lives of all citizens, all three branches of government will be involved in the establishment, administration, or adjudication of education in the state.

The state education clause typically defines the duty for the General Assembly to provide state support for education, and recognizes state level officers to oversee public education including a state superintendent or other executive level officer; a state board of education; and a state department of education to establish and administer regulations consistent with the state constitution and statutes governing education.

Interpreting Legislation

School officials are charged with following and administering applicable laws, including federal and state statutes, regulations, and court decisions. To follow and administer the laws, school officials must first know and understand the laws. And to effectively read and understand laws, it is useful to have a working knowledge of essential principles of legislation and judicial interpretation. If you can understand what legislators and regulators are communicating through statutes and regulations, and how courts are likely to interpret this legislation, you will have a much more thorough and accurate understanding of the law and its application.

Under the U.S. system of governance the legislative branch is vested with the power to make laws. All laws must, however, remain within constitutional limitations protecting individual rights, respecting separation of powers, and sufficiently reflecting the will of the electorate. But otherwise state lawmakers have broad authority to legislate on all issues legitimately under the authority of the state. When legislators have spoken clearly through their written laws, those laws speak for themselves to readers. When legislation is unclear, however, it is the responsible of the courts to interpret and clarify the law and its application.

Since *Marbury v. Madison*, 5 U.S. 137 (1803), the judicial branch has been recognized as vested with the power to interpret the constitution and laws. There is, however, a much longer common law history of judicial interpretation, and a continuing practice and reliance on judicial interpretation of constitutional provisions, statutes, and regulations when ambiguity requires further interpretation for lawful application.

The only way to truly understand a statute is to personally read it carefully, paying close attention to its text, structure, purposes, scope of applicability, etc. Lawmakers may structure a statute any way they choose. But a common form for legislation is to start with a general prohibition or mandate and then list exceptions legislators deem appropriate (*e.g.*, a general prohibition against carrying designated weapons in a school safety zone, followed by a list of persons or objects excepted from the general statutory prohibition). Lawmakers may include a section concerning legislative findings; a section defining key terms in the statute; a severability clause (*i.e.*, clarifying that if one section of the statute is declared unconstitutional the remainder is intended to stand); sections defining duties, penalties, etc.

> ***The Most Important Step in Understanding a Statute is***
> ***Simply to Carefully Read the Statute***

The section below reviews the fundamental principles of judicial interpretation of legislation as a guide to better interpreting, understanding, and applying statutes and regulations. These principles of interpretation should, however, be regarded as useful tools and not absolute rules of interpretation. These rules are helpful in understanding the intent of lawmakers and to provide useful guidance in the lawful administration of legislation. But they must always be applied subject to common sense and in view of applicable facts and circumstances in each case. In reading, interpreting, and administering legislation:

Follow the plain meaning of the statutory text: When the plain meaning of the text is clear, further interpretation is unwarranted. The goal of statutory interpretation is to clarify and follow the intentions of lawmakers. When that intention is clearly expressed through unambiguous language, no further interpretation is necessary or appropriate. Absent clear evidence to the contrary, it is assumed that lawmakers said what they meant, and meant what they said.

Interpret and administer legislation to further clearly stated general purposes: When legislators have articulated clear general purposes in legislation, interpretation and administration of the legislation should seek to further the clearly stated legislative purposes.

Interpret the legislation as a harmonious whole: To clarify ambiguous sections, view all parts of the statute as working together in harmony to further the common purposes of the legislation. When two or more reasonable interpretations are possible, the interpretation that is in harmony with the purposes of the legislation is assumed to be the intent of legislators.

Give terms the appropriate meaning in the context: If a term is expressly defined in the statute, the internal statutory definition governs over other possible external meanings. If the term is not expressly defined in the statute or made clear in the context of the entire statute, it may be interpreted consistent with external meanings as a legal term of art; as having its plain meaning; or its historical meaning. A legal term of art is a word or phrase such as "due process of law" that is recognized as carrying with it all the well-established legal principles attached to this word or phrase. In the absence of an express legislative definition or a recognized term of art, the term is given its plain dictionary meaning, or its historical meaning if seeking the original intent of lawmakers in an historical document.

Pay careful attention to modifying language: It is important to pay careful attention to the use of shall/may; and/or; the/a; etc., in the statute. For example "shall" is mandatory while "may" is discretionary; "and" requires that all of the listed items must be satisfied while "or" requires only one item; "the" suggests applicability to a particular named item or person while "a" suggests a more generalized applicability (e.g., "the principal" versus "a principal").

Apply the rule of lenity: Rules carrying harsh punishments or other severe consequences should clearly state the rule, scope of applicability, and the specific consequences for breach, so that persons of ordinary intelligence can understand what is prohibited or required, and understand the clear consequences for non-compliance. If the rule or consequence is unclear and two or more reasonable interpretations are possible, the rule of lenity requires lenience in the application of the rule and that ambiguities should be resolved in favor of the person charged with violating the rule until the rule is clarified through unambiguous and timely public notice.

Apply the legislation from the time of its enactment forward: Unless clearly stated that the rule is applicable retroactively or beginning at a future date, it is presumed that the rule is applicable from the date it is enacted forward. *Ex post facto* criminal laws, however, are unconstitutional, and *ex post facto* civil laws are generally disfavored under the Due Process Clause.

Interpreting Case Law

This section provides a brief guide to reviewing case law, to assist readers in better understanding a judicial opinion, and in generally interpreting the applicability of case law and its potential impact on professional practice. To better understand case law and its applicability:

Identify the jurisdiction of the court: Only decisions from courts with valid jurisdiction over your area constitute binding law (e.g., the Supreme Court of California has jurisdiction over California, while the U.S. Supreme Court has jurisdiction over the entire U.S.). Decisions from courts outside your jurisdiction may provide useful guidance, but they are not binding law in your jurisdiction. Courts must also have proper subject matter jurisdiction (e.g., juvenile courts generally have jurisdiction over juvenile laws, etc.). Is the decision binding in your jurisdiction?

Identify the legal issue addressed by the court: What was the specific legal issue(s) the court addressed in this case? The issue is the legal question the court is asked to decide. Some court opinions are very direct in stating the issue (e.g., "the issue we address in this case is"). In some opinions the court is less direct in stating the issue, but it can always be ascertained through careful reading. Is the question the court addressed applicable to your interests?

Identify the holding of the court: The holding is the court's answer to the legal question. Some courts are very direct in stating the holding (e.g., "today we hold that"), and in other opinions the court is less direct. The holding is only found in the majority opinion. Well-reasoned concurring or dissenting opinions may prove persuasive in future decisions. But only the holding of the majority of the court on the issue before the court constitutes a legally binding holding. Is the court's holding applicable to your interests?

Determine whether the holding is binding authority, persuasive authority, or distinguishable from your situation: Lawyers refer to a "case on all fours" as one in which the relevant facts and legal issues are virtually the same, or at least sufficiently close so that the prior decision serves as a clear, binding precedent in the current case. Lower courts must follow binding precedents from higher courts in the same jurisdiction. A lower court can only reach a different decision if the court can sufficiently distinguish facts or applicable law in the current case from prior cases. In litigation, parties present facts and legal authorities they believe favor their position, and attempt to distinguish their case from any facts or binding authorities that do not favor their position. Judges must then assess the weight of the facts and various legal authorities prior to making a decision. Judges must follow binding primary authorities or risk being overturned by a higher court. If no binding authority governs the case, however, judges have more discretion in following persuasive authorities. But judges may still risk having their opinions overturned if the reasoning is not sound or the authorities are not sufficiently strong. Because the strength of the legal authorities relied upon largely defines the strength of the opinion, it is important to understand the relative strength of legal authorities. From strongest to weakest these are:

>*Binding primary legal authority*: A relevant constitutional provision, statute, regulation, or higher court opinion in the same jurisdiction that must be followed.

Persuasive primary legal authority: A relevant lower court decision or any court decision from outside of the jurisdiction that may persuade the court.

Persuasive secondary legal authority: Other relevant legal opinions (*e.g.*, scholarly books, treatises, law reviews, etc.) that may be helpful or persuasive to the court.

On Target? Evaluating the Relative Strength of Legal Authorities in a Case

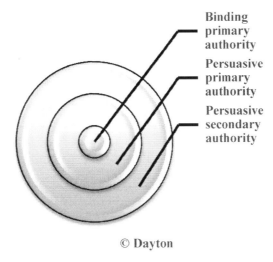

© Dayton

Selected Georgia Laws

Georgia Constitution

Article I, Section II: Origin and Structure of Government

Paragraph I: Origin and foundation of government. All government, of right, originates with the people, is founded upon their will only, and is instituted solely for the good of the whole. Public officers are the trustees and servants of the people and are at all times amenable to them.

Paragraph II: Object of government. The people of this state have the inherent right of regulating their internal government. Government is instituted for the protection, security, and benefit of the people; and at all times they have the right to alter or reform the same whenever the public good may require it.

Paragraph III: Separation of legislative, judicial, and executive powers. The legislative, judicial, and executive powers shall forever remain separate and distinct; and no person discharging the duties of one shall at the same time exercise the functions of either of the others except as herein provided.

Paragraph IV: Contempts. The power of the courts to punish for contempt shall be limited by legislative acts.

Paragraph V: What acts void. Legislative acts in violation of this Constitution or the Constitution of the United States are void, and the judiciary shall so declare them.

Paragraph VI: Superiority of civil authority. The civil authority shall be superior to the military.

Paragraph VII: Separation of church and state. No money shall ever be taken from the public treasury, directly or indirectly, in aid of any church, sect, cult, or religious denomination or of any sectarian institution.

Paragraph VIII: Lotteries and nonprofit bingo games.
(a) Except as herein specifically provided in this Paragraph VIII, all lotteries, and the sale of lottery tickets, and all forms of pari-mutuel betting and casino gambling are hereby prohibited; and this prohibition shall be enforced by penal laws.
(b) The General Assembly may by law provide that the operation of a nonprofit bingo game shall not be a lottery and shall be legal in this state. The General Assembly may by law define a nonprofit bingo game and provide for the regulation of nonprofit bingo games.
(c) The General Assembly may by law provide for the operation and regulation of a lottery or lotteries by or on behalf of the state and for any matters relating to the purposes or provisions of this subparagraph. Proceeds derived from the lottery or lotteries operated by or on behalf of the state shall be used to pay the operating expenses of the lottery or lotteries, including all prizes, without any appropriation required by law, and for educational programs and purposes as hereinafter provided . . . the Governor shall make specific recommendations as to educational programs and educational purposes to which said net proceeds shall be appropriated. In the

General Appropriations Act adopted by the General Assembly, the General Assembly shall appropriate all net proceeds of the lottery or lotteries by such separate budget category to educational programs and educational purposes. Such net proceeds shall be used to support improvements and enhancements for educational programs and purposes and such net proceeds shall be used to supplement, not supplant, non-lottery educational resources for educational programs and purposes. The educational programs and educational purposes for which proceeds may be so appropriated shall include only the following:

(1) Tuition grants, scholarships, or loans to citizens of this state to enable such citizens to attend colleges and universities located within this state, regardless of whether such colleges or universities are operated by the board of regents, or to attend institutions operated under the authority of the Department of Technical and Adult Education;
(2) Voluntary pre-kindergarten;
(3) One or more educational shortfall reserves in a total amount of not less than 10 percent of the net proceeds of the lottery for the preceding fiscal year;
(4) Costs of providing to teachers at accredited public institutions who teach levels K-12, personnel at public postsecondary technical institutes under the authority of the Department of Technical and Adult Education, and professors and instructors within the University System of Georgia the necessary training in the use and application of computers and advanced electronic instructional technology to implement interactive learning environments in the classroom and to access the state-wide distance learning network; and
(5) Capital outlay projects for educational facilities; provided, however, that no funds shall be appropriated for the items listed in paragraphs (4) and (5) of this subsection until all persons eligible for and applying for assistance as provided in paragraph (1) of this subsection have received such assistance, all approved pre-kindergarten programs provided for in paragraph (2) of this subsection have been fully funded, and the education shortfall reserve or reserves provided for in paragraph (3) of this subsection have been fully funded . . .

Article I, Section I: State Bill of Rights

Rights of Persons

Paragraph I: Life, liberty, and property. No person shall be deprived of life, liberty, or property except by due process of law.

Paragraph II: Protection to person and property; equal protection. Protection to person and property is the paramount duty of government and shall be impartial and complete. No person shall be denied the equal protection of the laws.

Paragraph III: Freedom of conscience. Each person has the natural and inalienable right to worship God, each according to the dictates of that person's own conscience; and no human authority should, in any case, control or interfere with such right of conscience.

Paragraph IV: Religious opinions; freedom of religion. No inhabitant of this state shall be molested in person or property or be prohibited from holding any public office or trust on account of religious opinions; but the right of freedom of religion shall not be so construed as to excuse acts of licentiousness or justify practices inconsistent with the peace and safety of the state.

Paragraph V: Freedom of speech and of the press guaranteed. No law shall be passed to curtail or restrain the freedom of speech or of the press. Every person may speak, write, and publish sentiments on all subjects but shall be responsible for the abuse of that liberty.

Paragraph VI: Libel. In all civil or criminal actions for libel, the truth may be given in evidence; and, if it shall appear to the trier of fact that the matter charged as libelous is true, the party shall be discharged.

Paragraph VII: Citizens, protection of. All citizens of the United States, resident in this state, are hereby declared citizens of this state; and it shall be the duty of the General Assembly to enact such laws as will protect them in the full enjoyment of the rights, privileges, and immunities due to such citizenship.

Paragraph VIII: Arms, right to keep and bear. The right of the people to keep and bear arms shall not be infringed, but the General Assembly shall have power to prescribe the manner in which arms may be borne.

Paragraph IX: Right to assemble and petition. The people have the right to assemble peaceably for their common good and to apply by petition or remonstrance to those vested with the powers of government for redress of grievances.

Paragraph X: Bill of attainder; ex post facto laws; and retroactive laws. No bill of attainder, ex post facto law, retroactive law, or laws impairing the obligation of contract or making irrevocable grant of special privileges or immunities shall be passed.

Paragraph XI: Right to trial by jury; number of jurors; selection and compensation of jurors.
(a) The right to trial by jury shall remain inviolate, except that the court shall render judgment without the verdict of a jury in all civil cases where no issuable defense is filed and where a jury is not demanded in writing by either party. In criminal cases, the defendant shall have a public and speedy trial by an impartial jury; and the jury shall be the judges of the law and the facts.
(b) A trial jury shall consist of 12 persons; but the General Assembly may prescribe any number, not less than six, to constitute a trial jury in courts of limited jurisdiction and in superior courts in misdemeanor cases.
(c) The General Assembly shall provide by law for the selection and compensation of persons to serve as grand jurors and trial jurors.

Paragraph XII: Right to the courts. No person shall be deprived of the right to prosecute or defend, either in person or by an attorney, that person's own cause in any of the courts of this state.

Paragraph XIII: Searches, seizures, and warrants. The right of the people to be secure in their persons, houses, papers, and effects against unreasonable searches and seizures shall not be violated; and no warrant shall issue except upon probable cause supported by oath or affirmation particularly describing the place or places to be searched and the persons or things to be seized.

Paragraph XIV: Benefit of counsel; accusation; list of witnesses; compulsory process. Every person charged with an offense against the laws of this state shall have the privilege and benefit of counsel; shall be furnished with a copy of the accusation or indictment and, on demand, with a list of the witnesses on whose testimony such charge is founded; shall have compulsory process to obtain the testimony of that person's own witnesses; and shall be confronted with the witnesses testifying against such person.

Paragraph XV: Habeas corpus. The writ of habeas corpus shall not be suspended unless, in case of rebellion or invasion, the public safety may require it.

Paragraph XVI: Self-incrimination. No person shall be compelled to give testimony tending in any manner to be self-incriminating.

Paragraph XVII: Bail; fines; punishment; arrest, abuse of prisoners. Excessive bail shall not be required, nor excessive fines imposed, nor cruel and unusual punishments inflicted; nor shall any person be abused in being arrested, while under arrest, or in prison.

Paragraph XVIII: Jeopardy of life or liberty more than once forbidden. No person shall be put in jeopardy of life or liberty more than once for the same offense except when a new trial has been granted after conviction or in case of mistrial.

Paragraph XIX: Treason. Treason against the State of Georgia shall consist of insurrection against the state, adhering to the state's enemies, or giving them aid and comfort. No person shall be convicted of treason except on the testimony of two witnesses to the same overt act or confession in open court.

Paragraph XX: Conviction, effect of. No conviction shall work corruption of blood or forfeiture of estate.

Paragraph XXI: Banishment and whipping as punishment for crime. Neither banishment beyond the limits of the state nor whipping shall be allowed as a punishment for crime.

Paragraph XXII: Involuntary servitude. There shall be no involuntary servitude within the State of Georgia except as a punishment for crime after legal conviction thereof or for contempt of court.

Paragraph XXIII: Imprisonment for debt. There shall be no imprisonment for debt.

Paragraph XXIV: Costs. No person shall be compelled to pay costs in any criminal case except after conviction on final trial.

Paragraph XXV: Status of the citizen. The social status of a citizen shall never be the subject of legislation.

Paragraph XXVI: Exemptions from levy and sale. The General Assembly shall protect by law from levy and sale by virtue of any process under the laws of this state a portion of the property of each person in an amount of not less than $1,600.00 and shall have authority to define to whom any such additional exemptions shall be allowed; to specify the amount of such exemptions; to provide for the manner of exempting such property and for the sale, alienation, and encumbrance thereof; and to provide for the waiver of said exemptions by the debtor.

Paragraph XXVII: Spouse's separate property. The separate property of each spouse shall remain the separate property of that spouse except as otherwise provided by law.

Paragraph XXVIII: Fishing and hunting. The tradition of fishing and hunting and the taking of fish and wildlife shall be preserved for the people and shall be managed by law and regulation for the public good.

Paragraph XXIX: Enumeration of rights not denial of others. The enumeration of rights herein contained as a part of this Constitution shall not be construed to deny to the people any inherent rights which they may have hitherto enjoyed.

Article VIII: Education

Section I: Public Education

Paragraph I: Public education; free public education prior to college or postsecondary level; support by taxation. The provision of an adequate public education for the citizens shall be a primary obligation of the State of Georgia. Public education for the citizens prior to the college or postsecondary level shall be free and shall be provided for by taxation. The expense of other public education shall be provided for in such manner and in such amount as may be provided by law.

Section II: State Board of Education

Paragraph I: State Board of Education.
(a) There shall be a State Board of Education which shall consist of one member from each congressional district in the state appointed by the Governor and confirmed by the Senate. The Governor shall not be a member of said board. The ten members in office on June 30, 1983, shall serve out the remainder of their respective terms. As each term of office expires, the Governor shall appoint a successor as herein provided. The terms of office of all members appointed after the effective date of this Constitution shall be for seven years. Members shall serve until their successors are appointed and qualified. In the event of a vacancy on the board by death, resignation, removal, or any reason other than expiration of a member's term, the Governor shall fill such vacancy; and the person so appointed shall serve until confirmed by the Senate and, upon confirmation, shall serve for the unexpired term of office.
(b) The State Board of Education shall have such powers and duties as provided by law.

(c) The State Board of Education may accept bequests, donations, grants, and transfers of land, buildings, and other property for the use of the state educational system.
(d) The qualifications, compensation, and removal from office of the members of the board of education shall be as provided by law.

Section III: State School Superintendent

Paragraph I: State School Superintendent. There shall be a State School Superintendent, who shall be the executive officer of the State Board of Education, elected at the same time and in the same manner and for the same term as that of the Governor. The State School Superintendent shall have such qualifications and shall be paid such compensation as may be fixed by law. No member of the State Board of Education shall be eligible for election as State School Superintendent during the time for which such member shall have been appointed.

Section IV: Board of Regents

Paragraph I: University System of Georgia; board of regents.
(a) There shall be a Board of Regents of the University System of Georgia which shall consist of one member from each congressional district in the state and five additional members from the state at large, appointed by the Governor and confirmed by the Senate. The Governor shall not be a member of said board. The members in office on June 30, 1983, shall serve out the remainder of their respective terms. As each term of office expires, the Governor shall appoint a successor as herein provided. All such terms of members shall be for seven years. Members shall serve until their successors are appointed and qualified. In the event of a vacancy on the board by death, resignation, removal, or any reason other than the expiration of a member's term, the Governor shall fill such vacancy; and the person so appointed shall serve until confirmed by the Senate and, upon confirmation, shall serve for the unexpired term of office.
(b) The board of regents shall have the exclusive authority to create new public colleges, junior colleges, and universities in the State of Georgia, subject to approval by majority vote in the House of Representatives and the Senate. Such vote shall not be required to change the status of a college, institution or university existing on the effective date of this Constitution. The government, control, and management of the University System of Georgia and all of the institutions in said system shall be vested in the Board of Regents of the University System of Georgia.
(c) All appropriations made for the use of any or all institutions in the university system shall be paid to the board of regents in a lump sum, with the power and authority in said board to allocate and distribute the same among the institutions under its control in such way and manner and in such amounts as will further an efficient and economical administration of the university system.
(d) The board of regents may hold, purchase, lease, sell, convey, or otherwise dispose of public property, execute conveyances thereon, and utilize the proceeds arising therefrom; may exercise the power of eminent domain in the manner provided by law; and shall have such other powers and duties as provided by law.
(e) The board of regents may accept bequests, donations, grants, and transfers of land, buildings, and other property for the use of the University System of Georgia.
(f) The qualifications, compensation, and removal from office of the members of the board of regents shall be as provided by law.

Section V: Local School Systems

Paragraph I: School systems continued; consolidation of school systems authorized; new independent school systems prohibited. Authority is granted to county and area boards of education to establish and maintain public schools within their limits. Existing county and independent school systems shall be continued, except that the General Assembly may provide by law for the consolidation of two or more county school systems, independent school systems, portions thereof, or any combination thereof into a single county or area school system under the control and management of a county or area board of education, under such terms and conditions as the General Assembly may prescribe; but no such consolidation shall become effective until approved by a majority of the qualified voters voting thereon in each separate school system proposed to be consolidated. No independent school system shall hereafter be established.

Paragraph II: Boards of education. Each school system shall be under the management and control of a board of education, the members of which shall be elected as provided by law. School board members shall reside within the territory embraced by the school system and shall have such compensation and additional qualifications as may be provided by law . .

Paragraph III: School superintendents. There shall be a school superintendent of each system appointed by the board of education who shall be the executive officer of the board of education and shall have such qualifications, powers, and duties as provided by general law . . .

Paragraph V: Power of boards to contract with each other.
(a) Any two or more boards of education may contract with each other for the care, education, and transportation of pupils and for such other activities as they may be authorized by law to perform.
(b) The General Assembly may provide by law for the sharing of facilities or services by and between local boards of education under such joint administrative authority as may be authorized.

Paragraph VI: Power of boards to accept bequests, donations, grants, and transfers. The board of education of each school system may accept bequests, donations, grants, and transfers of land, buildings, and other property for the use of such system.

Paragraph VII: Special schools.
(a) The General Assembly may provide by law for the creation of special schools in such areas as may require them and may provide for the participation of local boards of education in the establishment of such schools under such terms and conditions as it may provide; but no bonded indebtedness may be incurred nor a school tax levied for the support of special schools without the approval of a majority of the qualified voters voting thereon in each of the systems affected. Any special schools shall be operated in conformity with regulations of the State Board of Education pursuant to provisions of law. The state is authorized to expend funds for the support and maintenance of special schools in such amount and manner as may be provided by law.
(b) Nothing contained herein shall be construed to affect the authority of local boards of education or of the state to support and maintain special schools created prior to June 30, 1983.

Section VI: Local Taxation for Education

Paragraph I: Local taxation for education.
(a) The board of education of each school system shall annually certify to its fiscal authority or authorities a school tax not greater than 20 mills per dollar for the support and maintenance of education. Said fiscal authority or authorities shall annually levy said tax upon the assessed value of all taxable property within the territory served by said school system, provided that the levy made by an area board of education, which levy shall not be greater than 20 mills per dollar, shall be in such amount and within such limits as may be prescribed by local law applicable thereto.
(b) School tax funds shall be expended only for the support and maintenance of public schools, public vocational-technical schools, public education, and activities necessary or incidental thereto, including school lunch purposes.
(c) The 20 mill limitation provided for in subparagraph (a) of this Paragraph shall not apply to those school systems which are authorized on June 30, 1983, to levy a school tax in excess thereof.
(d) The method of certification and levy of the school tax provided for in subparagraph (a) of this Paragraph shall not apply to those systems that are authorized on June 30, 1983, to utilize a different method of certification and levy of such tax; but the General Assembly may by law require that such systems be brought into conformity with the method of certification and levy herein provided.

Paragraph II: Increasing or removing tax rate. The mill limitation in effect on June 30, 1983, for any school system may be increased or removed by action of the respective boards of education, but only after such action has been approved by a majority of the qualified voters voting thereon in the particular school system to be affected in the manner provided by law.

Paragraph III: School tax collection reimbursement. The General Assembly may by general law require local boards of education to reimburse the appropriate governing authority for the collection of school taxes, provided that any rate established may be reduced by local act.

Paragraph IV: Sales tax for educational purposes.
(a) The board of education of each school district in a county in which no independent school district is located may by resolution and the board of education of each county school district and the board of education of each independent school district located within such county may by concurrent resolutions impose, levy, and collect a sales and use tax for educational purposes of such school districts conditioned upon approval by a majority of the qualified voters residing within the limits of the local taxing jurisdiction voting in a referendum thereon. This tax shall be at the rate of 1 percent and shall be imposed for a period of time not to exceed five years, but in all other respects, except as otherwise provided in this Paragraph, shall correspond to and be levied in the same manner as the tax provided for by Article 3 of Chapter 8 of Title 48 of the Official Code of Georgia Annotated, relating to the special county 1 percent sales and use tax, as now or hereafter amended. Proceedings for the reimposition of such tax shall be in the same manner as proceedings for the initial imposition of the tax, but the newly authorized tax shall not be imposed until the expiration of the tax then in effect.

(b) The purpose or purposes for which the proceeds of the tax are to be used and may be expended include:

(1) Capital outlay projects for educational purposes;
(2) The retirement of previously incurred general obligation debt with respect only to capital outlay projects of the school system; provided, however, that the tax authorized under this Paragraph shall only be expended for the purpose authorized under this subparagraph (b)(2) if all ad valorem property taxes levied or scheduled to be levied prior to the maturity of any such then outstanding general obligation debt to be retired by the proceeds of the tax imposed under this Paragraph shall be reduced by a total amount equal to the total amount of proceeds of the tax imposed under this Paragraph to be applied to retire such bonded indebtedness. In the event of failure to comply with the requirements of this subparagraph (b)(2), as certified by the Department of Revenue, no further funds shall be expended under this subparagraph (b)(2) by such county or independent board of education and all such funds shall be maintained in a separate, restricted account and held solely for the expenditure for future capital outlay projects for educational purposes; or
(3) A combination of the foregoing.

(c) The resolution calling for the imposition of the tax and the ballot question shall each describe:

(1) The specific capital outlay projects to be funded, or the specific debt to be retired, or both, if applicable;
(2) The maximum cost of such project or projects and, if applicable, the maximum amount of debt to be retired, which cost and amount of debt shall also be the maximum amount of net proceeds to be raised by the tax; and
(3) The maximum period of time, to be stated in calendar years or calendar quarters and not to exceed five years.

(d) Nothing in this Paragraph shall prohibit a county and those municipalities located in such county from imposing as additional taxes local sales and use taxes authorized by general law.
(e) The tax imposed pursuant to this Paragraph shall not be subject to and shall not count with respect to any general law limitation regarding the maximum amount of local sales and use taxes which may be levied in any jurisdiction in this state.
(f) The tax imposed pursuant to this Paragraph shall not be subject to any sales and use tax exemption with respect to the sale or use of food and beverages which is imposed by law.
(g) The net proceeds of the tax shall be distributed between the county school district and the independent school districts, or portion thereof, located in such county according to the ratio the student enrollment in each school district, or portion thereof, bears to the total student enrollment of all school districts in the county or upon such other formula for distribution as may be authorized by local law. For purposes of this subparagraph, student enrollment shall be based on the latest FTE count prior to the referendum on imposing the tax.
(h) Excess proceeds of the tax which remain following expenditure of proceeds for authorized projects or purposes for education shall be used solely for the purpose of reducing any indebtedness of the school system. In the event there is no indebtedness, such excess proceeds

shall be used by such school system for the purpose of reducing its millage rate in an amount equivalent to the amount of such excess proceeds.

(i) The tax authorized by this Paragraph may be imposed, levied, and collected as provided in this Paragraph without further action by the General Assembly, but the General Assembly shall be authorized by general law to further define and implement its provisions including, but not limited to, the authority to specify the percentage of net proceeds to be allocated among the projects and purposes for which the tax was levied.

(j)(1) Notwithstanding any provision of any constitutional amendment continued in force and effect pursuant to Article XI, Section I, Paragraph IV (a) and except as otherwise provided in subparagraph (j)(2) of this Paragraph, any political subdivision whose ad valorem taxing powers are restricted pursuant to such a constitutional amendment may receive the proceeds of the tax authorized under this Paragraph or of any local sales and use tax authorized by general law, or any combination of such taxes, without any corresponding limitation of its ad valorem taxing powers which would otherwise be required under such constitutional amendment.

(2) The restriction on and limitation of ad valorem taxing powers described in subparagraph (j)(1) of this Paragraph shall remain applicable with respect to proceeds received from the levy of a local sales and use tax specifically authorized by a constitutional amendment in force and effect pursuant to Article XI, Section I, Paragraph IV (a), as opposed to a local sales and use tax authorized by this Paragraph or by general law.

Section VII: Educational Assistance

Paragraph I: Educational assistance programs authorized.
(a) Pursuant to laws now or hereafter enacted by the General Assembly, public funds may be expended for any of the following purposes:

> (1) To provide grants, scholarships, loans, or other assistance to students and to parents of students for educational purposes.
> (2) To provide for a program of guaranteed loans to students and to parents of students for educational purposes and to pay interest, interest subsidies, and fees to lenders on such loans. The General Assembly is authorized to provide such tax exemptions to lenders as shall be deemed advisable in connection with such program.
> (3) To match funds now or hereafter available for student assistance pursuant to any federal law.
> (4) To provide grants, scholarships, loans, or other assistance to public employees for educational purposes.
> (5) To provide for the purchase of loans made to students for educational purposes who have completed a program of study in a field in which critical shortages exist and for cancellation of repayment of such loans, interest, and charges thereon.

(b) Contributions made in support of any educational assistance program now or hereafter established under provisions of this section may be deductible for state income tax purposes as now or hereafter provided by law.

(c) The General Assembly shall be authorized by general law to provide for an education trust fund to assist students and parents of students in financing postsecondary education and to provide for contracts between the fund and purchasers for the advance payment of tuition by each purchaser for a qualified beneficiary to attend a state institution of higher education. Such general law shall provide for such terms, conditions, and limitations as the General Assembly shall deem necessary for the implementation of this subparagraph. Notwithstanding any provision of this Constitution to the contrary, the General Assembly shall be authorized to provide for the guarantee of such contracts with state revenues.

Paragraph II: Guaranteed revenue debt. Guaranteed revenue debt may be incurred to provide funds to make loans to students and to parents of students for educational purposes, to purchase loans made to students and to parents of students for educational purposes, or to lend or make deposits of such funds with lenders which shall be secured by loans made to students and to parents of students for educational purposes. Any such debt shall be incurred in accordance with the procedures and requirements of Article VII, Section IV of this Constitution.

Paragraph III: Public authorities. Public authorities or public corporations heretofore or hereafter created for such purposes shall be authorized to administer educational assistance programs and, in connection therewith, may exercise such powers as may now or hereafter be provided by law.

Paragraph IV: Waiver of tuition. The Board of Regents of the University System of Georgia shall be authorized to establish programs allowing attendance at units of the University System of Georgia without payment of tuition or other fees, but the General Assembly may provide by law for the establishment of any such program for the benefit of elderly citizens of the state.

Georgia Statutes

Local School Governance

§ 20-2-85: Legislative Intent re: School Councils

(a) The General Assembly recognizes the need to improve communication and participation of parents and the community in the management and operation of local schools. The General Assembly believes that parent and community support is critical to the success of students and schools. The intent of this article is to bring communities and schools closer together in a spirit of cooperation to solve difficult education problems, improve academic achievement, provide support for teachers and administrators, and bring parents into the school-based decision-making process. The establishment of school councils is intended to help local boards of education develop and nurture participation, bring parents and the community together with teachers and school administrators to create a better understanding of and mutual respect for each other's concerns, and share ideas for school improvement. School councils shall be reflective of the school community.
(b) The management and control of public schools shall be the responsibility of local boards of education, and the school leader shall be the principal. School councils shall provide advice, recommendations, and assistance and represent the community of parents and businesses. Each member of the council, as a community representative, shall be accorded the respect and attention deserving of such election.

§ 20-2-86: Establishment of School Councils

(a) By October 1, 2003, each local board of education shall have a school council operational in each of the schools under its jurisdiction. Local boards of education may by board policy allow an alternative to a school council at a charter school, an alternative school, or a psycho-education center if another governance body or advisory council exists that performs a comparable function.

(b) The local board of education shall provide a training program to assist schools in forming a school council and to assist school councilmembers in the performance of their duties. Such program shall address the organization of councils, their purpose and responsibilities, applicable laws, rules, regulations and meeting procedures, and important state and local school system program requirements and shall provide a model school council organization plan. Additional training programs shall be offered to school councilmembers annually. The State Board of Education shall develop and make available a model school council training program.

(c) Any member may withdraw from the council by delivering to the council a written resignation and submitting a copy to the secretary of the council or school principal. Should school councilmembers determine that a member of the council is no longer active in the council as defined by the bylaws of the council, the council may, by a majority vote, withdraw such person's membership status, effective as of a date determined by the council.

(d) The property and business of the council shall be managed by a minimum of seven school councilmembers of whom a majority shall constitute a quorum. The number of councilmembers shall be specified in the council's bylaws. Members of the school council shall include:

>(1) A number of parents or guardians of students enrolled in the school, excluding employees who are parents or guardians of such students, so that such parents or guardians make up a majority of the council and at least two of whom shall be businesspersons;
>
>(2) At least two certificated teachers, excluding any personnel employed in administrative positions, who are employed at least four of the six school segments at the school;
>
>(3) The school principal; and
>
>(4) Other members as specified in the council's bylaws, such as, but not limited to, students, staff, and representatives of school related organizations. Other businesspersons from the local business community may serve on the council and shall be selected by the other members of the school council. Selection procedures for these members and the business members shall be specified in the council's bylaws.

An employee of the local school system may serve as a parent representative on the council of a school in which his or her child is enrolled if such employee works at a different school. With the exception of the principal and the business representatives, members shall be elected by, and from among, the group they represent.

(e) Members of the council shall serve for a term of two years or for such other term as may be specified in the council's bylaws, except as provided in this subsection. The terms of the councilmembers shall be staggered. Upon the expiration of the terms of the two businessperson councilmembers in office on July 1, 2007, these member positions shall subsequently be filled by parent councilmembers; provided, however, that additional businesspersons may serve on the council if provided for in the council's bylaws in accordance with paragraph (4) of subsection (d) of this Code section. Councilmembers may serve more than one term. The office of school councilmember shall be automatically vacated:

(1) If a member shall resign;
(2) If the person holding the office is removed as a member by an action of the council pursuant to this Code section; or
(3) If a member no longer meets the qualifications specified in this Code section.

An election within the electing body for a replacement to fill the remainder of an unexpired term shall be held within 30 days, unless there are 90 days or less remaining in the term in which case the vacancy shall remain unfilled.

(f) All meetings of the school council shall be open to the public. The council shall meet at least four times annually and the number of meetings shall be specified in the council's bylaws. The council shall also meet at the call of the chairperson, or at the request of a majority of the members of the council. Notice by mail shall be sent to school councilmembers at least seven days prior to a meeting of the council and shall include the date, time, and location of the meeting. School councils shall be subject to Chapter 14 of Title 50, relating to open and public meetings, in the same manner as local boards of education. Each member is authorized to exercise one vote. A quorum must be present in order to conduct official council business. Members of the council shall not receive remuneration to serve on the council or its committees.

(g) After providing public notice at least two weeks before the meeting of each electing body, the principal of each school shall call a meeting of electing bodies for the purpose of selecting members of the school council as required by this Code section. The electing body for the parent members shall consist of all parents and guardians eligible to serve as a parent member of the school council, and the electing body for the teacher members shall consist of all certificated personnel eligible to serve as a teacher member of the school council. The school council shall specify in its bylaws the month in which elections are to be held and shall specify a nomination and election process.

(h) The school council shall adopt such bylaws as it deems appropriate to conduct the business of the council. The adoption of bylaws or changes thereto requires a two-thirds' affirmative vote. The State Board of Education shall develop and make available model school council bylaws.

(i) The school council shall have the same immunity as the local board of education in all matters directly related to the functions of the council.

(j)(1) The officers of the school council shall be a chairperson, vice chairperson, and secretary. Officers of the council shall be elected by the council at the first meeting of the council following the election of school councilmembers; provided, however, that the chairperson shall be a parent member. The officers of the council shall hold office for the term specified in the council's bylaws.

(2) The vice chairperson shall, in the absence or disability of the chairperson, perform the duties and exercise the powers of the chairperson and shall perform such other duties as shall be required by the council.

(3) The secretary shall attend all meetings, act as clerk of the council, and be responsible for recording all votes and minutes of all proceedings in the books to be kept for that purpose. The secretary shall give or cause to be given notice of all meetings of the council and shall perform such other duties as may be prescribed by the council.

(k) The members of the school council are accountable to the constituents they serve and shall:

>   (1) Maintain a school-wide perspective on issues;
>   (2) Regularly participate in council meetings;
>   (3) Participate in information and training programs;
>   (4) Act as a link between the school council and the community;
>   (5) Encourage the participation of parents and others within the school community; and
>   (6) Work to improve student achievement and performance.

(l) The minutes of the council shall be made available to the public, for inspection at the school office, and shall be provided to the councilmembers, each of whom shall receive a copy of such minutes within 20 days following each council meeting. All school councils shall be subject to Article 4 of Chapter 18 of Title 50, relating to the inspection of public records, in the same manner as local boards of education.

(m) At all meetings of the council every question shall be determined by a majority vote of members present, representing a quorum.

(n) The term of office of all councilmembers shall begin and end on the dates specified in the council's bylaws.

(o) The council may appoint committees, study groups, or task forces for such purposes as it deems helpful and may utilize existing or new school advisory groups.

(p) The local board of education shall provide all information not specifically made confidential by law, including school site budget and expenditure information and site average class sizes by grade, to the council as requested or as required by state law or state board rule. The local board shall also designate an employee of the school system to attend council meetings as requested by a school council for the purpose of responding to questions the council may have concerning information provided to it by the local board or actions taken by the local board. The central administration shall be responsive to requests for information from a school council.

(q) The local board of education shall receive and consider all recommendations of the school council, including the annual report, as follows:

>   (1) Public notice shall be given to the community of the local board's intent to consider school council reports or recommendations;

(2) Written notice shall be given to the members of the school council at least seven days prior to a local board meeting, along with a notice of intent to consider a council report or recommendation; and

(3) The members of the school council shall be afforded an opportunity to present information in support of the school council's report or recommendation.

The local board of education shall respond to recommendations of the school council within 60 days after being notified in writing of the recommendation.

(r) The school principal shall have the following duties pertaining to school council activities:

(1) Cause to be created a school council pursuant to this Code section by convening the appropriate bodies to select school councilmembers; setting the initial agenda, meeting time, and location; and notifying all school councilmembers of the same;

(2) Perform all of the duties required by law and the bylaws of the council;

(3) Communicate all council requests for information and assistance to the local school superintendent and inform the council of responses or actions of the local school superintendent;

(4) Develop the school improvement plan and school operation plan and submit the plans to the school council for its review, comments, recommendations, and approval; and

(5) Aid in the development of the agenda for each meeting of the council after taking into consideration suggestions of councilmembers and the urgency of school matters. An item may be added to the agenda at the request of three or more councilmembers.

(s) School councils are advisory bodies. The councils shall provide advice and recommendations to the school principal and, where appropriate, the local board of education and local school superintendent on any matter related to student achievement and school improvement, including, but not limited to, the following:

(1) School board policies;
(2) School improvement plans;
(3) Curriculum and assessments;
(4) Report cards issued or audits of the school conducted by the Office of Student Achievement;
(5) Development of a school profile which shall contain data as identified by the council to describe the academic performance, academic progress, services, awards, interventions, environment, and other such data as the council deems appropriate;
(6) School budget priorities, including school capital improvement plans;
(7) School-community communication strategies;
(8) Methods of involving parents and the community;
(9) Extracurricular activities in the school;
(10) School-based and community services;

(11) Community use of school facilities;
(12) Student discipline and attendance;
(13) Reports from the school principal regarding progress toward the school's student achievement goals, including progress within specific grade levels and subject areas and by school personnel; and
(14) The method and specifications for the delivery of early intervention services or other appropriate services for underachieving students.

(t) The role of the school council in the principal selection process shall be determined in policy written by the local board of education.

Chapter 2: Children, Families, and the State

It is the moral duty of adults to protect children. In recognition of this solemn obligation, all 50 U.S. states have enacted statutes mandating reports of suspected abuse or neglect of children to state officials. For persons subject to these statutes protecting children from abuse or neglect is not only a moral obligation, it is a legal duty. These statutes provide criminal sanctions if mandated reporters fail to make a timely report of child abuse or neglect.

> *If the Facts and Circumstances would have caused a Reasonable Person to Suspect Child Abuse or Neglect, there is a Legal Duty to Report*

Mandatory reporting statutes were enacted in recognition of the general duty of adults, and child services professionals in particular, to protect children. In enacting these statutes lawmakers made a policy decision that when children may be in danger it is better to have too many reports rather than too few. Over-reporting consumes resources, and sometimes causes unnecessary intrusions. But under-reporting presents a serious danger that children may be unprotected. Therefore the legal standard is generally knowledge of "suspected" abuse and not just "known" abuse. There is a legal duty to make a report when a reasonable person would have suspected abuse under the facts and circumstances within the knowledge of the individual.

This is an objective legal standard, not a subjective standard. The "reasonable person" standard is based on the expected conduct of the ordinary person under the circumstances, a person with average knowledge, skills, and judgment. If a reasonable person would have made a report under those facts and circumstances, there is a legal duty to report. Further, the report should be made as soon as practicable avoiding any unnecessary delay that could interfere with the timely provision of help for the child.

Levels of Evidence of Abuse or Neglect and the Duty to Report

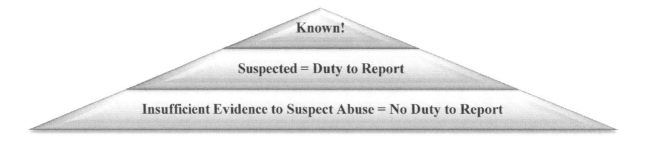

© Dayton

If there is insufficient evidence to cause a reasonable person to suspect abuse there is no duty to report. If there is evidence sufficient to cause a reasonable person to suspect child abuse, there is a legal duty to report and willful failure to do so may be subject to criminal punishments. Known abuse calls for immediate action to protect the child including a referral to law enforcement officials.

If abuse or neglect are suspected the witness must comply with state laws for reporting abuse or neglect. For failing to report suspected abuse or neglect child care professionals could lose their professional licenses and be convicted of a misdemeanor. But if it can be proven that an adult actually knew about child abuse and allowed the abuse to continue by failing to report, that person could be subject to prosecution as an accessory to the crime. In cases of child sexual abuse this could be a felony level crime punishable by significantly more than a year in prison.

When a report is made under the state reporting statute state child protection services personnel will investigate the report and make an initial determination whether the child is in danger or whether the child and family are in need of services, acting to protect the child as indicated. If the report turns out to be unfounded, however, as long as the report was made in good faith, persons reporting suspected abuse or neglect are generally shielded from any liability under state law by good faith immunity. Knowingly making a false report, however, is a crime. A person who knowingly makes a false report for purposes of harassment or defamation could be subject to both criminal prosecution and civil liability for defamation.

Abusers rarely abuse children in public view. Instead, child care professionals and community members may see signs and behaviors indicating that a child may be abused or neglected. It is also important to remember that while children must be protected from abuse or neglect, parents may also be in need of counseling, social services, or support. Not all marginal or bad parenting is legally actionable abuse or neglect.

Continuum of Parental Care

© **Dayton**

Optimal care for all children is ideal. Due to family, parental, or economic circumstances, however, optimal child care will not occur in many families. Child abuse and neglect laws seek to strike a proper balance between family privacy and public concern; parental autonomy and legal accountability; private economic realities and available public resources. Limited public resources mean that the state must establish a system of triage, directing resources to the children in greatest danger and need first. An essential tool in this system is a mandatory system for reporting suspected child abuse or neglect so that children in need of public services can be identified, helped, and protected.

Child care professionals are on the front lines of defense in protecting children from abuse or neglect. For this reason it is essential that child care professionals recognize signs of abuse or neglect. Below are examples of warning signs and red flags. Note that the lists below are only illustrative lists intended to raise awareness of possible signs of abuse or neglect. These are not the only indicators of abuse or neglect, nor does an indicator of possible abuse or neglect necessarily mean a child is being abused or neglected. Each case must be independently evaluated in consideration of the totality of the circumstances.

General Indicators of Child Abuse or Neglect:

- Sudden behavioral changes
- Dramatic declines in school performance
- Becoming socially withdrawn
- Unexplained anxiety or anger
- Troubling conduct when with a parent
- Unusual desire to stay at school
- Substance abuse
- Bullying or abusing other children
- Running away
- Self-harm or attempted suicide

Indicators of Child Neglect:

- Unsupervised
- Poor hygiene
- Dirty or insufficient clothing
- Stealing or begging food or money
- Untreated dental or medical problems
- Excessive school absences
- Falling asleep in school
- Frequent illnesses or injuries

Indicators of verbal or emotional abuse are too often dismissed as merely regrettable. A child can be severely and permanently harmed, however, without anyone touching the child physically. In severe cases psychological and emotional pain can be worse than physical pain, and leave deeper and longer lasting scars. Severe verbal or emotional abuse may also drive a child to self-injury or other reactions to abuse that may endanger the child or others.

Indicators of Verbal or Emotional Abuse:

- Low self-esteem
- The child repeating abusive comments
- Public disparagement of the child
- Intentional humiliation of the child
- Grossly disproportionate punishments
- Exposure to domestic abuse
- Displays of extreme anger directed at the child
- Throwing or destroying objects near the child
- Threats, intimidation, or attempts to frighten the child
- Threats to withhold necessities, abandon, or force the child out of the home
- Threatening to harm loved personal possessions or pets
- Other evidence of emotional manipulation of the child or intentional cruelty

Indicators of Physical Abuse:

- Unexplained marks (bruises; cuts; scalds; burns; bite marks)
- Any suspicious injury (broken ribs; spiral fracture on long bone; cigarette burn)
- Any suspicious pattern of recurrent minor injuries
- Bruise in the shape of an object
- Bruises on both sides of the face or body (accidents generally injure only one side)
- Injury in protected/hidden area (foot sole; mouth; inner thigh; buttocks; back)
- Fingertip marks on neck (choking)
- Fingertip marks on upper arm or inside underarm (shaking)
- Rope burns or bruise marks on wrists or ankles suggesting restraint
- Broken or missing teeth
- Eye injury or hemorrhage
- Bruised outer ear (from being pulled or "boxed")
- Missing patch of hair (from pulling)
- Sickness or diarrhea from being forced to eat soap, salt, or other substances

Indicators of Sexual Abuse:

- Sudden change in behavior
- Low self-esteem
- Unexplained crying, anxiety, anger, social withdrawal
- Age-inappropriate sexual knowledge
- Overreaction to normal physical contact
- Inappropriate interactions with adults
- Sexual abuse of other children
- Discomfort in sitting or walking
- Sudden reluctance to disrobe for P.E. or showers
- Self-injury or attempted suicide
- Venereal disease or pregnancy

Based on an evaluation of the evidence and the totality of the circumstances concerning the child, the child care professional must decide on an appropriate course of action. Appropriate responses may range from an immediate emergency report to continued monitoring of the circumstances.

Emergency or imminent danger: Report to police for immediate intervention.

No emergency but red flags indicate abuse or neglect: Report as soon as possible consistent with statutory mandates for reporting.

No emergency or red flags but the totality of the circumstances would lead a reasonable person to suspect abuse or neglect: Make a timely report consistent with the mandatory reporting statute.

Suspicious circumstance noticed but does not meet reporting criteria: Ask appropriate, reasonable questions, engaging in a non-intrusive investigation to assure child safety.

Questioning children concerning suspicious circumstances:

- Ask open-ended questions (e.g., "are you alright?"; "what happened?")
- Follow up with more focused questions (e.g., what; how; who; why)
- Give the child time to respond
- Do not suggest conclusions
- Do not suggest abuse or neglect
- Do not act shocked
- Make the child feel safe and assure protection if needed

When possible, have another child care professional present to verify events and the child's statements. If at any point evidence of abuse or neglect exceeds the legal threshold under the reporting statute, make a report. Child protective services agents, law enforcement officers, or medical personnel may need to engage in a more thorough and intrusive interview or search. Do not exceed the appropriate bounds of your professional role in questioning or searching a child.

Uncertain what to do: Call child protective services for a consultation.

Child, parent, or family is in need of assistance but there is no abuse or neglect: Direct to support services and resources in the community.

No current evidence of abuse or neglect, but a lingering concern remains: Continue to appropriately and discreetly monitor the child's health and safety.

The parent's reaction to an injury may provide important clues in separating naturally occurring injuries from abuse. Factors that may enhance suspicion are an intentional delay in seeking medical treatment when obviously needed; the explanation of the child's injury is vague;

the parent seems more concerned about personal issues than the child's health and safety; the parent is curiously evasive or hostile; or the parent and child provided conflicting accounts.

Parental problems with money, lifestyle, or physical or mental health issues may increase risks for abuse or neglect. Parents' incomes of course have no correlation with their love for their children. But extreme poverty or homelessness can increase family stress and make it very difficult for parents to properly care for children.

Concerning lifestyle choices, a parent's lifestyle can have severe impacts on the health and safety of the child. Unhealthy or unsafe home conditions threaten the health and safety of the child. A parent's promiscuity or engaging in prostitution in the home may bring strangers into private contact with the child. To gain private access to a child, pedophiles sometimes target a parent with young children under the guise of a relationship with the parent. Substance abuse or drug dealing may also introduce dangerous people and conditions into the home. Domestic violence is a further threat to the child's mental and physical health and safety.

A parent struggling with serious mental health issues may be more prone to neglect and abuse or may be unfit to care for the child. If the parent is capable of child care, support should be provided to preserve the family when possible. But if the child is endangered by the parent's mental health problems the child must be protected.

For example, an uncommon by serious danger that must be recognized when present is Munchausen Syndrome by Proxy. This is a psychiatric disorder where the parent, most commonly the mother, causes or falsely claims injury or illness of the child. The parent may inflict an injury on the child, fabricate a "mystery" illness, or falsely claim to have observed seizures, high fevers, signs of internal bleeding or other medical concerns that cannot currently be proven or disproven, often with an over-eagerness to have medical tests and procedures conducted on the child. Medical records may be falsified and test samples intentionally contaminated by the parent. The parent's behavior may be motivated by acquiring personal sympathy or attention, or a desire to "save" the child and be a hero while actually endangering the child. A parent with serious mental illness needs help, but the child must be protected first.

Selected Georgia Laws

Georgia Statutes

§ 19-7-5: Mandatory Reporting of Suspected Child Abuse

(a) The purpose of this Code section is to provide for the protection of children whose health and welfare are adversely affected and further threatened by the conduct of those responsible for their care and protection. It is intended that the mandatory reporting of such cases will cause the protective services of the state to be brought to bear on the situation in an effort to prevent further abuses, to protect and enhance the welfare of these children, and to preserve family life wherever possible. This Code section shall be liberally construed so as to carry out the purposes thereof.

(b) As used in this Code section, the term:

(1) "Abortion" shall have the same meaning as set forth in Code Section 15-11-111.
(2) "Abused" means subjected to child abuse.
(3) "Child" means any person under 18 years of age.
(4) "Child abuse" means:

(A) Physical injury or death inflicted upon a child by a parent or caretaker thereof by other than accidental means; provided, however, that physical forms of discipline may be used as long as there is no physical injury to the child;
(B) Neglect or exploitation of a child by a parent or caretaker thereof;
(C) Sexual abuse of a child; or
(D) Sexual exploitation of a child.

However, no child who in good faith is being treated solely by spiritual means through prayer in accordance with the tenets and practices of a recognized church or religious denomination by a duly accredited practitioner thereof shall, for that reason alone, be considered to be an "abused" child.

(5) "Child service organization personnel" means a person employed by or volunteering at a business or an organization, whether public, private, for profit, not for profit, or voluntary, that provides care, treatment, education, training, supervision, coaching, counseling, recreational programs, or shelter to children.
(6) "Clergy" means ministers, priests, rabbis, imams, or similar functionaries, by whatever name called, of a bona fide religious organization.
(7) "Pregnancy resource center" means an organization or facility that:

(A) Provides pregnancy counseling or information as its primary purpose, either for a fee or as a free service;
(B) Does not provide or refer for abortions;
(C) Does not provide or refer for FDA approved contraceptive drugs or devices; and
(D) Is not licensed or certified by the state or federal government to provide medical or health care services and is not otherwise bound to follow federal Health Insurance Portability and Accountability Act of 1996, P.L. 104-191, or other state or federal laws relating to patient confidentiality.

(8) "Reproductive "health care facility" means any office, clinic, or any other physical location that provides abortions, abortion counseling, abortion referrals, or gynecological care and services.

(9) "School" means any public or private pre-kindergarten, elementary school, secondary school, technical school, vocational school, college, university, or institution of postsecondary education.

(10) "Sexual abuse" means a person's employing, using, persuading, inducing, enticing, or coercing any minor who is not that person's spouse to engage in any act which involves:

(A) Sexual intercourse, including genital-genital, oral-genital, anal-genital, or oral-anal, whether between persons of the same or opposite sex;
(B) Bestiality;
(C) Masturbation;
(D) Lewd exhibition of the genitals or pubic area of any person;
(E) Flagellation or torture by or upon a person who is nude;
(F) Condition of being fettered, bound, or otherwise physically restrained on the part of a person who is nude;
(G) Physical contact in an act of apparent sexual stimulation or gratification with any person's clothed or unclothed genitals, pubic area, or buttocks or with a female's clothed or unclothed breasts;
(H) Defecation or urination for the purpose of sexual stimulation; or
(I) Penetration of the vagina or rectum by any object except when done as part of a recognized medical procedure.

"Sexual abuse" shall not include consensual sex acts involving persons of the opposite sex when the sex acts are between minors or between a minor and an adult who is not more than five years older than the minor. This provision shall not be deemed or construed to repeal any law concerning the age or capacity to consent.

(11) "Sexual exploitation" means conduct by any person who allows, permits, encourages, or requires that child to engage in:

(A) Prostitution, as defined in Code Section 16-6-9; or

(B) Sexually explicit conduct for the purpose of producing any visual or print medium depicting such conduct, as defined in Code Section 16-12-100.

(c)(1) The following persons having reasonable cause to believe that a child has been abused shall report or cause reports of that abuse to be made as provided in this Code section:

(A) Physicians licensed to practice medicine, interns, or residents;

(B) Hospital or medical personnel;

(C) Dentists;

(D) Licensed psychologists and persons participating in internships to obtain licensing pursuant to Chapter 39 of Title 43;

(E) Podiatrists;

(F) Registered professional nurses or licensed practical nurses licensed pursuant to Chapter 24 of Title 43 or nurse's aides;

(G) Professional counselors, social workers, or marriage and family therapists licensed pursuant to Chapter 10A of Title 43;

(H) School teachers;

(I) School administrators;

(J) School guidance counselors, visiting teachers, school social workers, or school psychologists certified pursuant to Chapter 2 of Title 20;

(K) Child welfare agency personnel, as that agency is defined pursuant to Code Section 49-5-12;

(L) Child-counseling personnel;

(M) Child service organization personnel;

(N) Law enforcement personnel; or

(O) Reproductive health care facility or pregnancy resource center personnel and volunteers.

(2) If a person is required to report child abuse pursuant to this subsection because that person attends to a child pursuant to such person's duties as an employee of or volunteer at a hospital, school, social agency, or similar facility, that person shall notify the person in charge of the facility, or the designated delegate thereof, and the person so notified shall report or cause a report to be made in accordance with this Code section. An employee or volunteer who makes a report to the person designated pursuant to this paragraph shall be deemed to have fully complied with this subsection. Under no circumstances shall any person in charge of such hospital, school, agency, or facility, or the designated delegate thereof, to whom such notification has been made exercise any control, restraint, modification, or make other change to the information provided by the reporter, although each of the aforementioned persons may be consulted prior to the making of a report and may provide any additional, relevant, and necessary information when making the report.

(d) Any other person, other than one specified in subsection (c) of this Code section, who has reasonable cause to believe that a child is abused may report or cause reports to be made as provided in this Code section.

(e) An oral report shall be made immediately, but in no case later than 24 hours from the time there is reasonable cause to believe a child has been abused, by telephone or otherwise and followed by a report in writing, if requested, to a child welfare agency providing protective services, as designated by the Department of Human Services, or, in the absence of such agency, to an appropriate police authority or district attorney. If a report of child abuse is made to the child welfare agency or independently discovered by the agency, and the agency has reasonable cause to believe such report is true or the report contains any allegation or evidence of child abuse, then the agency shall immediately notify the appropriate police authority or district attorney. Such reports shall contain the names and addresses of the child and the child's parents or caretakers, if known, the child's age, the nature and extent of the child's injuries, including any evidence of previous injuries, and any other information that the reporting person believes might be helpful in establishing the cause of the injuries and the identity of the perpetrator. Photographs of the child's injuries to be used as documentation in support of allegations by hospital employees or volunteers, physicians, law enforcement personnel, school officials, or employees or volunteers of legally mandated public or private child protective agencies may be taken without the permission of the child's parent or guardian. Such photographs shall be made available as soon as possible to the chief welfare agency providing protective services and to the appropriate police authority.

(f) Any person or persons, partnership, firm, corporation, association, hospital, or other entity participating in the making of a report or causing a report to be made to a child welfare agency providing protective services or to an appropriate police authority pursuant to this Code section or any other law or participating in any judicial proceeding or any other proceeding resulting therefrom shall in so doing be immune from any civil or criminal liability that might otherwise be incurred or imposed, provided such participation pursuant to this Code section or any other law is made in good faith. Any person making a report, whether required by this Code section or not, shall be immune from liability as provided in this subsection.

(g) Suspected child abuse which is required to be reported by any person pursuant to this Code section shall be reported notwithstanding that the reasonable cause to believe such abuse has occurred or is occurring is based in whole or in part upon any communication to that person which is otherwise made privileged or confidential by law; provided, however, that a member of the clergy shall not be required to report child abuse reported solely within the context of confession or other similar communication required to be kept confidential under church doctrine or practice. When a clergy member receives information about child abuse from any other source, the clergy member shall comply with the reporting requirements of this Code section, even though the clergy member may have also received a report of child abuse from the confession of the perpetrator.

(h) Any person or official required by subsection (c) of this Code section to report a suspected case of child abuse who knowingly and willfully fails to do so shall be guilty of a misdemeanor.

(i) A report of child abuse or information relating thereto and contained in such report, when provided to a law enforcement agency or district attorney pursuant to subsection (e) of this Code section or pursuant to Code Section 49-5-41, shall not be subject to public inspection under Article 4 of Chapter 18 of Title 50 even though such report or information is contained in or part of closed records compiled for law enforcement or prosecution purposes unless:

> (1) There is a criminal or civil court proceeding which has been initiated based in whole or in part upon the facts regarding abuse which are alleged in the child abuse reports and the person or entity seeking to inspect such records provides clear and convincing evidence of such proceeding; or
>
> (2) The superior court in the county in which is located the office of the law enforcement agency or district attorney which compiled the records containing such reports, after application for inspection and a hearing on the issue, shall permit inspection of such records by or release of information from such records to individuals or entities who are engaged in legitimate research for educational, scientific, or public purposes and who comply with the provisions of this paragraph. When those records are located in more than one county, the application may be made to the superior court of any one of such counties. A copy of any application authorized by this paragraph shall be served on the office of the law enforcement agency or district attorney which compiled the records containing such reports. In cases where the location of the records is unknown to the applicant, the application may be made to the Superior Court of Fulton County. The superior court to which an application is made shall not grant the application unless:
>
> > (A) The application includes a description of the proposed research project, including a specific statement of the information required, the purpose for which the project requires that information, and a methodology to assure the information is not arbitrarily sought;
> >
> > (B) The applicant carries the burden of showing the legitimacy of the research project; and
> >
> > (C) Names and addresses of individuals, other than officials, employees, or agents of agencies receiving or investigating a report of abuse which is the subject of a report, shall be deleted from any information released pursuant to this subsection unless the court determines that having the names and addresses open for review is essential to the research and the child, through his or her representative, gives permission to release the information.

§ 20-2-780: Unlawful Change of Custody at School

(a) No person shall make or attempt to make a change of custody of a minor child by removing the child from the premises of a private or public elementary or secondary school without the permission of the person who enrolled the child in the school, notwithstanding the fact that the person seeking to obtain custody of the child from the school has a court order granting custody of the child to such person.
(b) This Code section shall not apply with respect to the following:

(1) Persons seeking to enforce court orders that specifically authorize or direct the release of custody by the school; or
(2) State or local officials acting under the express authority of this state's child protection laws.

(c) Any person violating this Code section shall be guilty of a misdemeanor.
(d) School officials when acting in their official capacities in preventing or attempting to prevent a violation of this Code section shall be immune from civil or criminal liability that otherwise might be incurred or imposed.

§ 20-2-720: Education Records; Parents Right to Inspect

No local school system, whether county, independent, or area, shall have a policy of denying, or which effectively prevents, the parents of students who are in attendance at or who have been enrolled in any facility within such system the right to inspect and review the education records of their child. A parent shall be entitled to inspect and review only information relating to his or her own child and if any material or document in a child's record includes information on another student, such information regarding any other student shall not be made available for inspection or review except to the parents of that student. Both parents of a child shall be entitled to inspect and review the education records of their child or to be provided information concerning their child's progress. Information concerning a child's education record shall not be withheld from the noncustodial parent unless a court order has specifically removed the right of the noncustodial parent to such information or unless parental rights have been terminated. For purposes of this Code section, "education records" shall include attendance reports and records.

§ 20-2-150. Eligibility to Enroll in Public Education Programs

(a) Except as otherwise provided by subsection (b) of this Code section, all children and youth who have attained the age of five years by September 1 shall be eligible for enrollment in the appropriate general education programs authorized in this part unless they attain the age of 20 by September 1 or they have received high school diplomas or the equivalent. This shall specifically include students who have reenrolled after dropping out and who are married, parents, or pregnant. Special education students shall also be eligible for enrollment in appropriate education programs through age 21 or until they receive high school or special education diplomas or the equivalent; provided, however, they were enrolled during the preceding school year and had an approved Individualized Education Program (IEP) which indicated that a successive year of enrollment was needed. Other students who have not yet attained age 21 by September 1 or received high school diplomas or the equivalent shall be eligible for enrollment in appropriate education programs, provided they have not dropped out of school for one quarter or more. Each local unit of administration shall have the authority to assign students who are married, parents, or pregnant or who have reenrolled after dropping out one quarter or more to programs of instruction within its regular daytime educational program, provided that a local unit of administration may develop and implement special programs of instruction limited to such students within the regular daytime educational program or, at the option of the student, in an alternative program beyond the regular daytime program; provided, further, that such programs of instruction are designed to enable such students to earn course credit toward receiving high school diplomas. These programs may include instruction in prenatal care and child care. Each local unit of administration shall have the authority to provide alternative programs beyond the regular daytime educational program. Unless otherwise provided by law, the State Board of Education shall have the authority to determine the eligibility of students for enrollment. It is declared to be the policy of this state that general and occupational education be integrated into a comprehensive educational program which will contribute to the total development of the individual.

(b) A child who was a legal resident of one or more other states for a period of two years immediately prior to moving to this state and who was legally enrolled in a public kindergarten or first grade, or a kindergarten or first grade accredited by a state or regional association, shall be eligible for enrollment in the appropriate general or special education programs authorized in this part if such child will attain the age of five for kindergarten or six for first grade by December 31 and is otherwise qualified.

(c) All children enrolled for 20 school days or more in the public schools of this state prior to their seventh birthday shall become subject to all of the provisions of this article, the provisions of Code Sections 20-2-690 through 20-2-701, and the rules and regulations of the State Board of Education relating to compulsory school attendance even though they have not attained seven years of age.

(d) No child or youth shall be admitted to any public school of the state until the parent or guardian provides to the proper school authorities an official copy of that child's social security number which shall be incorporated into the official school records pertaining to that child or youth. Each local unit of administration shall establish and implement a plan for providing the public appropriate notice of the information required of every student under its jurisdiction prior to the beginning of each school year. School authorities may provisionally admit a child for whom an official social security number has not been provided if the parent or guardian completes a postage-paid application for a social security number at the time of enrollment. A parent or guardian who objects to the incorporation of the social security number into the school records of a child may have the requirement waived by signing a statement objecting to the requirement.

§ 20-2-690.1: Mandatory School Attendance

(a) Mandatory attendance in a public school, private school, or home school program shall be required for children between their sixth and sixteenth birthdays. Such mandatory attendance shall not be required where the child has successfully completed all requirements for a high school diploma.

(b) Every parent, guardian, or other person residing within this state having control or charge of any child or children during the ages of mandatory attendance as required in subsection (a) of this Code section shall enroll and send such child or children to a public school, a private school, or a home study program that meets the requirements for a public school, a private school, or a home study program; and such child shall be responsible for enrolling in and attending a public school, a private school, or a home study program that meets the requirements for a public school, a private school, or a home study program under such penalty for noncompliance with this subsection as is provided in Chapter 11 of Title 15, unless the child's failure to enroll and attend is caused by the child's parent, guardian, or other person, in which case the parent, guardian, or other person alone shall be responsible; provided, however, that tests and physical exams for military service and the National Guard and such other approved absences shall be excused absences. The requirements of this subsection shall apply to a child during the ages of mandatory attendance as required in subsection (a) of this Code section who has been assigned by a local board of education or its delegate to attend an alternative public school program established by that local board of education, including an alternative public school program provided for in Code Section 20-2-154.1, regardless of whether such child has been suspended or expelled from another public school program by that local board of education or its delegate, and to the parent, guardian, or other person residing in this state who has control or charge of such child. Nothing in this Code section shall be construed to require a local board of education or its delegate to assign a child to attend an alternative public school program rather than suspending or expelling the child.

(c) Any parent, guardian, or other person residing in this state who has control or charge of a child or children and who shall violate this Code section shall be guilty of a misdemeanor and, upon conviction thereof, shall be subject to a fine not less than $25.00 and not greater than $100.00, imprisonment not to exceed 30 days, community service, or any combination of such penalties, at the discretion of the court having jurisdiction. Each day's absence from school in violation of this part after the child's school system notifies the parent, guardian, or other person who has control or charge of a child of five unexcused days of absence for a child shall constitute a separate offense. After two reasonable attempts to notify the parent, guardian, or other person who has control or charge of a child of five unexcused days of absence without response, the school system shall send a notice to such parent, guardian, or other person by certified mail, return receipt requested. Public schools shall provide to the parent, guardian, or other person having control or charge of each child enrolled in public school a written summary of possible consequences and penalties for failing to comply with compulsory attendance under this Code section for children and their parents, guardians, or other persons having control or charge of children. The parent, guardian, or other person who has control or charge of a child or children shall sign a statement indicating receipt of such written statement of possible consequences and penalties; children who are age ten years or older by September 1 shall sign a statement indicating receipt of such written statement of possible consequences and penalties. After two reasonable attempts by the school to secure such signature or signatures, the school shall be considered to be in compliance with this subsection if it sends a copy of the statement, via certified mail, return receipt requested, to such parent, guardian, other person who has control or charge of a child, or children. Public schools shall retain signed copies of statements through the end of the school year.

(d) Local school superintendents in the case of private schools or home study programs and visiting teachers and attendance officers in the case of public schools shall have authority and it shall be their duty to file proceedings in court to enforce this subpart.

(e) An unemancipated minor who is older than the age of mandatory attendance as required in subsection (a) of this Code section who has not completed all requirements for a high school diploma who wishes to withdraw from school shall have the written permission of his or her parent or legal guardian prior to withdrawing. Prior to accepting such permission, the school principal or designee shall convene a conference with the child and parent or legal guardian within two school days of receiving notice of the intent of the child to withdraw from school. The principal or designee shall make a reasonable attempt to share with the student and parent or guardian the educational options available, including the opportunity to pursue a general educational development (GED) diploma and the consequences of not having earned a high school diploma, including lower lifetime earnings, fewer jobs for which the student will be qualified, and the inability to avail oneself of higher educational opportunities. Every local board of education shall adopt a policy on the process of voluntary withdrawal of unemancipated minors who are older than the mandatory attendance age. The policy shall be filed with the Department of Education no later than January 1, 2007. The Department of Education shall provide annually to all local school superintendents model forms for the parent or guardian signature requirement contained in this subsection and updated information from reliable sources relating to the consequences of withdrawing from school without completing all requirements for a high school diploma. Such form shall include information relating to the opportunity to pursue a general educational development (GED) diploma and the consequences of not having earned a high school diploma, including lower lifetime earnings, fewer jobs for which the student will be qualified, and the inability to avail oneself of higher educational opportunities. Each local school superintendent shall provide such forms and information to all of its principals of schools serving grades six through twelve for the principals to use during the required conference with the child and parent or legal guardian.

§ 20-2-690: Requirements for Private Schools and Home Study Programs

(a) This subpart recognizes the existence of public schools, private schools, and home study programs as educational entities.

(b) As used in this subpart, the term "private school" means an institution meeting the following criteria or requirements:

(1) The primary purpose of the institution is to provide education or, if the primary purpose of the institution is religious in nature, the institution shall provide the basic academic educational program specified in paragraph (4) of this subsection;

(2) The institution is privately controlled and operates on a continuing basis;

(3) The institution provides instruction each 12 months for the equivalent of 180 school days of education with each school day consisting of at least four and one-half school hours;

(4) The institution provides a basic academic educational program which includes, but is not limited to, reading, language arts, mathematics, social studies, and science;

(5) Within 30 days after the beginning of each school year, it shall be the duty of the administrator of each private school to provide to the school superintendent of each local public school district which has residents enrolled in the private school a list of the name, age, and residence of each resident so enrolled. At the end of each school month, it shall be the duty of the administrator of each private school to notify the school superintendent of each local public school district of the name, age, and residence of each student residing in the public school district who enrolls or terminates enrollment at the private school during the immediately preceding school month. Such records shall indicate when attendance has been suspended and the grounds for such suspension. Enrollment records and reports shall not be used for any purpose except providing necessary enrollment information, except with the permission of the parent or guardian of a child, pursuant to the subpoena of a court of competent jurisdiction, or for verification of attendance by the Department of Public Safety for the purposes set forth in subsection (a.1) of Code Section 40-5-22; and

(6) Any building used by the institution for private school purposes meets all health and safety standards established under state law and local ordinances.

(c) Parents or guardians may teach their children at home in a home study program which meets the following requirements:

(1) The parent, parents, or guardian must submit within 30 days after the establishment of a home study program and by September 1 annually thereafter a declaration of intent to utilize a home study program to the Department of Education, which may provide for electronic submittal of such declaration of intent;

(2) The declaration shall include a list of the names and ages of the students who are enrolled in the home study program, the address where the home study program is located, and a statement of the 12 month period that is to be considered the school year for that home study program. Enrollment records and reports shall not be used for any purpose except providing necessary enrollment information, except with the permission of the parent or guardian of a child, pursuant to the subpoena of a court of competent jurisdiction, or for verification of attendance by the Department of Public Safety for the purposes set forth in subsection (a.1) of Code Section 40-5-22;

(3) Parents or guardians may teach only their own children in the home study program, provided the teaching parent or guardian possesses at least a high school diploma or a general educational development diploma, but the parents or guardians may employ a tutor who holds a high school diploma or a general educational development diploma to teach such children;

(4) The home study program shall provide a basic academic educational program which includes, but is not limited to, reading, language arts, mathematics, social studies, and science;

(5) The home study program must provide instruction each 12 months to home study students equivalent to 180 school days of education with each school day consisting of at least four and one-half school hours unless the child is physically unable to comply with the rule provided for in this paragraph;

(6) Attendance records for the home study program shall be kept and shall be submitted annually to the Department of Education and additionally, in accordance with department regulations for purposes of verification of attendance by the Department of Public Safety, for the purposes set forth in subsection (a.1) of Code Section 40-5-22. The department may provide for electronic submittal of such records. Attendance records and reports shall not be used for any purpose except providing necessary attendance information, except with the permission of the parent or guardian of a child, pursuant to the subpoena of a court of competent jurisdiction, or for verification of attendance by the Department of Public Safety for the purposes set forth in subsection (a.1) of Code Section 40-5-22;

(7) Students in home study programs shall be subject to an appropriate nationally standardized testing program administered in consultation with a person trained in the administration and interpretation of norm reference tests to evaluate their educational progress at least every three years beginning at the end of the third grade and records of such tests and scores shall be retained but shall not be required to be submitted to public educational authorities; and

(8) The home study program instructor shall write an annual progress assessment report which shall include the instructor's individualized assessment of the student's academic progress in each of the subject areas specified in paragraph (4) of this subsection, and such progress reports shall be retained by the parent, parents, or guardian of children in the home study program for a period of at least three years.

(d) Any person who operates a private school without complying with the requirements of subsection (b) of this Code section or any person who operates a home study program without complying with the requirements of subsection (c) of this Code section shall be guilty of a misdemeanor and, upon conviction thereof, shall be punished by a fine not to exceed $100.00.

(e) The State Board of Education shall devise, adopt, and make available to local school superintendents, who shall in turn make available to administrators of private schools and parents or guardians with children in home study programs, such printed forms and procedures as may be reasonably necessary to carry out efficiently the reporting provisions of this Code section, but such printed forms and procedures shall not be inconsistent with or exceed the requirements of this Code section.

Georgia Regulations

160-4-8-.04: Child Abuse and Neglect Reporting

(1) Requirements:
(a) Local boards of education shall adopt and implement a policy and procedures on the identification and reporting of child abuse according to the provisions of O.C.G.A. 19-7-5.
(b) All school system personnel who have reasonable cause to believe that any student under 18 years of age has been abused shall report the suspected abuse to the school social worker/visiting teacher or another person designated by the local superintendent to receive such reports.
(c) The school social worker/visiting teacher or other designee who receives reports shall immediately report in turn to the Department of Family and Children Services of the county in which the student lives and shall notify the school system superintendent of all referrals.
(d) All school personnel who have contact with students shall receive training in the identification and reporting of child abuse and neglect with annual updates in the form of memoranda, directives or other written information.

Authority O.C.G.A. § 19-7-5

160-4-8-.01: Student Support Services

(1) Definitions:
(a) Alternative Education Program (AEP): an educational program that serves students who are eligible to remain in the regular classroom but are more likely to succeed in a nontraditional setting such as that provided in an alternative education program, as well as students who are excluded from the regular classroom because of disciplinary reasons.
(b) Counseling: a process where some students receive assistance from professionals who assist them to overcome emotional and social problems or concerns which may interfere with learning.
(c) Guidance: a process of regular assistance that all students receive from parents, teachers, school counselors, and others to assist them in making appropriate educational and career choices.
(d) School Climate Management: systematic plan for addressing the factors that affect school climate including a consistent management style and leadership by the principal, a code of expected behavior, a code of disciplinary responses, a code of ethics for educators, a Student Support Team, delivery of counseling and psychological mental health services, methods to reduce absences and increase attendance, physical health support services, efforts to enlist parent and community support, utilization of volunteers, support by and for the parent teacher organization, a preventive safety plan and a crisis

response plan, staff development, and the maintenance program for the school's physical plant.

(e) School Counseling and Guidance Services: guidance program planning, implementation and evaluation; individual and group counseling; classroom and small group guidance; career and educational development; parent and teacher consultation; and referral.

(f) School Health Services: a process to address medically related health and safety issues and address requests by parents and physicians that the school provide appropriate health procedures to allow students to remain in school and increase opportunities for academic success.

(g) School Psychological Services: psycho-educational evaluation; crisis intervention; case study; consultation to student support teams, parents, teachers, and administrators; behavioral observations and analysis; and psychological counseling.

(h) School Social Work/Visiting Teacher Services: technical assistance on school climate issues; assessment and intervention, including written social histories; individual, group, and family counseling; and networking of appropriate home, school, and community services to address identified student problems.

(i) Student Support Services (SSS): integrated and collaborative programs of school counseling and guidance services, school climate management and student discipline, school health services, school psychology services, alternative education programs, and school social work/visiting teacher services, provided individually or through a team approach, to all students at all grade levels.

(2) Requirements:

(a) Each local school system shall develop a Student Services Plan that prescribes and identifies programs and services that incorporate school climate improvement and management processes.

(b) Each Student Services Plan must minimally include guidelines for the systematic provision of the following components:

    (1) Alternative education programs;
    (2) School psychological services;
    (3) School climate management;
    (4) School counseling and guidance services;
    (5) School health services;
    (6) School social work/visiting teacher services.

(c) The local board of education (LBOE) shall provide for a School Climate Management Process to include improved student behavior and discipline in accordance with state and federal laws and State Board of Education rules regarding the Improved Student Learning Environment and Discipline Act of 1999.

(d) The LBOE shall provide for School Guidance and Counseling Services in accordance with state and federal laws, State Board of Education rules, and department guidelines.

(e) The LBOE shall provide School Social Work/Visiting Teacher Services by promoting home, school, and community cooperation to address the needs of the at-risk student population characterized by poverty, high absenteeism, academic failure, pregnancy, disruptive behavior or other student dysfunctions.

(f) The LBOE shall provide for School Psychological Services sufficient to satisfy federal and state regulations and additional legal obligations incurred through court agreement.
(g) The LBOE shall provide an Alternative Education Program in accordance with state and federal laws, State Board of Education rules, and department guidelines.
(h) The LBOE shall provide for a School Health Nurse Program and must establish policies and procedures regarding a School Health Nurse Program in accordance with state and federal laws.

Authority O.C.G.A. §§ 19-7-5; 20-2-140; 20-2-150; 20-2-151; 20-2-154.1; 20-2-155; 20-2-180; 20-2-182; 20-2-184; 20-2-185; 20-2-186; 20-2-187; 20-2-200; 20-2-201; 20-2-202; 20-2-203; 20-2-240; 20-2-300; 20-2-690; 20-2-693; 20-2- 695; 20-2-696; 20-2-735; 20-2-740; 20-2-741; 20-2-771.2

160-4-8-.05: Guidance Counselors

(1) Definitions:
(a) Counseling: a process where some students receive assistance from professionals who assist them to overcome emotional and social problems or concerns which may interfere with learning.
(b) Guidance: a process of regular assistance that all students receive from parents, teachers, school counselors, and others to assist them in making appropriate educational and career choices.
(c) School Counseling and Guidance Services: guidance, program planning, implementation and evaluation; individual and group counseling; classroom and small group guidance; career and educational development; parent and teacher consultation; and referral.
(2) Requirements:
(a) The local board of education (LBOE) shall provide for school guidance and counseling services in accordance with state and federal laws, State Board of Education rules, and department guidelines by:

(1) Insuring that each school counselor is engaged in counseling or guidance activities, including advising students, parents, or guardians, for a minimum of five of six fulltime segments or the equivalent.
(2) Including the following as duties of the school counselor:

(i) Program design, planning, and leadership:

(I) Develops a written school-based guidance and counseling program.
(II) Implements an individual plan of action.

(ii) Counseling:

(I) Coordinates and implements delivery of counseling services in areas of self-knowledge, educational and occupational exploration, and career planning to facilitate academic achievement.
(II) Schedules time to provide opportunities for various types of counseling.
(III) Counsels learners individually by actively listening, identifying and defining issues, discussing alternative solutions, and formulating a plan of action.
(IV) Adheres to established system policies and procedures in scheduling appointments and obtaining parental permission.
(V) Leads counseling or support groups for learners experiencing similar problems.
(VI) Evaluates effectiveness of group counseling and makes revisions as necessary.

(iii) Guidance and collaboration.

(I) Coordinates with school staff to provide supportive instructional guidance activities that relate to students' self-knowledge, educational and occupational exploration, and career planning to facilitate academic achievement.
(II) Conducts classroom guidance activities related to identified goals and objectives.
(III) Gathers and evaluates data to determine effectiveness of classroom and student comprehension, making revisions when necessary.
(IV) Provides direct/indirect educationally based guidance assistance to learners preparing for test taking.
(V) Provides information to students, parents, teachers, administrators, and, when appropriate, to the community on student test scores.
(VI) Provides information to students and parents on career planning.

(iv) Consultation and coordination.

(I) Consults, as needed or requested, with system/staff, parents, and community about issues and concerns.
(II) Collaborates with school staff in developing a strategy or plan for improving school climate.
(III) Follows up on counseling and consultative referrals.
(IV) Consults with school system in making referrals to community agencies.
(V) Implementation of a comprehensive and developmental guidance and counseling curriculum to assist all students.

(v) Insuring that each school counselor is engaged in other functions for no more than one of the six program segments or the equivalent.

Authority O.C.G.A. § 20-2-182

Chapter 3: First Amendment Freedoms and Religion

State constitutions may guarantee positive rights (e.g., a state right to a publicly funded education) in addition to protecting the negative rights also secured under the U.S. Constitution. State constitutions may further protect negative rights (e.g., rights not to have intrusions by government agents on religious freedoms, free speech, and other fundamental rights) at higher levels than they are protected under the federal constitution. State actions cannot, however, fall below the level of protected rights under the U.S. Constitution.

> *The U.S. Constitution Established a Floor-level for Protected Rights. State Constitutions may, however, protect these Rights at Higher Levels and Provide Additional Rights*

Among state constitutional provisions that may provide greater protections against establishment of religion at the state level are the "Blaine Amendments" found in many state constitutions. Blaine Amendments are named after James Blaine, a member of the U.S. Congress who introduced an amendment to the U.S. Constitution in 1875 that stated:

> No State shall make any law respecting an establishment of religion, or prohibiting the free exercise thereof; and no money raised by taxation in any State for the support of public schools, or derived from any public fund therefor, nor any public lands devoted thereto, shall ever be under the control of any religious sect; nor shall any money so raised or lands so devoted be divided between religious sects or denominations.

Blaine's proposed amendment passed overwhelmingly in the U.S. House of Representatives. In the U.S. Senate, however, the amendment fell four votes short of the two-thirds majority required by Article V of the U.S. Constitution for a successful constitutional amendment.

Nearly a century and a half later Blaine Amendments remain controversial, with some condemning them as remnants of anti-Catholic religious bigotry, and others praising them as protectors of church-state separation and religious liberty. Notwithstanding the failure at the federal level, supporters of these amendments were far more successful at the state level. Over two-thirds of the states adopted Blaine Amendments into their state constitutions.

The exact text of the state amendments varies. But what state-level Blaine Amendments have in common is a prohibition against using public tax dollars for private religious purposes. Exactly what is prohibited, however, depends on judicial interpretations of these amendments by state courts. State courts are free to interpret their state constitution's religion clauses in any otherwise lawful manner they elect. Nonetheless, many state courts continue to closely follow the federal models for interpreting establishment and free exercise related provisions in their constitutions. Summaries of these federal models are provided below:

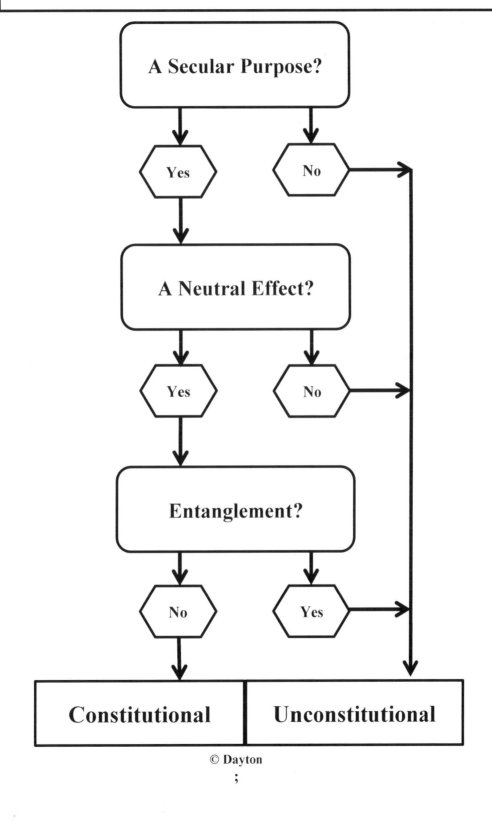

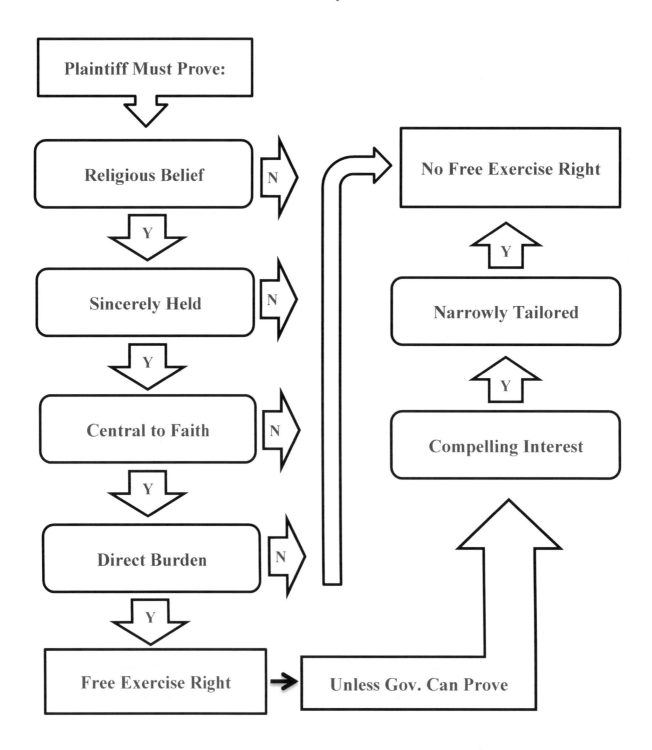

Selected Georgia Laws

Georgia Constitution

Article I, Section II

Paragraph III: Freedom of conscience. Each person has the natural and inalienable right to worship God, each according to the dictates of that person's own conscience; and no human authority should, in any case, control or interfere with such right of conscience.

Paragraph IV: Religious opinions; freedom of religion. No inhabitant of this state shall be molested in person or property or be prohibited from holding any public office or trust on account of religious opinions; but the right of freedom of religion shall not be so construed as to excuse acts of licentiousness or justify practices inconsistent with the peace and safety of the state.

Article I, Section II ("Blaine Amendment")

Paragraph VII: Separation of church and state. No money shall ever be taken from the public treasury, directly or indirectly, in aid of any church, sect, cult, or religious denomination or of any sectarian institution.

Georgia Statutes

§ 20-2-1050 Moment of Silence in Public Schools

(a) In each public school classroom, the teacher in charge shall, at the opening of school upon every school day, conduct a brief period of quiet reflection for not more than 60 seconds with the participation of all the pupils therein assembled.
(b) The moment of quiet reflection authorized by subsection (a) of this Code section is not intended to be and shall not be conducted as a religious service or exercise but shall be considered as an opportunity for a moment of silent reflection on the anticipated activities of the day.
(c) The provisions of subsections (a) and (b) of this Code section shall not prevent student initiated voluntary school prayers at schools or school related events which are nonsectarian and nonproselytizing in nature.

§ 20-2-1051 Freedom of Belief Protected

No teacher, principal, school board, or any other person may require or prescribe any particular method or manner in which a child shall participate in any period of silent prayer or meditation, but each child shall be absolutely free to participate therein or not, in such manner or way as such child shall personally desire, consistent with his or her beliefs.

§ 20-2-319: Prayers Prior to Athletic Events at Private Schools

(a) No law or regulation of this state shall prohibit or be construed as prohibiting or discouraging a private school from conducting a prayer prior to an athletic event held on the campus of the private school.

(b) No athletic team from any public school in this state shall be prohibited by state law or regulation from participating in an athletic event held on the campus of a private school in this state for the reason that the private school conducts a prayer prior to such athletic event.

(c) No school which receives funding under this article shall participate in, sponsor, or provide coaching staff for interscholastic sports events which are conducted under the authority of, conducted under the rules of, or scheduled by any athletic association which prohibits or discourages a private school from conducting a prayer prior to an athletic event held on the campus of the private school.

(d) As used in this Code section, the term "athletic association" means any association of schools or any other similar organization which acts as an organizing, sanctioning, scheduling, or rule-making body for interscholastic athletic events in which public schools in this state participate.

§ 20-2-148: Course in the History and Literature of the Old and New Testaments

(a) All public schools with grade nine or above may make available to eligible students in grades nine through 12 an elective course in the History and Literature of the Old Testament Era and an elective course in the History and Literature of the New Testament Era. The purpose of such courses shall be to accommodate the rights and desires of those teachers and students who wish to teach and study the Old and New Testaments and to familiarize students with the contents of the Old and New Testaments, the history recorded by the Old and New Testaments, the literary style and structure of the Old and New Testaments, the customs and cultures of the peoples and societies recorded in the Old and New Testaments, and the influence of the Old and New Testaments upon law, history, government, literature, art, music, customs, morals, values, and culture.

(b)(1) No later than February 1, 2007, the State Board of Education shall adopt a curriculum for each course, including objectives, reading materials, and lesson plans, which has been prepared in accordance with the requirements of this subsection.

(2) The book or collection of books commonly known as the Old Testament shall be the basic text for the course in the History and Literature of the Old Testament Era, and the book or collection of books commonly known as the New Testament shall be the basic text for the course in the History and Literature of the New Testament Era. In addition, students may be assigned a range of reading materials for the courses, including selections from secular historical and cultural works and selections from other religious and cultural traditions. The courses shall familiarize students with the customs and cultures of the times and places referred to in the Old and New Testaments. The courses shall familiarize the students with the methods and tools of writing at the times the Old and New Testament books were written, the means by which they were preserved, the languages in which they were written and into which they were translated, and the historical and cultural events which led to the translation of the Old and New Testaments

into the English language. The local board of education may recommend which version of the Old or New Testament may be used in the course; provided, however, that the teacher of the course shall not be required to adopt that recommendation but may use the recommended version or another version. No student shall be required to use one version as the sole text of the Old or New Testament. If a student desires to use as the basic text a different version of the Old or New Testament from that chosen by the local board of education or teacher, he or she shall be permitted to do so.

(3) The courses provided for in this Code section shall:

(A) Be taught in an objective and non-devotional manner with no attempt made to indoctrinate students as to either the truth or falsity of the biblical materials or texts from other religious or cultural traditions;

(B) Not include teaching of religious doctrine or sectarian interpretation of the Bible or of texts from other religious or cultural traditions; and

(C) Not disparage or encourage a commitment to a set of religious beliefs.

(c) The provisions of this chapter relating to personnel employed by local units of administration, including without limitation certification requirements, employment, and supervision, shall apply to persons who teach the courses provided for in this Code section. In addition, no person shall be assigned to teach such courses based in whole or in part on any religious test, profession of faith or lack thereof, prior or present religious affiliation or lack of affiliation, or criteria involving particular beliefs or lack thereof about the Bible. Except for these requirements, the qualifications and training of teachers shall be determined by the local boards of education.

(d) On and after July 1, 2007, for the purpose of earning Carnegie unit curriculum credits at the high school level, satisfactory completion of the course in the History and Literature of the Old Testament Era shall be accepted by the State Board of Education for one-half unit of elective credit, and satisfactory completion of the course in the History and Literature of the New Testament Era shall be accepted by the State Board of Education for one-half unit of elective credit; provided, however, that such courses are taught in strict compliance with the requirements of this Code section.

(e) A local board of education may make such arrangements for monitoring the content and teaching of the course in the History and Literature of the Old Testament Era and the course in the History and Literature of the New Testament Era as it deems appropriate.

(f) Nothing in this Code section shall be construed to limit the authority of a local board of education to offer courses regarding the Old Testament or the New Testament that are not in compliance with this Code section; provided, however, that no state funds distributed pursuant to this article shall be expended in connection with such a course that does not meet the requirements of this Code section.

(g) Nothing in this Code section shall be construed to prohibit local boards of education from offering elective courses based upon the books of other religions or societies. In determining whether to offer such courses, the local board may consider various factors including, but not limited to, student and parent demand for such courses and the impact such books have had upon history and culture.

§ 20-2-771: Immunization Required; Medical or Religious Exemption

(a) As used in this Code section, the term:

(1) "Certificate of immunization" means certification by a physician licensed under the laws of this state or by an appropriate official of a local board of health, on a form provided by the Department of Public Health, that a named person has been immunized in accordance with the applicable rules and regulations of the Department of Public Health.
(2) "Facility" means any public or private day-care center or nursery intended for the care, supervision, or instruction of children.
(3) "Responsible official" means a county school superintendent, a school principal, or a chief operating officer of a school or facility.
(4) "School" means any public or private educational program or institution instructing children at any level or levels, kindergarten through twelfth grade, or children of ages five through 19 if grade divisions are not used.

(b) No child shall be admitted to or attend any school or facility in this state unless the child shall first have submitted a certificate of immunization to the responsible official of the school or facility. The responsible official of any school or facility may grant a 30 calendar day waiver of the certification requirement for a justified reason. The waiver may be extended from the date of first admittance or of first attendance, whichever is earlier, for up to 90 calendar days provided documentation is on file at the school or facility from the local health department or a physician specifying that an immunization sequence has been started and that this immunization time schedule can be completed within the 90 day waiver period, provided confirmation is received during the waiver period from the health department or physician that immunizations are being received as scheduled, and provided the student under waiver is a transfer student, who is defined as a student who moves from an out-of-state school system to a Georgia school system, or a student entering kindergarten or first grade from out of state. The waiver may not be extended beyond 90 calendar days; and upon expiration of the waiver, the child shall not be admitted to or be permitted to attend the school or facility unless the child submits a certificate of immunization.

(c) The Department of Public Health shall promulgate rules and regulations specifying those diseases against which immunization is required and the standards for such immunizations. The school or facility shall maintain on file the certificates of immunization for all children attending the school or facility. All facilities shall file a report annually with the Department of Public Health. The report shall be filed on forms prepared by the Department of Public Health and shall state the number of children attending the school or facility, the number of children who did not submit certificates of immunization within the waiver period, and the number of children who are exempted from the certification requirement for medical or religious reasons.

(d) If, after examination by the local board of health or any physician licensed under the laws of this state or of any other state having comparable laws governing the licensure of physicians, any child to whom this Code section applies is found to have any physical disability which may make vaccination undesirable, a certificate to that effect issued by the local board of health or such physician licensed under the laws of this or such other state may be accepted in lieu of a certificate of immunization and shall exempt the child from the requirement of obtaining a certificate of immunization until the disability is relieved.

(e) This Code section shall not apply to a child whose parent or legal guardian objects to immunization of the child on the grounds that the immunization conflicts with the religious beliefs of the parent or guardian; however, the immunization may be required in cases when such disease is in epidemic stages. For a child to be exempt from immunization on religious grounds, the parent or guardian must first furnish the responsible official of the school or facility an affidavit in which the parent or guardian swears or affirms that the immunization required conflicts with the religious beliefs of the parent or guardian.

(f) During an epidemic or a threatened epidemic of any disease preventable by an immunization required by the Department of Public Health, children who have not been immunized may be excluded from the school or facility until (1) they are immunized against the disease, unless they present valid evidence of prior disease, or (2) the epidemic or threat no longer constitutes a significant public health danger . . .

(h) Any responsible official permitting any child to remain in a school or facility in violation of this Code section, and any parent or guardian who intentionally does not comply with this Code section, shall be guilty of a misdemeanor and, upon conviction thereof, shall be punished by a fine of not more than $100.00 or by imprisonment for not more than 12 months. The Department of Public Health may adopt rules and regulations for the enforcement of this Code section. The Department of Public Health and the local board of health, or either of them, may institute a civil action in the superior court of the county in which the defendant resides for injunctive relief to prevent a threatened or continuing violation of any provision of this Code section.

Chapter 4: First Amendment Freedoms and Speech

Free speech is the essential means through which citizens must protect all other rights. It is a necessary tool for perpetuating and advancing democracy and the Rule of Law. Public schools serve an important role in teaching the lessons of the First Amendment, citizenship, and democracy. But if public schools are to act as the functional nurseries of an enduring democracy, students' free speech rights must be protected, respected, and encouraged so that students may mature into citizens well prepared to actively discuss ideas; ask necessary questions; speak out on important public matters; vote wisely; and participate fully in a democratic society.

Education, free speech, civility, and civic courage are the four pillars of democracy. Totalitarian regimes are only possible when the people are kept ignorant, silenced, divided, and fearful of speaking up and making their own decisions. A closed culture of retaliation, fear, and silence is a breeding ground for corruption. The broad protection of free speech is the best means of shining the light of truth into every corner of common society to assure honesty and accountability. As Justice Brandeis said: "Sunlight is the best disinfectant."

To protect essential First Amendment rights, the general rule under the free speech provisions is that government cannot limit individual speech and expression of ideas. The scope of potential expression protected by the First Amendment is as broad as the universe of human thought and human ability to express those thoughts. At the core of these rights are protections for religious and political speech. Philosophical, satirical, commercial, and an infinite variety of other types of expression are also protected. However, in the potential universe of protected expression speech that is illegal, obscene, defaming, or in a non-public forum does not receive First Amendment protection.

In summary, while the general rule under the First Amendment is that speech is protected, the scope of protection necessarily involves balancing the rights of the individual with the legitimate interests of the public. Accordingly, the Court recognizes some special exceptions to general First Amendment protections for free speech. Government officials can limit speech if it is:

    a) Illegal or subversive speech, which can be controlled if it is:

        i) Directed towards inciting illegal or subversive action; and is
        ii) Likely to incite imminent lawless action (includes "fighting words" and "yelling fire in crowded theatre").

    b) Obscene.
    c) Defamatory.
    d) Commercial speech.
    e) Speech in a non-public forum: Regulations must be reasonable in light of the purposes of the forum.

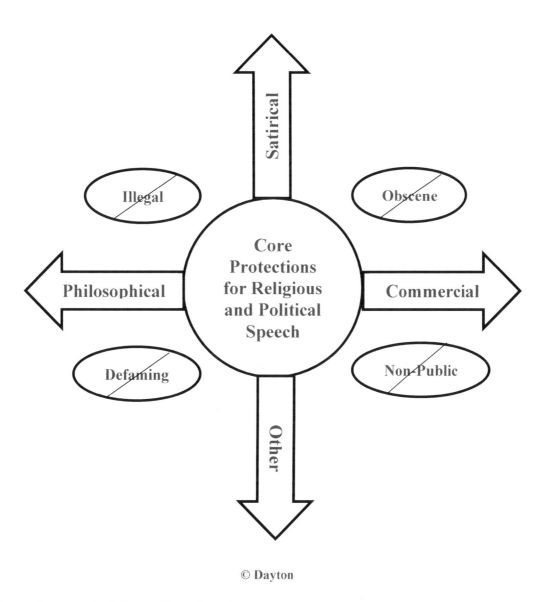

First Amendment principles re: Free Speech:

- First Amendment protections are potentially as broad as the universe of human thought and human ability to express those thoughts.
- At the core these protections are protections for religious and political speech.
- Philosophical, satirical, commercial, and an infinite variety of other types of expression are also protected, balancing individual rights and public needs.
- However, in the potential universe of protected expression speech that is illegal, obscene, defaming, or in a non-public forum does not receive First Amendment protection.

Student Speech Rights

In *Tinker v. Des Moines*, 393 U.S. 503 (1969), the Court declared:

> It can hardly be argued that either students or teachers shed their constitutional rights to freedom of speech or expression at the schoolhouse gate . . . In our system, state-operated schools may not be enclaves of totalitarianism. School officials do not possess absolute authority over their students. Students in school as well as out of school are "persons" under our Constitution. They are possessed of fundamental rights which the State must respect, just as they themselves must respect their obligations to the State. In our system, students may not be regarded as closed-circuit recipients of only that which the State chooses to communicate. They may not be confined to the expression of those sentiments that are officially approved. In the absence of a specific showing of constitutionally valid reasons to regulate their speech, students are entitled to freedom of expression of their views.

In harmonizing constitutional ideals with concrete realities the Court must strike a proper balance between essential individual freedoms and the legitimate needs of the public. Democracy is incompatible with both chaos and oppression. The school culture must be both free and orderly; both candid and civil. The Court has consistently recognized the authority and obligation of school officials to protect order and discipline in schools, while appropriately respecting free speech rights.

Concerning free speech in public schools the Court has distinguished between two different types of student expression: a) Individual student expression; and b) Public school sponsored student expression:

> a) *Individual student expression* is speech not sponsored, controlled, or reasonably perceived as attributable to the school. The *Tinker* standard governs individual student speech. School officials must show through evidence of facts and circumstances that student expression would "materially and substantially interfere with the requirements of appropriate discipline in the operation of the school." Avoiding minor disruptions, discomforts, and unpleasantness are not sufficient justifications to limit individual expression.

> b) *School sponsored expression* (e.g., school newspapers, forums, performances, etc.) that are sponsored, controlled, or reasonably perceived as attributable to the school. The *Fraser* and *Hazelwood* decisions govern school sponsored speech. School officials have wide discretion to control content where the expression is sponsored by the school. Limitations can be based on any legitimate educational rationale (e.g., age appropriateness; fit with the educational mission; etc.).

Student Speech: *Tinker* & *Fraser/Hazelwood* Tests

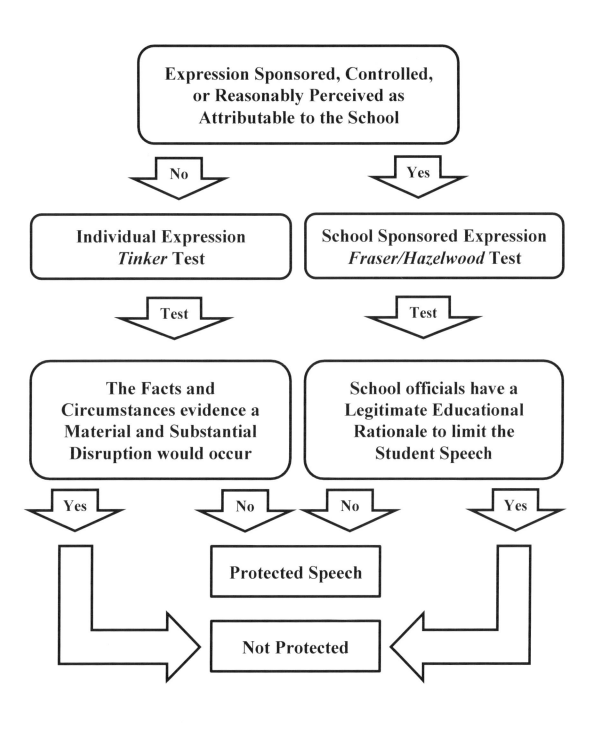

© Dayton

Employee Speech Rights

Generally, public employees have the same free speech rights as all citizens. If public school officials wish to sanction speech by school employees, including dismissal or other employment sanctions, school officials must be prepared to show that the speech negatively impacted the employment relationship, and that the speech was unprotected in the context. The *Pickering* test is used to distinguish between protected and unprotected speech by public employees:

> The *Pickering* Test: To determine whether speech is protected, courts generally balance the employee's speech rights against the employer's legitimate interests in efficient operation of the public institution. Questions considered in this balance include:
>
> 1) *Was the speech related to a legitimate matter of public concern?* Speech regarding legitimate public concerns generally receives First Amendment protection.
>
> 2) *Was the speech true?* True statements receive more protection than false statements.
>
>> Note: Even if the speech is true, courts will also consider public officials' legitimate needs for: 1) Regular close contact and a working relationship of loyalty and trust with the speaker; 2) Appropriate office discipline; and 3) Harmony among co-workers.
>
> 3) *If false, was the false statement merely negligently made by the public employee?* False statements made only negligently may still receive First Amendment protection.

PURPOSELY
KNOWINGLY
RECKLESSLY
-----*Pickering Line*-----
NEGLIGENTLY

> Note: Courts will also consider whether the false statements interfere with the performance of duties or the regular operations of the institution.

In "mixed motive" cases (there is both a legitimate basis for termination and a controversy over free speech) if a teacher merits termination independent of a subsequent free speech controversy, school officials do not have to continue the employment of an otherwise unfit teacher.

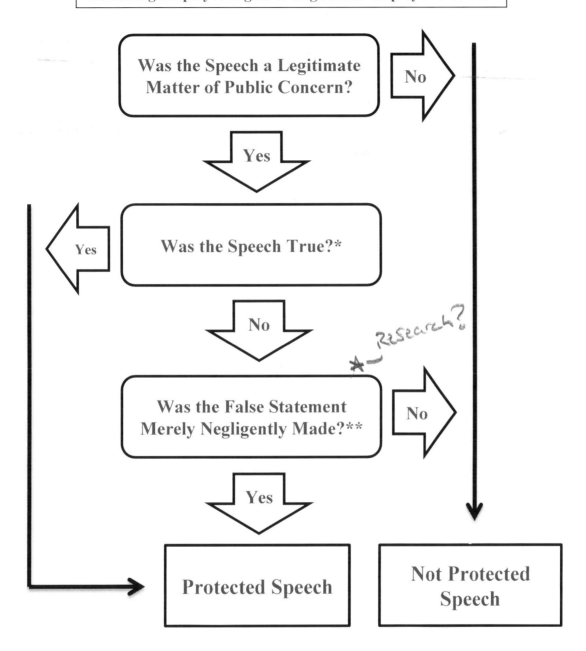

* *N.B*: Even if the speech is true, courts will also consider public officials' legitimate needs for: 1) Regular close contact and a working relationship of loyalty and trust with the speaker; 2) Appropriate office discipline; and 3) Harmony among co-workers.
** *N.B*: Courts will also consider whether the false statements interfere with the performance of duties or the regular operations of the institution.

© Dayton

Lawful Limitations on Speech

The Court recognizes some universal exceptions to First Amendment protections, and these limitations are always available to government officials:

a) Government officials can always apply reasonable time, place, and manner (TPM) restrictions on speech. TPM restrictions are held reasonable if they are:
    i) Content neutral;
    ii) Narrowly tailored to serve a significant governmental interest; and
    iii) Leave open an adequate alternative channel of communication.
b) Government officials can always limit free speech by establishing a compelling governmental interest for the intrusion on freedom of expression, and that no less restrictive alternative exists.

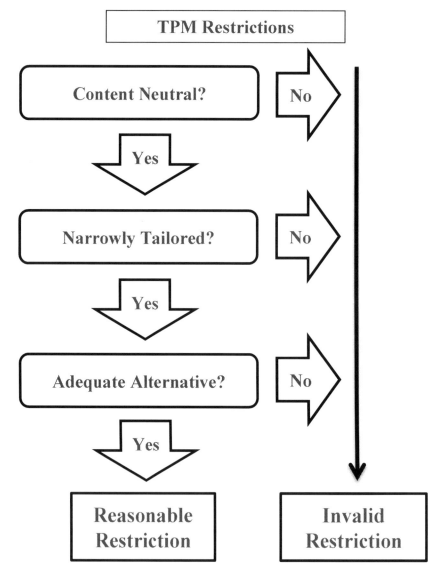

© Dayton

Selected Georgia Laws

Georgia Constitution

Article I, Section I

Paragraph V: Freedom of speech and of the press guaranteed. No law shall be passed to curtail or restrain the freedom of speech or of the press. Every person may speak, write, and publish sentiments on all subjects but shall be responsible for the abuse of that liberty.

Paragraph VI: Libel. In all civil or criminal actions for libel, the truth may be given in evidence; and, if it shall appear to the trier of fact that the matter charged as libelous is true, the party shall be discharged.

Paragraph IX: Right to assemble and petition. The people have the right to assemble peaceably for their common good and to apply by petition or remonstrance to those vested with the powers of government for redress of grievances.

Georgia Statutes

§ 20-2-705: Clubs and Organizations; Parental Permission

(a) As used in this Code section, the term:

(1) "Clubs and organizations" means clubs and organizations comprised of students who wish to organize and meet for common goals, objectives, or purposes and which is directly under the sponsorship, direction, and control of the school. This term shall include any activities reasonably related to such clubs and organizations, but shall not include competitive interscholastic activities or events.
(2) "Competitive interscholastic activity" means functions held under the auspices or sponsorship of a school that involves its students in competition between individuals or groups representing two or more schools. This term shall include cheerleading, band, and chorus.

(b) Each local board of education shall include in the student code of conduct distributed annually at the beginning of each school year pursuant to Code Section 20-2-736 information regarding school clubs and organizations. Such information shall include without limitation the name of the club or organization, mission or purpose of the club or organization, name of the club's or organization's faculty advisor, and a description of past or planned activities. On the form included in the student code of conduct, as required in Code Section 20-2-751.5, the local board of education shall provide an area for a parent or legal guardian to decline permission for his or her student to participate in a club or organization designated by him or her.

(c) For clubs or organizations started during the school year, the local board of education shall require written permission from a parent or guardian prior to a student's participation.

Chapter 5: Search and Seizure

The Fourth Amendment to the U.S. Constitution was intended to protect against abuses of government power involving unreasonable searches and seizure. The Fourth Amendment states:

> The right of the people to be secure in their persons, houses, papers, and effects, against unreasonable searches and seizures, shall not be violated, and no Warrants shall issue, but upon probable cause, supported by Oath or affirmation, and particularly describing the place to be searched, and the persons or things to be seized.

State constitutions generally include similar provisions protecting against unreasonable searches and seizures. State provisions must at least protect individual rights at the level protected by federal law. State constitutions may, however, provide greater protections against unreasonable searches and seizures under state law.

The Core Right of Privacy and other Associated Fourth Amendment Rights

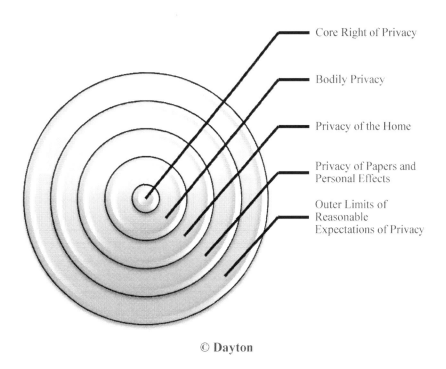

© Dayton

Protections against unreasonable searches only apply when there is a reasonable expectation of privacy. Whenever there is a reasonable expectation of privacy, the Fourth Amendment and similar state constitutional provisions protect against unreasonable intrusions by government agents. Outside of that reasonable expectation of privacy, however, there is no protection. Individuals do not, for example, have any reasonable expectation of privacy in anything they place in plain view, leave unsupervised or abandoned in public areas, or otherwise fail to maintain reasonable privacy or control over.

To protect public safety and order government agents must sometimes conduct searches for evidence of prohibited activity or contraband, and seize property or persons. The command of the Fourth Amendment and similar state constitutional provisions is that these searches and seizures must be reasonable under the totality of the circumstances, appropriately balancing the rights of individuals with legitimate governmental needs.

Prior to conducting a search the government is generally required to prove to a reviewing magistrate that there is probable cause for the search:

Elements of Proof Leading to Probable Cause

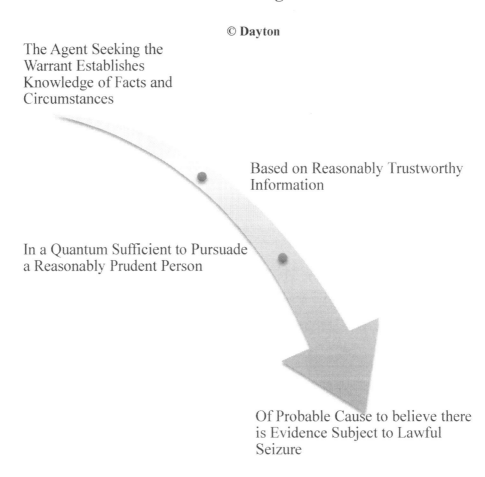

Exceptions to these general requirements include:

1) Searches incident to arrest;
2) Emergency situations;
3) Searches by consent;
4) International border searches; and
5) Seizure of items in plain view.

Establishing probable cause requires a relatively high burden of proof. In *New Jersey v. T.L.O.*, 469 U.S. 325 (1985), however, the Court held that because of the special context of public schools only "reasonable suspicion" of a violation of the law or school rules was required to conduct a reasonable search in schools, not the higher standard of probable cause:

Elements of Proof Leading to Reasonable Suspicion under *T.L.O.*

© Dayton

School Officials Establish the Challenged Search was Justified in its Inception, with Reasonable Grounds to Believe that the Search would Produce Evidence of Wrongdoing

School Officials Establish that the Search was Reasonably Related in Scope to the Objectives of the Search, and not Excessively Instrusive in light of the Age and Sex of the Student and the Nature of the Infraction

School Officials had Reasonable Suspicion of a Violation of the Law or School Rules Suficient to Justify the Search by School Officials as Reasonable under the Fourth Amendment

In summary, the federal and state constitutions protect reasonable expectations of individual privacy from unwarranted governmental intrusions, and prohibit unreasonable searches and seizures by government officials. To justify a challenged search, government officials must establish sufficient cause for the search (i.e. probable cause or reasonable suspicion). Courts evaluate these claims by weighing the individual's reasonable expectation of privacy under the circumstances against the government's legitimate need to search. Police searches are subject to the higher standard of "probable cause." But public school officials generally need only show that their searches of students were based on the lower standard of "reasonable suspicion" defined by the *T.L.O.* test. To be reasonable under the *T.L.O.* test the search must be:

1) *Justified in its inception*: The school agent had reasonable grounds to believe that a search would produce evidence of wrong doing (i.e., illegal activity or a breach of school rules).
2) *Reasonably related in scope to the objectives of the search and not excessively intrusive in light of the*:

   a) Age of the student
   b) Sex of the student
   c) Nature of the infraction

In all searches, school officials should carefully weigh the intrusiveness of the search against the legitimate need for the search. If the intrusiveness of the search outweighs the need for the search, the search is unreasonable and therefore unlawful.

Strip Searches of Students

Strip searches of children should be strongly avoided. As the U.S. Supreme Court noted in *Safford v. Redding*, 557 U.S. 364 (2009), strip searches of children are recognized as a distinct category of searches generally disfavored by courts. These highly intrusive searches require additional elements of proof beyond the *T.L.O.* test. For a strip search to satisfy the requirements of the second prong of the *T.L.O.* test (that the search be reasonably related in scope to the objectives of the search) the *Redding* test further requires that strip searches must be based on:

1) A reasonable suspicion of danger and;
2) A reasonable basis for believing that the danger is hidden in an intimate area.

A genuine need for urgency in preventing the danger (e.g., seizing an imminently dangerous weapon; explosives; etc.) would also bolster the case for an intrusive search by school officials. Strip searches falling short of these standards may result not only in institutional liability, but also individual liability for public school officials conducting strip searches contrary to well established law after *T.L.O.* and *Redding*.

Strip searches are those searches that go beyond a search of personal belongings and outer clothing to reveal intimate garments and private bodily areas. In *Redding* the Court noted that if a strip search by school officials is ever lawful it would have to satisfy the *T.L.O.* test that "the search as actually conducted be reasonably related in scope to the circumstances which justified the interference in the first place" and "not excessively intrusive in light of the age and sex of the student and the nature of the infraction."

Theoretically then, a strip search of a very young student may be less intrusive than the search of a post-pubescent student; a search by a same-sex school official may be less intrusive than an opposite sex search; and a search for dangerous weapons, explosives, or hazardous drugs may provide greater license to search than searches for more trivial items.

That said, in *Redding* the Court was very clear that strip searches are highly disfavored, noting that strip searches are "so degrading that a number of communities have decided that strip searches in schools are never reasonable and have banned them no matter what the facts may be." Strip searches should only be resorted to in extraordinary circumstances and only where there is a reasonable suspicion of danger; and a reasonable basis for believing the danger is hidden in an intimate area.

School Locker Searches

School lockers are school property owned by the school and controlled by school officials. Unless a right of privacy is established by state law, policy, or local practice, there is generally no reasonable expectation of privacy in property owned and controlled by the school. Further, school officials commonly provide students with official notice through student handbooks or signed consent forms that school lockers are the property of the school, and that there is therefore no reasonable expectation of privacy in items that students choose to place in school lockers.

School officials may routinely examine the contents of school lockers for custodial, safety, or other legitimate purposes. Even where a reasonable expectation of privacy in the locker is recognized, under *T.L.O.*, a search by school officials would only require reasonable suspicion of a violation of the law or a school rule. Contraband items found in the process of a lawful inspection of the locker may be seized and used as evidence in school disciplinary and law enforcement proceedings.

Metal Detectors and Administrative Searches

Government searches of individuals generally require: 1) Individualized suspicion; and 2) Sufficient cause to justify the search under the circumstances. Courts have, however, recognized legitimate "administrative searches" as an exception to these general rules. To qualify as an administrative search, the search must be:

1) Aimed at a general danger (e.g., keeping weapons out of public gathering areas); and
2) Nonintrusive.

Metal detectors may be used for administrative searches, and when properly administered, the detectors may help prevent general dangers and do so in a nonintrusive manner.

Example Use of a Door-Frame Style Metal Detector in an Administrative Search:

• Used in response to a credible general danger in the area.
• Not used to search for evidence of individual misconduct.
• Strategically placed so that all persons choosing to enter must pass through the detector.
• Persons are notified in advance to remove metal objects.
• There are no further intrusions on individuals unless the detector "alerts" or an individual's conduct independently warrants further action.

Responding to an "Alert" by the Metal Detector:

• Detector alerts are common and mostly benign (e.g., metal belt buckles; steel shanks in shoes; keys; coins; medical implants; etc.). Nonetheless, have a lawful emergency

response plan prepared and practiced in the event of an imminent danger (e.g., drawing or use of a weapon by a suspect).
- Observe the individual's reaction to the alert and his or her subsequent demeanor.
- If there is no cause for immediate intervention, the individual is simply asked to pass through the detector again to confirm the alert. Otherwise no bodily contact or unnecessary intrusions or delays are imposed.
- After a confirmed alert, a hand-held detector is used to pin-point the metal object.
- A properly trained school official asks appropriate questions about the detected object.
- A further lawful search may occur if warranted by the facts and circumstances.
- Assure that back-up security can be quickly contacted in the event of an emergency.

Under the Fourth Amendment suspicionless administrative searches are limited to what is reasonably necessary to guard against an immediate general danger (e.g., nonintrusive screening for weapons, explosives, etc., in a public gathering area; not an intrusive search for marijuana, etc.). A search exceeding the lawful limits of an administrative search must be justified as an individual suspicion-based search, or fall within a recognized exception under the Fourth Amendment (e.g., a search by consent, etc.)

After a metal detector alert is confirmed, any more intrusive follow-up search of an individual student by public school officials must comply with the *T.L.O.* test, and the *Redding* test (when applicable). Metal detector alerts may, however, serve as key elements in establishing a lawful basis for a follow-up search, supplemented with other relevant factors showing sufficient reason for the search under the totality of the circumstances (e.g., the metal detector alerted; the alert was confirmed; a hand-held detector also confirmed the presence of a metal object; the shape and location of the object was consistent with a concealed weapon; the suspect's explanation was not credible; the demeanor of the suspect indicated deception and extreme nervous tension; etc.). Adequately document any searches exceeding the scope of an administrative search including all relevant facts and circumstances that made the search reasonable under the totality of the circumstances. Until the law is clarified, assume that the standard for searches of non-student adults and all searches involving law enforcement officers is probable cause.

Administrative searches cannot be a pretext for unlawful blanket searches or "fishing expeditions" aimed at finding general individual violations of the law or school rules. The focus must remain on deterring the presence of serious common dangers such as weapons. Further, metal detectors should not be used arbitrarily. The use of metal detectors should be in response to a demonstrable legitimate need. School officials may wish to make factual findings documenting a need to protect a common area (e.g., prior instances of weapons in the area); adopt a lawful policy for the use of metal detectors; and assure that assigned personnel are adequately trained in the lawful, non-discriminatory application of the policy.

In summary, to qualify as an administrative search the genuine purpose cannot be to find non-dangerous individual misconduct. The purpose must be a nonintrusive means of preventing a serious common danger (e.g., preventing anyone from bringing a dangerous weapon into the area). However, contraband found in the process of a lawful administrative search may be seized and used as evidence in subsequent school disciplinary and law enforcement proceedings.

Security Cameras

Conduct in plain view of the public is not within any reasonable expectation of privacy protected under the Fourth Amendment or similar state provisions. Government officials, including school officials, can place security cameras in public areas to promote public safety, security, and to record evidence of misconduct. Cameras should not, however, be placed in areas in which there may be a legitimate expectation of privacy such as restrooms, showering and changing areas, etc. Other more private and appropriate means of supervision and security may be used in these areas.

In addition to the use of security cameras in school entrances, hallways, cafeterias, and other common areas, security cameras are increasingly being used on school buses. Uses on buses include supervision and discipline of students on the bus, and also cameras aimed at vehicles near the bus. Bus cameras aimed at surrounding traffic are used to document evidence of dangerous illegal passing of the school bus while stopped and children are crossing the road, and to generally deter unsafe driving that endangers students. Public streets are public areas, and there is generally no reasonable expectation of privacy concerning conduct in public areas.

Electronic Privacy

There is generally a legitimate expectation of privacy in the contents of personal electronic devices. The contents stored in individuals' personal electronic devices are the modern electronic equivalents of their "papers, and effects" protected under the Fourth Amendment and similar state laws. These electronic files receive the same legal protections accorded to hard copies of private documents.

While the contents of electronic devices may be protected, consistent with state law and local policy school officials may lawfully prohibit students from having or using cell phones or other electronic devises in school. If a cell phone or other device is lawfully confiscate during school hours, however, that does not grant school officials a legal license to go on a "fishing expedition" through private electronic devices.

School officials may only search the contents of students' personal electronic devices if there is sufficient justification to do so under the guidelines established in *T.L.O.* The scope of the search cannot exceed the parameters of the justification for the search. If there is only reasonable suspicion for searching recent text messages, for example, older saved messages or stored photos should not be searched. If there is no valid cause to search the electronic device, the device should be secured and returned to the student or parent consistent with school policy.

Materials that students or teachers post on-line, however, are not protected by any reasonable expectation of privacy. To legitimately claim any reasonable expectation of privacy, the individual's actions must be consistent with the maintenance of privacy. By posting materials on-line and available to the general public, any reasonable expectation of privacy is waived, and school officials may search these materials without violating the Fourth Amendment. Further, any reasonable expectation of privacy is limited to private electronic devices. There is no reasonable expectation of privacy when using public school computers, school e-mail, or other school owned and controlled electronic devices and systems.

Dog Searches

The U.S. Supreme Court has not yet directly addressed the legality of dog searches in public schools, and lower courts have issued conflicting opinions. The Court has, however, addressed dog searches in other contexts. By viewing these cases in conjunction with the Court's articulated Fourth Amendment standards in public schools, some general principles can be reasonably deduced in this still evolving area of the law:

General Principles Governing Dog Searches:

• Anything search dogs can smell in the open air of public areas falls under the "plain view" doctrine; no search was involved; the Fourth Amendment is inapplicable.
• Search dogs should not be allowed to poke and jab their noses into students.
• Search dogs should remain a reasonable distance from students.
• Individuals should not be required to submit to very close smelling of their person by search dogs.
• Individuals should not be detained for an unreasonable time.
• A search using dogs must not be administered in a way that is unreasonable, frightening, or embarrassing to students or other persons.

If the search dog "alerts" to an individual this action by a trained canine may serve as the basis for the individual suspicion and cause necessary for a further lawful search. The reasonableness of the subsequent search is determined by balancing the intrusiveness of the search against the government's legitimate justification for the search under the totality of the circumstances.

To help assure that any searches involving search dogs are lawful under the Fourth Amendment, school officials should:

• Be prepared to explain why search dogs were necessary under the circumstances.
• Searches should be aimed at protecting the health and safety of students.
• Plan adequately and appropriately prior to initiating dog searches.
•Take steps to minimize the intrusiveness of the searches as much as is practicable under the circumstances.
• The search should be conducted by well trained and tested dogs and professional handlers.

Searches of School Employees

Like many other issues under the Fourth Amendment, the law governing searches of school employees remains unsettled. Some argue that the *T.L.O.* standard should apply to all school searches, even those of adult school employees. Others argue that the rules concerning private employers should apply when the government is merely acting as an employer and not with police powers. And yet others argue that government searches of adults with adult consequences should be subject to the general standard of probable cause under the Fourth Amendment. The Court addressed this issue in *O'Connor v. Ortega*, 480 U.S. 709 (1987), but in a 5-4 decision that produced no majority opinion, the standard of law remained unsettled. The Court again failed to settle this issue in *City of Ontario v. Quon*, 560 U.S. 746 (2010).

Nonetheless, many lower courts have applied Justice O'Connor's plurality opinion standard in *Ortega*, holding that when the government conducts a search in its capacity as employer the relevant standard is whether that intrusion on the privacy of the employee is one that a reasonable employer might follow in the ordinary conduct of business, or whether it is unreasonable in the context. Others suggest that until the law is more clearly settled in this area, following the higher standard of probable cause is a safer practice.

What is currently clear is that a search of a government employee (including their private papers and effects) by a government supervisor or other government agent is in fact a search within the protections of the Fourth Amendment. It is the standard of proof required to justify these searches that remains unsettled. When the law remains uncertain, complying with the higher standard of law is the safest option, as you cannot lose a lawsuit by providing more constitutional protection than was required. For this reason, school officials may choose to assume that the standard of law for searches of adult employees is probable cause until this issue is finally resolved by the U.S. Supreme Court. It is also clear that there is no reasonable expectation of privacy in items left in plain view in the work place, or in communications sent through the school district's publicly controlled e-mail system or other school controlled media.

The Court has also recognized that "operational realities" may reduce or remove any reasonable expectation of privacy in certain circumstances. For example, there is a lower reasonable expectation of privacy in an office or desk that is shared, open, and commonly used by other employees, than in an office or desk that is assigned solely to the employee, locked, or otherwise objectively regarded as privately used. The scope of the expectation of privacy must be determined on a case-by-case basis, considering the unique circumstances and balancing the individual's legitimate privacy interests against the employer's legitimate interests in work-place supervision, safety, and efficiency.

Seizure and Bailment

Seizure of students should only occur when doing so is necessary to protect health, safety, or order in the school, and any seizure or restraint of students must be consistent with state law. Seized students must be supervised in a safe area, treated appropriately, and only detained for the time necessary. Concerning seized property, school officials hold seized property in bailment. School officials must use ordinary care in protecting the seized property from damage, loss, or theft. And they must provide students and/or parents with a fair process for redeeming items of value.

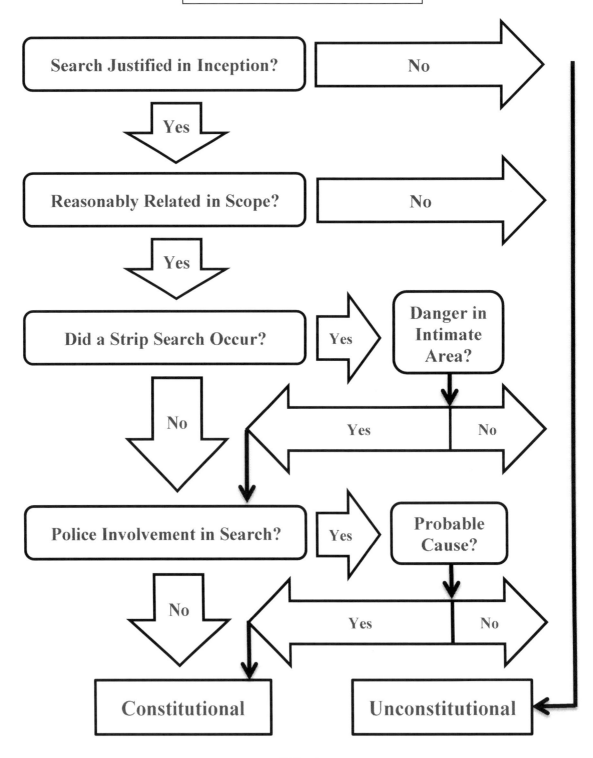

Selected Georgia Laws

Georgia Constitution

Article I, Section I

Paragraph XIII: Searches, seizures, and warrants. The right of the people to be secure in their persons, houses, papers, and effects against unreasonable searches and seizures shall not be violated; and no warrant shall issue except upon probable cause supported by oath or affirmation particularly describing the place or places to be searched and the persons or things to be seized.

Georgia Regulations

160-5-1-.35 Seclusion and Restraint for All Students

(1) Definitions:
(a) *Chemical restraint* – any medication that is used to control behavior or restrict the student's freedom of movement that is not a prescribed treatment for the student's medical or psychiatric condition. Use of chemical restraint is prohibited in Georgia public schools and educational programs.
(b) *Mechanical restraint* – the use of any device or material attached to or adjacent to a student's body that is intended to restrict the normal freedom of movement and which cannot be easily removed by the student. The term does not include an adaptive or protective device recommended by a physician or therapist when used as recommended by the physician or therapist to promote normative body positioning and physical functioning, and/or to prevent self-injurious behavior. The term also does not include seatbelts and other safety equipment when used to secure students during transportation. Use of Mechanical restraint is prohibited in Georgia public schools and educational programs.
(c) *Physical restraint* – direct physical contact from an adult that prevents or significantly restricts a student's movement. The term physical restraint does not include prone restraint, mechanical restraint, or chemical restraint. Additionally, physical restraint does not include: providing limited physical contact and/or redirection to promote student safety, providing physical guidance or prompting when teaching a skill, redirecting attention, providing guidance to a location, or providing comfort.
(d) *Prone restraint* – a specific type of restraint in which a student is intentionally placed face down on the floor or another surface, and physical pressure is applied to the student's body to keep the student in the prone position. Use of prone restraint is prohibited in Georgia public schools and educational programs.
(e) *Seclusion* – a procedure that isolates and confines the student in a separate area until he or she is no longer an immediate danger to himself/herself or others. The seclusion occurs in a specifically constructed or designated room or space that is physically isolated from common areas and from which the student is physically prevented from leaving. Seclusion may also be referred to as monitored seclusion, seclusion timeout, or isolated timeout. Seclusion does not include situations in which a staff member trained in the use of de-escalation techniques or restraint is physically present in the same unlocked room

as the student, time-out as defined in paragraph (1)(g) of this rule, in-school suspension, detention, or a student-requested break in a different location in the room or in a separate room. Use of seclusion is prohibited in Georgia public schools and educational programs.

[Editor's Note: There is no section (f) in the published state regulation].

(g) *Time-out* – a behavioral intervention in which the student is temporarily removed from the learning activity but in which the student is not confined.

(2) Requirements:

(a) The use of seclusion is prohibited in Georgia public schools and educational programs.

(b) The use of prone restraint is prohibited in Georgia public schools and educational programs.

(c) The use of mechanical restraint is prohibited in Georgia public schools and educational programs.

(d) The use of chemical restraint is prohibited in Georgia public schools and educational programs.

(e) The use of physical restraint is prohibited in Georgia public schools and educational programs except in those situations in which the student is an immediate danger to himself or others and the student is not responsive to less intensive behavioral interventions including verbal directives or other de-escalation techniques.

   (1) Notwithstanding the foregoing, physical restraint is prohibited in Georgia public schools and educational programs:

      (i) As a form of discipline or punishment,
      (ii) When the student cannot be safely restrained, and
      (iii) When the use of the intervention would be contraindicated due to the student's psychiatric, medical, or physical conditions as described in the student's educational records.

(f) All physical restraint must be immediately terminated when the student is no longer an immediate danger to himself or others or if the student is observed to be in severe distress.

(g) Schools and programs that use physical restraint in accordance with paragraph (2)(e) of this rule must develop and implement written policies to govern the use of physical restraint. Parents must be provided information regarding the school or program's policies governing the use of physical restraint. The written policies must include the following provisions:

   (1) Staff and faculty training on the use of physical restraint and the school or programs policy and procedures.
   (2) Written parental notification when physical restraint is used to restrain their student within a reasonable time not to exceed one school day from the use of restraint.
   (3) Procedures for observing and monitoring the use of physical restraint.

(4) The use of physical restraint to be documented by staff or faculty participating in or supervising the restraint for each student in each instance in which the student is restrained.

(5) Procedures for the periodic review of the use of restraint and the documentation described in paragraph (2)(g)(4).

(h) Schools and programs that use physical restraints in accordance with paragraph (2)(e) of this rule, must ensure that staff and faculty are trained in the use of physical restraint. This training shall be provided as a part of a program which addresses a full continuum of positive behavioral intervention strategies as well as prevention and de-escalation techniques. Schools and programs must maintain written or electronic documentation on training provided and the list of participants in each training. Records of such training must be made available to the Georgia Department of Education or any member of the public upon request.

(i) Nothing in this rule shall be construed to interfere with a school system, school or program, or school or program employee's authority to utilize time-out as defined in paragraph (1)(g) of this rule or any other classroom management technique or approach, including a student's removal from the classroom, that is not specifically addressed in this rule.

(j) Nothing in this rule shall be construed to prohibit a school system, school, or program employee from taking appropriate action to diffuse a student fight or altercation.

(k) Nothing in this rule shall be construed to eliminate or restrict the ability of an employee of a school system, school or program to use his or her discretion in the use of physical restraint to protect students or others from imminent harm or bodily injury. Nothing in this rule shall be construed to impose ministerial duties on individual employees of a school system, school or program when acting to protect students or others from imminent harm or bodily injury.

(l) In some instances in which a student is an immediate danger to himself or herself or others, the school or program must determine when it becomes necessary to seek assistance from law enforcement and/or emergency medical personnel. Nothing in these rules shall be construed to interfere with the duties of law enforcement or emergency medical personnel.

(1) Parents must be immediately informed when students are removed from the school or program setting by emergency medical or law enforcement personnel.

Authority: O.C.G.A. § 20-2-240

Chapter 6: Due Process of Law

Due process is the framework and lifeblood of any legitimate legal system, establishing substantive standards for fundamental fairness and a procedural system for conducting impartial hearings. In schools, due process plays an essential role in the just resolution of disputes over student discipline, personnel issues, and other significant controversies between individuals and school officials.

To achieve professional competence and comply with legal mandates in managing these disputes, school officials must master the essential principles of due process under the U.S. Constitution, and the specific due process requirements established by their State's statutes and local policies. School officials are ultimately responsible for assuring compliance with due process of law in their schools. When state laws or local policies mandate certain due process procedures, it is difficult to defend against charges that school officials representing the state and the local school district failed to follow their own rules in these proceedings. School officials must be able to find, understand, and apply legal rules governing due process proceedings in their schools.

Federal standards of due process guarantee certain rights to parties in hearings. For example, during hearings parties will have the right to present witnesses and evidence on their behalf. They will also have the right to examine and contest all witnesses and evidence presented against them. State and local rules vary as to how closely these hearings must comply with formal rules of evidence. Nonetheless, school officials should understand the basic principles of questioning and evidence so that they can more effectively participate in the hearing process, and better understand and assist legal counsel in preparing the school's case.

Generally, because the school hearing is not a formal courtroom trial, it is not necessary that school officials have extensive expertise in the rules of evidence. But great care should be taken to assure that the hearing process is fundamentally fair, as justice is the core purpose of the rules of evidence. For example, there should be no surprise evidence or unannounced ambush witnesses. These surprise revelations unfairly advantage one party and deny the other party a fair opportunity to prepare a response, which is of course the real purpose of the "surprise" evidence or witness, to catch the other party unprepared to fairly respond. To guard against such unfair surprises, a list of evidence to be introduced must be revealed in advance, and a list of witnesses and a summary of the issues they will testify on must be disclosed.

Irrelevant or prejudicial evidence or testimony should not be allowed in the hearing. Evidence is irrelevant if it does not prove or disprove any unresolved issue in the proceedings, or only tends to prove that the charged party is a "bad person" generally, whether or not the charges are true. To determine whether evidence should be admitted, a tribunal should weigh the probative value of the evidence (i.e., the degree to which it proves or disproves an unresolved issue) against the prejudicial effect (i.e., the degree to which it simply prejudices the trier of fact or superfluously attacks the character of the accused). It must always be remembered that the hearing is about whether the party actually committed the alleged violation in this instance. Irrelevant prior history, personal beliefs, or the fundamental character of the accused are not on trial. Legal relevancy is determined by weighing probative value against prejudicial effect.

Weighing Admissibility: Probative Value v. Prejudicial Effect

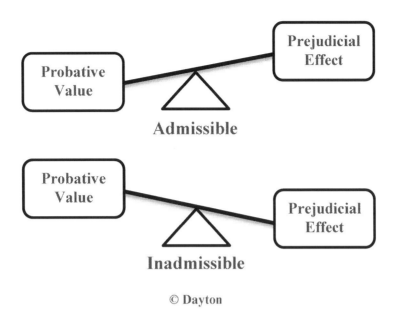

© Dayton

Although most student disciplinary proceedings are not rigidly bound by the legal rules of evidence, "hearsay" evidence (i.e., an out-of-hearing statement offered in evidence as proof of the matter asserted, including repeated rumors, second-hand statements, etc.) may be problematic if the admission of an out-of-hearing statement denies the tribunal an opportunity to assess the demeanor and honesty of the person making the statement, or denies the charged party any meaningful opportunity to cross-examine and contest the out-of-hearing statement.

Below are summaries of some of the most important aspects of managing investigations and hearings, including conducting investigations and interviewing witnesses; preparing for a successful hearing; questioning and evidence; a summary of the essential rules of evidence; an overview of the appeals process; and selected state law provisions concerning due process.

Conducting Investigations and Interviewing Witnesses

Most investigations begin when school officials receive a complaint, observe suspicious behavior, hear a rumor, etc., concerning student or employee misconduct or a danger or disruption to the school community. Developing good skills in conducting investigations and interviewing witnesses can prove invaluable in keeping the school a safe and productive place for everyone. Below are some useful considerations in conducting investigations and interviewing witnesses:

Prioritize investigations: Time and resources are always limited, so school officials must necessarily make triage decisions in allocating time and resources. Investigations affecting the safety and well-being of students and personnel must be given the highest priority. Imminent dangers must be addressed immediately.

Act quickly to secure evidence and statements: Time is the investigator's enemy. As time passes memories become weaker; evidence may be lost or destroyed; witnesses may become unavailable; hostile witnesses have more opportunities to collude; and perpetrators have more time to cover their tracks. Act quickly to secure essential documents and evidence; record initial statements from important witnesses; and secure a crime scene as soon as possible to assure safety and prevent the destruction of evidence.

Properly plan from the beginning: The formal investigation process should begin with a sound plan. The plan must address the exigencies of the specific situation: What persons or agencies should be involved in the investigation? What steps are necessary to assure a fair and effective investigation? What is the best order of events? Modifications will be necessary as the investigation evolves, but sound initial planning will save significant time and resources, and help to assure a fair, efficient, and effective investigation.

Document effectively: Cases are often won or lost based on documentation. The process and results of an investigation must be thoroughly, accurately, and professionally documented, keeping in mind that the investigation may lead to litigation.

Remain professional and objective: As an investigator, do not become emotionally involved in events or take sides in disputes. To conduct a fair investigation an investigator must remain objective until the investigation is completed.

Separate witnesses: Separate witnesses in interviews to avoid the unconscious construction of a group consensus, or giving untruthful witnesses an opportunity to "fit" their statements to those of others. The truth is far more likely to emerge from the investigator's triangulation of independent sources. Further, genuinely independent witnesses provide the most reliable corroboration.

Do not prejudice or influence witnesses: Be careful not to prejudice witnesses directly (i.e., by revealing what you really want to hear), or influence witnesses indirectly (e.g., through facial expressions or body language indicating approval/disapproval). The investigator needs candid statements and unfiltered facts, not witnesses motivated to confirm the investigator's well-intentioned but preconceived assumptions.

Focus on the facts: Focus questions on what the witnesses actually detected with their own senses (e.g., what did you see; hear; smell; etc.). Do not ask witnesses to give opinions, draw conclusions, or speculate. Focus on gathering direct eye-witness accounts; physical evidence; documents; and provable events. And then the investigator draws conclusions based on the facts and not opinions and speculation.

Weigh the status and credibility of potential witnesses: Many people may have witnessed an event. Focus your interviews on the most valuable and credible potential witnesses. An ideal witness is mature, lucid, convincing, and unflappable. Very young children may not yet grasp the boundaries between fantasy and reality; a witness who was drinking, distracted, etc., at the time of the event is going to be less credible; a witness with a reputation for lying or dishonesty is less credible; as is a witness with a strong personal bias or a motive to lie. Witnesses that are psychologically or emotionally fragile are also likely to be more vulnerable during cross-examinations. The reality is, however, that your choices are always limited to only the witnesses you actually have available. Among available witnesses, focus on the most credible potential witnesses needed to testify on the most important elements in the case.

Corroborate testimony: Whenever possible attempt to corroborate important testimony. Ask potential witnesses for any confirmation of important facts (e.g., "do you know anyone who can confirm that?"; "do you have any records, receipts, pictures, saved or recorded messages, or other additional evidence confirming this?").

Guard information during a pending investigation: Tell individuals only what they need to know and no more. Once information is disclosed, it may reach hostile parties or aid perpetrators in intimidating witnesses or covering up evidence. Further, providing witnesses with details of the case may unduly influence their recollections and testimony. A witness whose understanding of events is based more on what others think and said than on personal knowledge is likely to be a weak and vulnerable witness in the hearing. While the investigation is pending, sensitive information should be shared only on a need to know basis, and investigation records and evidence should be kept in a secured area.

Appropriately respect individual privacy and confidentiality: If you have established a trust-worthy reputation in the community, and potential witnesses know you will appropriately respect their privacy and confidentiality, they are much more likely to fully cooperate in the investigation process. Always respect legal and ethical boundaries of privacy in the investigation process and keep all legally and professionally confidential information confidential. If you leak a piece of gossip acquired in the investigation, it may harm your case, the cooperating party who shared it with you, and your professional reputation for maintaining privacy and confidentiality. Further, a breach of privacy or confidentiality may expose you to potential legal and professional sanctions.

Properly manage documents, reports, and the media: Remember that all documents and reports may be subject to open records laws or the discovery process in litigation. Everything recorded in these documents must be objective, professional, and lawful. Before releasing any potentially sensitive documents, be certain to comply with FERPA and other applicable privacy laws through redaction or other appropriate means. Members of the media should work through a single contact school official who understands relevant laws and rules concerning media access to hearings and records, and what can and cannot be communicated to the media during a pending investigation.

Preparing for a Successful Hearing

Good planning and preparation are the keys to a successful hearing. Below are some useful considerations in preparing for a successful hearing:

Start with the big picture and then systematically fill in the necessary details: Start with the conclusion required by the law and justice, based on the totality of the facts and circumstances (e.g. the student willfully committed an assault in clear violation of state law and the applicable discipline code; presents a continuing danger; and must be expelled from school). What testimony and evidence are necessary to convince the trier of fact to reach that conclusion? Envision the story you need to communicate to the tribunal from the beginning to the end. When the theory and vision of the case is clear in your mind, and you are confident that the fundamental arguments are persuasive, planning a convincing sequence of testimony and evidence becomes relatively easy.

In communication, less is generally more effective: Remember that the tribunal is made up of people with ordinary human limitations on their attention and memory. Your plan for the hearing must take these realities into account. Plan your case and your arguments for a presentation that is concise and focused. Be careful not to dilute the power of your case with superfluous evidence or excessive oration.

Carefully plan the sequence of events: Unless another approach is warranted, general, the sequence of witnesses and evidence follows the chronological sequence of events related to the charges and disposition (e.g., the events leading up to the incident; the incident; consequences; relevant future implications). When possible, however, there may be a strategic advantage to carefully ordering your witnesses (i.e., starting with a strong witness or evidence and finishing with a strong witness or evidence). The triers of fact are likely to form initial and lasting impressions of the case very early in the hearing, and they may also be disproportionately influenced by events near the close of the hearing.

Carefully weigh the cost-benefits of any discretionary witnesses: Some witnesses are essential, requiring you to play the hand you have been dealt. Some witnesses may be discretionary, in that they may bolster other testimony and evidence, but they are not absolutely essential to the case. For any discretionary witnesses, carefully weigh the cost-benefits of including this witness in your case (e.g., the value and impact of the witness' testimony versus risks that the witness may lack credibility; be easily impeached; open the door to unwanted issues; or otherwise damage the case).

Be aware of special concerns with child witnesses: Child witnesses require special consideration and planning, and the younger and less mature the child, the more care and preparation is needed. Children generally have more limited comprehension, life experiences, and vocabulary. They also often have a desire to cooperate and please adults, even if they have to alter their memories to do so. Children can be easily overwhelmed or frightened in hearings. It is important to remember that a child is not an adult, and to treat the child appropriately. In the hearing, be prepared to establish a friendly rapport with the child prior to more serious questioning. Prepare clear questions using simple words. Be certain the child understands the question (e.g., the child may be reluctant to admit he or she does not understand the question). Allow for longer pauses in questioning, giving the child sufficient time to think and respond. Very young children may need more close-ended and leading questions when testifying. Their answers may be corroborated or rehabilitated with documented consistent answers to more open-ended questions under the less stressful conditions of a previous interview with the child.

Good questions are the key to good testimony: You cannot get the right answer unless you ask the right question. Carefully plan and write down questions you need to ask of each witness. Questions should be written in a simple conversational style. Follow the overall written plan, making sure all essential questions are asked and answered in the hearing and on the record. Because the hearing is interactive it will sometimes be necessary to improvise. Do so, however, with great caution. Do not ask a question unless you already know how the witness will respond. You do not want any surprises in the hearing: Only ask a question when you already know the answer.

Plan persuasive opening and closing statements: Make a powerful case by assuring that everyone hears the essential evidence proving the charges three times: In the opening statement; in the presentation of testimony and evidence; and in the closing statement. The opening and closing statements should concisely and powerfully summarize all the essential elements of the charges and the evidence proving the charges. The opening and closing statements are intentionally repetitive (i.e., the opening statement tells the tribunal what you will prove; the testimony and evidence provide the promised proof; and the closing statement summarizes what you proved). The opening and closing statements must be concise and to the point. Generally, the longer the statement; the less is remembered. Do not dilute the main message with unnecessary rhetoric.

Questioning and Evidence

Skillful investigation, interviews of witnesses, and planning will lay the essential foundation for a successful hearing. Below are considerations in conducting the hearing with effective questioning and presentations of evidence:

Introduce the witness and establish a basis for credibility: Begin by establishing the witness' identify and a basis for credibility (e.g., "please introduce yourself to the tribunal members and tell them who you are"). Follow up with close-ended questions to solidly establish the witness' credibility and the relevance of testimony (e.g., "Do you know Johnny?"; "Did you witness the event in question?"). Answering these easy yes/no questions also helps the witness to relax and get used to testifying. When the witness' credibility and basis for knowledge of the events has been established the direct examination can begin with more open-ended questions.

Conduct an effective direct-examination: The goal is have the witness testify truthfully and persuasively. With open-ended questions guide the witness through a chronological account of the events witnessed. Stay focused on important, relevant events and testimony. Allowing the witness to ramble dilutes the testimony and may open opportunities for detrimental distractions or an unnecessary impeachment of the witness on cross-examination.

Asking open-ended questions: Open-ended questions encourage witnesses to tell the story in their own words. In general use open-ended questions on direct-examination. A helpful technique in asking open-ended, non-leading questions, is to begin the question with what, when, where, who, why, or how. Remember that although you ask the questions, only witnesses testify. The tribunal needs to hear the testimony of the witnesses, not just your conclusions confirmed with a yes or no from the witnesses.

When necessary, however, be prepared to guide a straying witness back to relevant testimony with a more focused open-ended question (e.g., "please tell us exactly what you saw happen to Mary at the time of the incident").

Conduct effective cross-examinations/question hostile witnesses: The goal concerning cross-examinations and hostile witnesses is to reveal significant inaccuracies and to impeach the credibility of the witness. Close-ended questions and leading the witness are appropriate, calling for yes/no and other short answers (e.g., "Isn't it true that you personally never entered that room?"). Close-ended questions limit the hostile witness' ability to ignore the direct question, diminish or excuse damaging testimony, or introduce unwanted statements Without badgering the witness or appearing rude to members of the tribunal, rapidly move from one question to the next to minimize open space for a hostile witness.

Asking close-ended leading questions: Close-ended leading questions only call for a yes/no type response or for a single word or short answer. Leading questions are permissible on cross-examination or when questioning a hostile witness. But you may generally also use close-ended leading questions on direct-examination to quickly get through undisputed facts or information for the record; to redirect the witness to relevant areas; to refresh the witness' memory; etc.

Impeachment of the witness: The goal is to raise significant doubts concerning the testimony or credibility of the witness. This may include, for example, comparing the witness' current testimony with prior statements and showing relevant inconsistencies (e.g., "You just testified that [quote testimony]. But didn't you previously state [quote directly from prior statement to highlight contradictions]?); comparing the witness' statement to provable facts (e.g., "you testified you witnessed the event, but here are police records proving you were arrested and jailed on a DUI charge over two hours prior to the event"); introduce evidence that the witness is biased and slanting testimony, etc. If the witness denies making a contradictory statement, be prepared to show proof that the statement was in fact made by the witness. And always directly ask if the witness made the statement. Do not ask if the witness remembers making the statement, as doing so may allow the witness to use a "memory lapse" to avoid accountability

Rehabilitation of your witness: The goal in rehabilitating your witness in the hearing is to repair damage from the cross-examination. This may merely require giving the witness an opportunity to clarify and explain important testimony that was called into question during cross-examination. Caution should be exercised, however, to assure that the scope of questioning in your rehabilitation of the witness does not exceed issues covered on direct-examination, or you may be opening the door to additional issues for the opposing party to challenge. In the planning and execution of the hearing, an ounce of prevention is worth many pounds of cure. It is best to conduct a solid and well-planned direct-examination, leaving little opportunity for damage in cross-examination, thereby minimizing chances that rehabilitation of the witness will even be necessary.

Types of questions to avoid:

Factually irrelevant questions: Questions that do not address an issue in dispute.

Legally irrelevant questions: Questions for which the prejudicial effect outweighs the probative value.

Questions calling for hearsay: Questions that call for the witness to testify about another person's out-of-hearing statements (e.g., "What did Johnny say he saw her do?").

Compound questions: Two or more questions fused together (e.g., "Did you know Johnny was at the party and did Jimmy leave?"). Compound questions are confusing, especially when answered by the witness with a single yes or no, leaving everyone to guess as to what exactly the witness meant. Further, asking a hostile witness a compound question offers the hostile witness an opportunity to choose which question to answer or claim answering a different part of the question if later confronted with perjury.

Confusing questions: Avoid questions that are too long; too complex; vaguely worded, or otherwise ambiguous.

Questions that assume facts not already in evidence: These questions contain statements of fact that have not yet been put in evidence (e.g., "Did you talk to Johnny before he attacked Mary at the party?" when it has not been established that Johnny was at the party, attacked anyone, or that Mary was attacked).

Argumentative questions: These "questions" may end with a question mark, but an argumentative question isn't really a question at all, and is instead rhetorical or gratuitously hostile (e.g., "When you came to school that day, had you already decided you were going to annoy everyone?").

Questions that have already been asked and answered: Repeating a question that has previously been clearly answered by the witness, and either wasting time or attempting to unduly call attention to an issue.

Questions that misstate the testimony or evidence: A question containing a relevant factual misstatement of testimony or the evidence.

Asking leading questions, when not appropriate: Questions that give the witness the answer. The questioner should not testify, with the witness only affirming the testimony of the questioner (e.g., to a friendly witness "Johnny was the one who did it, right?"). However, leading questions may be used on cross-examination; with a hostile witness; to aid a very young child; refresh a witness' memory; or other appropriate and limited uses.

Questions calling for conclusions: Questions that invite the witness to draw conclusions are problematic because they present the witness' speculation or personal opinion and not facts (e.g., "what was Johnny thinking at that time" requiring the witness to speculate about Johnny's thoughts).

Using non-verbal demonstrations: Remembering that a picture can be worth a thousand words, and that visual images are often remembered more vividly than words, consider incorporating non-verbal demonstrations and evidence when appropriate (e.g., "Please show the tribunal where Johnny put his hands"; presenting a picture of property damage; a scaled map of the location; etc.).

Remember that the record is officially the totality of the case: Make sure all the necessary testimony and evidence is entered into the formal record. In the appeals process, the case is considered solely on the basis of what was actually recorded in the official record. So if something is not in the record, it doesn't exist on appeal. A sure way to lose an appeal is to leave an essential element of proof out of the record of the hearing.

Summary of the Essential Rules of Evidence

School tribunals are not judicial trials. The rules of evidence are generally more relaxed in school tribunals, and a hearing officer or the chair of the tribunal has great discretion concerning what evidence will be allowed. Nonetheless, a good working knowledge of the essential rules of evidence can be very helpful for school officials in assuring that the evidence admitted is fair and that it will likely survive challenges in the appeals process.

The rules of evidence are intended to promote fairness in the hearing process, and the paramount goal of school officials must always be a fair hearing for all parties. Understanding and generally following the essential rules of evidence will help insure that the evidence introduced in the hearing is fair. Further, because any gross breach of the rules of evidence opens school officials to the possibility of challenges and losing on appeal, assuring that the evidence introduced is fundamentally fair, as guided by the essential rules of evidence, helps to assure that school officials' case will likely withstand an appeal.

Moreover, understanding the essential rules of evidence will enable school officials to know when to object to the admission of inappropriate evidence by an opposing party. If no objection is made to the attempted admission of inappropriate or unfair evidence and testimony, the evidence is generally admitted, and the right to appeal the admission of this evidence may be waived. And finally, understanding the essential rules of evidence can assist school officials in more effectively working with legal counsel when necessary. The essential rules of evidence in brief summary are as follows:

Evidence: Presented to prove or disprove disputed facts in a hearing.

Types of Evidence:

Direct evidence: Directly proves a fact, requiring no inferences (e.g., "I saw Johnny stab Mary"). Direct evidence is almost always admissible.

Indirect (circumstantial) evidence: Does not directly prove a fact but presents evidence of circumstances inferring that the fact is true as charged (e.g., "I saw Johnny with a knife running away from the area where Mary was stabbed"). Most objections to admissibility address indirect evidence and assertions that its probative value is outweighed by its prejudicial effect.

Forms of Evidence:

Testimonial evidence: Sworn statements from witnesses.

Tangible evidence: Real objects such as a weapon, garment, map, visual aid, etc., Tangible evidence should be: a) Identified for the record; b) Authenticated (i.e., proven genuine); c) Offered to the opposing party for inspection; and d) Admitted into evidence with the permission of the tribunal. Concerning documents to be entered into evidence have an official copy available for review, but an electronic copy for use with an overhead projector or power-point may be helpful for simultaneous viewing by all parties in the tribunal.

Factual relevancy: Must tend to prove or disprove facts in dispute in the hearing.

Legal relevancy: Determined by weighing the probative value of the evidence against the prejudicial effect.

Competency: Concerns whether the witness is competent to testify. The witness must: a) Have direct knowledge of relevant issues (e.g., the witness directly saw, heard, etc.); and b) Be capable of truthful communication (i.e., the witness understands the duty to tell the truth and can competently communicate).

Appropriate questioning on direct-examination: Questioning of a friendly witness, generally using open-ended questions based on what, when, who, where, etc., (e.g., "Can you tell us what happened after you arrived at the party?").

Appropriate questioning on cross-examination: Questioning of a hostile witness following direct exam by the opposing party. Close-ended leading questions are allowed. Questioning is generally limited to the issues discussed on direct examination, but may include relevant issues, impeachment, etc.

Impeachment of a witness: Challenging the witness' testimony or credibility. This may be achieved through cross-examination or the presentation of contradictory evidence (e.g., prior inconsistent statements; lack of knowledge or capacity; conflicts of interest; bias; dishonesty; etc.). The basis for impeachment must be relevant to the proceedings and not simply gratuitous.

Rehabilitation of a witness: A re-direct examination to rebut the opposing party's effort to impeach the witness or give the witness an opportunity to clarify statements.

Objection: A complaint from parties in the hearing concerning the proceedings, usually an objection to the admissibility of testimonial or tangible evidence. Objections must be made in a timely manner or the right to object may be waived. A timely and continuing objection may also be necessary to preserve the issue for appeal. The objection will either be "sustained" (i.e., the tribunal expressing agreement with the objection and excluding the evidence) or "overruled" (i.e., the tribunal expressing disagreement with the objection and allowing the evidence to be admitted).

Hearsay: In-hearing testimony about another party's out-of-hearing statement offered as evidence in the hearing (e.g., "Jimmy said that he saw Johnny do it"). The fundamental concern is to protect the fairness of the proceedings, and to give the opposing party a fair opportunity to cross-examine all witnesses (i.e., the evidence is based on Jimmy's statement but Jimmy is not subject to cross-examination or an assessment of his demeanor and honesty by the tribunal). Hearsay evidence should be avoided when possible. But the tribunal generally has the discretion to allow hearsay evidence if the evidence appears trustworthy and its admission does not deny the opposing party a fair hearing. An important exception to the hearsay rule is that relevant official records by public employees are generally deemed trustworthy and admissible.

Authentication: Proof that the object offered into evidence is genuine and that it is what it is asserted to be. Official government documents are self-authenticating. Other documents may be authenticated by presenting the document for verification to a person who authored the document, saw it written, can identify the signature, responded to the document, etc. Other objects may be verified as authentic by a party in the hearing or connected to the location of the event in question. This may be achieved by having a witness identify a unique characteristic of the object (e.g., "I recognize this because it has a unique mark here"), or by establishing the chain of custody from the time and location when the object was seized to its presentation into evidence.

Privilege: A rule of law permitting a witness to withhold otherwise compelled testimony or allowing another party to prevent a witness from revealing confidential information. Possible privileges include the right not to answer incriminating questions, and confidences disclosed in the attorney-client; physician-patient; psychotherapist-patient; clergy-penitent; or marital relationship.

Burden of proof: In student discipline hearings and employment hearings initiated by school officials, the burden of proof rests with school officials who must prove the charges by a preponderance of the evidence (i.e., the evidence established that it was more probable than not that the charges are true).

Basic Guide to Questioning

Asking Non-Leading Questions (Direct-Examination): Begin with what; when; where; who; why; etc., and ask an open-ended question.

Asking Leading Questions (Cross-Examination/Hostile Witness): Begin with didn't; isn't; wasn't . . . or end with right?; correct? true?, and ask a close-ended question.

Basic Guide to Objections

"Objection, the question is . . . "

factually irrelevant . . .	does not address an issue in dispute in the hearing
legally irrelevant . . .	the prejudicial effect outweighs the probative value
calling for hearsay . . .	asking the witness to testify about someone else's out-of-hearing statements
compound question . . .	presenting the witness with more than a single question to answer
confusing . . .	too long/complex/vaguely worded/ambiguous
assumes a fact not in evidence . . .	it has not been established that . . .
argumentative . . .	rhetorical/gratuitously hostile/badgering the witness
asked and answered . . .	question was already asked and the witness has answered
misstates testimony/evidence . . .	question contains a significant misstatement of the testimony/evidence
leading the witness . . .	the questioner should not testify with the witness only affirming the questioner's statements
calls for conclusions . . .	asks for speculation/personal opinions and not facts

© Dayton

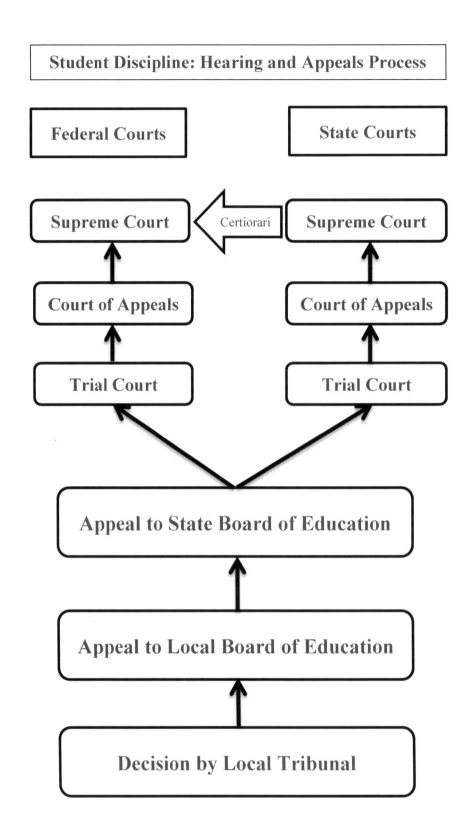

Selected Georgia Laws

Georgia Constitution

Article I, Section I

Paragraph I: Life, liberty, and property. No person shall be deprived of life, liberty, or property except by due process of law.

Paragraph X: Bill of attainder; ex post facto laws; and retroactive laws. No bill of attainder, ex post facto law, retroactive law, or laws impairing the obligation of contract or making irrevocable grant of special privileges or immunities shall be passed.

Paragraph XIV: Benefit of counsel; accusation; list of witnesses; compulsory process. Every person charged with an offense against the laws of this state shall have the privilege and benefit of counsel; shall be furnished with a copy of the accusation or indictment and, on demand, with a list of the witnesses on whose testimony such charge is founded; shall have compulsory process to obtain the testimony of that person's own witnesses; and shall be confronted with the witnesses testifying against such person.

Paragraph XV: Habeas corpus. The writ of habeas corpus shall not be suspended unless, in case of rebellion or invasion, the public safety may require it.

Paragraph XVI: Self-incrimination. No person shall be compelled to give testimony tending in any manner to be self-incriminating.

Paragraph XVIII: Jeopardy of life or liberty more than once forbidden. No person shall be put in jeopardy of life or liberty more than once for the same offense except when a new trial has been granted after conviction or in case of mistrial.

Georgia Statutes

§ 20-2-1160: Local School Board as School Court

(a) Every county, city, or other independent board of education shall constitute a tribunal for hearing and determining any matter of local controversy in reference to the construction or administration of the school law, with power to summon witnesses and take testimony if necessary. When such local board has made a decision, it shall be binding on the parties; provided, however, that the board shall notify the parties in writing of the decision and of their right to appeal the decision to the State Board of Education and shall clearly describe the procedure and requirements for such an appeal which are provided in subsection (b) of this Code section.

(b) Any party aggrieved by a decision of the local board rendered on a contested issue after a hearing shall have the right to appeal therefrom to the State Board of Education. The appeal shall be in writing and shall distinctly set forth the question in dispute, the decision of the local board, and a concise statement of the reasons why the decision is complained of; and the party taking the appeal shall also file with the appeal a transcript of testimony certified as true and correct by the local school superintendent. The appeal shall be filed with the superintendent within 30 days of the decision of the local board, and within ten days thereafter it shall be the duty of the superintendent to transmit a copy of the appeal together with the transcript of evidence and proceedings, the decision of the local board, and other matters in the file relating to the appeal to the state board. The state board shall adopt regulations governing the procedure for hearings before the local board and proceedings before it.

(c) Where an appeal is taken to the state board, the state board shall notify the parties in writing of its decision within 25 days after hearing thereon and of their right to appeal the decision to the superior court of the county wherein the local board of education is located and shall clearly describe the procedure and requirements for such an appeal which are provided in this subsection and in subsection (d) of this Code section. Any party aggrieved thereby may appeal to the superior court of the county wherein the local board of education is situated. Such appeal shall be filed in writing within 30 days after the decision of the state board. Within ten days after filing of such appeal, it shall be the duty of the State School Superintendent to transmit to the superior court a copy of the record and transcript sent up from the local board as well as the decision and any order of the state board, certified as true and correct.

(d) The following form shall be sufficient for an appeal:

"In re _____

_____ hereby appeals to the _____ from the decision of _____ rendered in the above-stated matter on _____.

This _____ day of _____, _____."

(e) Neither the state board nor the superior court shall consider any question in matters before the local board nor consider the matter de novo, and the review by the state board or the superior court shall be confined to the record. In the superior court, the appeal shall be determined by the judge sitting without a jury.

(f) The procedures provided in subsections (a) through (e) of this Code section shall not be applicable to disabled children when a hearing is necessary to decide a complaint made under the federal Education for All Handicapped Children Act of 1975.[1]

---

[1] *The state board shall promulgate by rules and regulations an impartial due process procedure for hearing and determining any matter of local controversy in reference to the construction or administration of the school law with respect to disabled children as such term is defined by the state board. Any tribunal which the state board shall empower to hear such cases shall have the power to summon witnesses and take testimony as such tribunal deems it necessary. In promulgating such rules and regulations, the state board shall consult with local boards of education and other local school officials in order to establish procedures required by this subsection which will coordinate, to the extent practicable, with the administrative practices of such local boards.*

§ 20-2-751.5: Student Code of Conduct; Mandated Provisions

(a) Each student code of conduct shall contain provisions that address the following conduct of students during school hours, at school related functions, and on the school bus in a manner that is appropriate to the age of the student:

(1) Verbal assault, including threatened violence, of teachers, administrators, and other school personnel;
(2) Physical assault or battery of teachers, administrators, and other school personnel;
(3) Disrespectful conduct toward teachers, administrators, and other school personnel, including use of vulgar or profane language;
(4) Verbal assault of other students, including threatened violence or sexual harassment as defined pursuant to Title IX of the Education Amendments of 1972;
(5) Physical assault or battery of other students, including sexual harassment as defined pursuant to Title IX of the Education Amendments of 1972;
(6) Disrespectful conduct toward other students, including use of vulgar or profane language;
(7) Verbal assault of, physical assault or battery of, and disrespectful conduct, including use of vulgar or profane language, toward persons attending school related functions;
(8) Failure to comply with compulsory attendance as required under Code Section 20-2-690.1;
(9) Willful or malicious damage to real or personal property of the school or to personal property of any person legitimately at the school;
(10) Inciting, advising, or counseling of others to engage in prohibited acts;
(11) Marking, defacing, or destroying school property;
(12) Possession of a weapon, as provided for in Code Section 16-11-127.1;
(13) Unlawful use or possession of illegal drugs or alcohol;
(14) Willful and persistent violation of the student code of conduct;
(15) Bullying as defined by Code Section 20-2-751.4;
(16) Marking, defacing, or destroying the property of another student; and
(17) Falsifying, misrepresenting, omitting, or erroneously reporting information regarding instances of alleged inappropriate behavior by a teacher, administrator, or other school employee toward a student.

With regard to paragraphs (9), (11), and (17) of this subsection, each student code of conduct shall also contain provisions that address conduct of students during off-school hours.

(b)(1) In addition to the requirements contained in subsection (a) of this Code section, each student code of conduct shall include comprehensive and specific provisions prescribing and governing student conduct and safety rules on all public school buses. The specific provisions shall include but not be limited to:

(A) Students shall be prohibited from acts of physical violence as defined by Code Section 20-2-751.6, bullying as defined by subsection (a) of Code Section 20-2-751.4, physical assault or battery of other persons on the school bus, verbal assault of other persons on the school bus, disrespectful conduct toward the school bus driver or other persons on the school bus, and other unruly behavior;

(B) Students shall be prohibited from using any electronic devices during the operation of a school bus, including but not limited to cell phones; pagers; audible radios, tape or compact disc players without headphones; or any other electronic device in a manner that might interfere with the school bus communications equipment or the school bus driver's operation of the school bus; and

(C) Students shall be prohibited from using mirrors, lasers, flash cameras, or any other lights or reflective devises in a manner that might interfere with the school bus driver's operation of the school bus.

(2) If a student is found to have engaged in physical acts of violence as defined by Code Section 20-2-751.6, the student shall be subject to the penalties set forth in such Code section. If a student is found to have engaged in bullying as defined by subsection (a) of Code Section 20-2-751.4 or in physical assault or battery of another person on the school bus, the local school board policy shall require a meeting of the parent or guardian of the student and appropriate school district officials to form a school bus behavior contract for the student. Such contract shall provide for progressive age-appropriate discipline, penalties, and restrictions for student misconduct on the bus. Contract provisions may include but shall not be not limited to assigned seating, ongoing parental involvement, and suspension from riding the bus. This subsection is not to be construed to limit the instances when a school code of conduct or local board of education may require use of a student bus behavior contract.

(c) Each student code of conduct shall also contain provisions that address any off-campus behavior of a student which could result in the student being criminally charged with a felony and which makes the student's continued presence at school a potential danger to persons or property at the school or which disrupts the educational process.

(d) Local board policies relating to student codes of conduct shall provide that each local school superintendent shall fully support the authority of principals and teachers in the school system to remove a student from the classroom pursuant to Code Section 20-2-738, including establishing and disseminating procedures. It is the policy of this state that it is preferable to reassign disruptive students to alternative educational settings rather than to suspend or expel such students from school.

(e) Any student handbook which is prepared by a local board or school shall include a copy of the student code of conduct for that school or be accompanied by a copy of the student code of conduct for that school as annually distributed pursuant to Code Section 20-2-736. When distributing a student code of conduct, a local school shall include a form for acknowledgment of the student's parent or guardian's receipt of the code, and the local school shall solicit or require that the form be signed and returned to the school.

§ 20-2-754: Procedures for Student Disciplinary Hearings

(a) The provisions of Code Section 20-2-1160 shall apply to disciplinary proceedings under this subpart.

(b) A disciplinary officer, panel, or tribunal of school officials appointed as required by Code Section 20-2-753 shall, in addition to any other requirements imposed by rules and regulations which may have been promulgated pursuant to Code Section 20-2-752, ensure that:

>(1) All parties are afforded an opportunity for a hearing after reasonable notice served personally or by mail. This notice shall be given to all parties and to the parent or guardian of the student or students involved and shall include a statement of the time, place, and nature of the hearing; a short and plain statement of the matters asserted; and a statement as to the right of all parties to present evidence and to be represented by legal counsel;
>
>(2) The hearing is held no later than ten school days after the beginning of the suspension unless the school system and parents or guardians mutually agree to an extension;
>
>(3) All parties are afforded an opportunity to present and respond to evidence and to examine and cross-examine witnesses on all issues unresolved;
>
>(4) Any teacher who is called as a witness by the school system shall be given notice no later than three days prior to the hearing; and
>
>(5) A verbatim electronic or written record of the hearing shall be made and shall be available to all parties.

(c) If appointed to review an instance pursuant to Code Section 20-2-753, the disciplinary officer, panel, or tribunal shall conduct the hearing and, after receiving all evidence, render its decision, which decision shall be based solely on the evidence received at the hearing. The decision shall be in writing and shall be given to all parties within ten days of the close of the record. Any decision by such disciplinary officer, panel, or tribunal may be appealed to the local board of education by filing a written notice of appeal within 20 days from the date the decision is rendered. Any disciplinary action imposed by such officer, panel, or tribunal may be suspended by the school superintendent pending the outcome of the appeal.

(d) The local board of education shall review the record and shall render a decision in writing. The decision shall be based solely on the record and shall be given to all parties within ten days, excluding weekends and public and legal holidays provided for in Code Section 1-4-1, from the date the local board of education receives the notice of appeal. The board may take any action it determines appropriate, and any decision of the board shall be final. All parties shall have the right to be represented by legal counsel at any such appeal and during all subsequent proceedings.

(e) Either or both parents or guardians or legal counsel of the student involved may obtain a copy of any documents relating to a disciplinary proceeding conducted pursuant to this Code section.

§ 20-2-755: Dispositions and Appeals

The disciplinary officer, panel, or tribunal of school officials, when appointed as required in Code Section 20-2-753, shall determine what, if any, disciplinary action shall be taken. Such action may include, but is not limited to, expulsion, long-term suspension, or short-term suspension. Any action taken by such officer, panel, or tribunal shall be subject to modification by the local school board on appeal.

§ 20-2-764. Definitions

As used in this subpart, the term:

(1) "Chronic disciplinary problem student" means a student who exhibits a pattern of behavioral characteristics which interfere with the learning process of students around him or her and which are likely to recur.
(2) "Expulsion" means expulsion of a student from a public school beyond the current school quarter or semester.
(3) "Suspension" means the short-term suspension of a student from a public school for not more than ten days or long-term suspension for more than ten days pursuant to Code Section 20-2-751.

§ 20-2-756: Reporting Alleged Criminal Actions to Police

(a) The school administration, disciplinary hearing officer, panel, tribunal of school officials, or the local board of education may, when any alleged criminal action by a student occurs, report the incident to the appropriate law enforcement agency or officer for investigation to determine if criminal charges or delinquent proceedings should be initiated.
(b) No individual reporting any incident under this subpart to a law enforcement agency or officer shall be subject to any action for malicious prosecution, malicious abuse of process, or malicious use of process.

§ 20-2-757: Student Hearings; Student Privacy Protected

(a) All proceedings and hearings conducted under this subpart shall be confidential and shall not be subject to the open meetings requirement of Code Section 50-14-1 or other open meetings laws.
(b) All electronic or other written records of all hearings conducted under this subpart; all statements of charges; all notices of hearings; and all written decisions rendered by a hearing officer, tribunal, the local board of education, or the State Board of Education shall not be subject to public inspection or other disclosure under Article 4 of Chapter 18 of Title 50 or other public disclosure laws; provided, however, the board of education shall prepare a written summary of any proceeding conducted under this subpart, which summary shall include a description of the incident and the disposition thereof but shall not contain the names of any party to the incident. The summary shall be a public record.

§ 20-2-758: Right to other Causes of Action

Nothing in this subpart shall be construed to prohibit, restrict, or limit in any manner any cause of action otherwise provided by law and available to any teacher, school official, employee, or student. The provisions of subsections (b) through (f) of Code Section 20-2-1160 shall apply to all proceedings under this subpart.

§ 20-2-765: Chronic Disciplinary Problems; Parental Conference

Any time a teacher or principal identifies a student as a chronic disciplinary problem student, the principal shall notify by telephone call and by either certified mail or statutory overnight delivery with return receipt requested or first-class mail the student's parent or guardian of the disciplinary problem, invite such parent or guardian to observe the student in a classroom situation, and request at least one parent or guardian to attend a conference with the principal or the teacher or both to devise a disciplinary and behavioral correction plan.

§ 20-2-766: Parental Attendance at Conference

Before any chronic disciplinary problem student is permitted to return from an expulsion or suspension, the school to which the student is to be readmitted shall request by telephone call and by either certified mail or statutory overnight delivery with return receipt requested or first-class mail at least one parent or guardian to schedule and attend a conference with the principal or his or her designee to devise a disciplinary and behavioral correction plan. Failure of the parent or guardian to attend shall not preclude the student from being readmitted to the school. At the discretion of the principal, a teacher, counselor, or other person may attend the conference. The principal shall ensure that a notation of the conference is placed in the student's permanent file.

§ 20-2-766.1: Court Order for Parental Participation

The local board of education may, by petition to the juvenile court, proceed against a parent or guardian as provided in this Code section. If the court finds that the parent or guardian has willfully and unreasonably failed to attend a conference requested by a principal pursuant to Code Section 20-2-765 or 20-2-766, the court may order the parent or guardian to attend such a conference, order the parent or guardian to participate in such programs or such treatment as the court deems appropriate to improve the student's behavior, or both. After notice and opportunity for hearing, the court may impose a fine, not to exceed $500.00, on a parent or guardian who willfully disobeys an order of the court entered under this Code section. The court may use its contempt and other powers specified in Code Section 15-11-5 to enforce any order entered under this Code section.

§ 20-2-731: Use of Corporal Punishment in Public Schools

An area, county, or independent board of education may, upon the adoption of written policies, authorize any principal or teacher employed by the board to administer, in the exercise of his sound discretion, corporal punishment on any pupil or pupils placed under his supervision in order to maintain proper control and discipline. Any such authorization shall be subject to the following requirements:

(1) The corporal punishment shall not be excessive or unduly severe;

(2) Corporal punishment shall never be used as a first line of punishment for misbehavior unless the pupil was informed beforehand that specific misbehavior could occasion its use; provided, however, that corporal punishment may be employed as a first line of punishment for those acts of misconduct which are so antisocial or disruptive in nature as to shock the conscience;

(3) Corporal punishment must be administered in the presence of a principal or assistant principal, or the designee of the principal or assistant principal, employed by the board of education authorizing such punishment, and the other principal or assistant principal, or the designee of the principal or assistant principal, must be informed beforehand and in the presence of the pupil of the reason for the punishment;

(4) The principal or teacher who administered corporal punishment must provide the child's parent, upon request, a written explanation of the reasons for the punishment and the name of the principal or assistant principal, or designee of the principal or assistant principal, who was present; provided, however, that such an explanation shall not be used as evidence in any subsequent civil action brought as a result of the corporal punishment; and

(5) Corporal punishment shall not be administered to a child whose parents or legal guardian has upon the day of enrollment of the pupil filed with the principal of the school a statement from a medical doctor licensed in Georgia stating that it is detrimental to the child's mental or emotional stability.

§ 20-2-732: Good Faith Immunity from Liability

No principal or teacher who shall administer corporal punishment to a pupil or pupils under his care and supervision in conformity with the policies and regulations of the area, county, or independent board of education employing him and in accordance also with this subpart shall be held accountable or liable in any criminal or civil action based upon the administering of corporal punishment where the corporal punishment is administered in good faith and is not excessive or unduly severe.

§ 20-2-751.4: Anti-Bullying Policies Mandated

(a) As used in this Code section, the term "bullying" means an act which occurs on school property, on school vehicles, at designated school bus stops, or at school related functions or activities, or by use of data or software that is accessed through a computer, computer system, computer network, or other electronic technology of a local school system, that is:

(1) Any willful attempt or threat to inflict injury on another person, when accompanied by an apparent present ability to do so;

(2) Any intentional display of force such as would give the victim reason to fear or expect immediate bodily harm; or

(3) Any intentional written, verbal, or physical act which a reasonable person would perceive as being intended to threaten, harass, or intimidate, that:

- (A) Causes another person substantial physical harm within the meaning of Code Section 16-5-23.1 or visible bodily harm as such term is defined in Code Section 16-5-23.1;
- (B) Has the effect of substantially interfering with a student's education;
- (C) Is so severe, persistent, or pervasive that it creates an intimidating or threatening educational environment; or
- (D) Has the effect of substantially disrupting the orderly operation of the school.

(b) No later than August 1, 2011:

(1) Each local board of education shall adopt a policy that prohibits bullying of a student by another student and shall require such prohibition to be included in the student code of conduct for schools in that school system;

(2) Each local board policy shall require that, upon a finding by the disciplinary hearing officer, panel, or tribunal of school officials provided for in this subpart that a student in grades six through 12 has committed the offense of bullying for the third time in a school year, such student shall be assigned to an alternative school;

(3) Each local board of education shall establish and publish in its local board policy a method to notify the parent, guardian, or other person who has control or charge of a student upon a finding by a school administrator that such student has committed an offense of bullying or is a victim of bullying; and

(4) Each local board of education shall ensure that students and parents of students are notified of the prohibition against bullying, and the penalties for violating the prohibition, by posting such information at each school and by including such information in student and parent handbooks.

(c) No later than January 1, 2011, the Department of Education shall develop a model policy regarding bullying, that may be revised from time to time, and shall post such policy on its website in order to assist local school systems. Such model policy shall include:

(1) A statement prohibiting bullying;

(2) A requirement that any teacher or other school employee who has reliable information that would lead a reasonable person to suspect that someone is a target of bullying shall immediately report it to the school principal;

(3) A requirement that each school have a procedure for the school administration to promptly investigate in a timely manner and determine whether bullying has occurred;

(4) An age-appropriate range of consequences for bullying which shall include, at minimum and without limitation, disciplinary action or counseling as appropriate under the circumstances;

(5) A procedure for a teacher or other school employee, student, parent, guardian, or other person who has control or charge of a student, either anonymously or in such person's name, at such person's option, to report or otherwise provide information on bullying activity;

(6) A statement prohibiting retaliation following a report of bullying; and

(7) Provisions consistent with the requirements of subsection (b) of this Code section.

(d) The Department of Education shall develop and post on its website a list of entities and their contact information which produce anti-bullying training programs and materials deemed appropriate by the department for use in local school systems.

(e) Any person who reports an incident of bullying in good faith shall be immune from civil liability for any damages caused by such reporting.

(f) Nothing in this Code section or in the model policy promulgated by the Department of Education shall be construed to require a local board of education to provide transportation to a student transferred to another school as a result of a bullying incident.

(g) Any school system which is not in compliance with the requirements of subsection (b) of this Code section shall be ineligible to receive state funding pursuant to Code Sections 20-2-161 and 20-2-260.

§ 20-2-751.6: Student Acts of Violence against School Employees

(a) As used in this Code section, the term "physical violence" means:

(1) Intentionally making physical contact of an insulting or provoking nature with the person of another; or

(2) Intentionally making physical contact which causes physical harm to another unless such physical contacts or physical harms were in defense of himself or herself, as provided in Code Section 16-3-21.

(b) Local board of education policies and student codes of conduct shall provide for the penalties to be assessed against a student found by a disciplinary hearing officer, panel, or tribunal pursuant to Code Section 20-2-752 to have committed any act of physical violence against a teacher, school bus driver, or other school official or employee. Such disciplinary hearing officer, panel, or tribunal shall hold any disciplinary hearing in accordance with the provisions of Code Section 20-2-754. Any student alleged to have committed an act of physical violence shall be suspended pending the hearing by the disciplinary hearing officer, panel, or tribunal. The decision of the disciplinary hearing officer, panel, or tribunal may be appealed to the local school board pursuant to Code Section 20-2-754. If appropriate under paragraph (1) of subsection (c) of this Code section, the decision of the disciplinary hearing officer, panel, or tribunal shall include a recommendation as to whether a student may return to public school and, if return is recommended, a recommended time for the student's return to public school. The local school board may impose penalties not recommended by the disciplinary hearing officer, panel, or tribunal.

(c)(1) A student found by a disciplinary hearing officer, panel, or tribunal to have committed an act of physical violence as defined in paragraph (2) of subsection (a) of this Code section against a teacher, school bus driver, school official, or school employee shall be expelled from the public school system. The expulsion shall be for the remainder of the student's eligibility to attend public school pursuant to Code Section 20-2-150. The local school board at its discretion may permit the student to attend an alternative education program for the period of the student's expulsion. If the student who commits an act of physical violence is in kindergarten through grade eight, then the local school board at its discretion and on the recommendation of the disciplinary hearing officer, panel, or tribunal may permit such a student to reenroll in the regular public school program for grades nine through 12. If the local school board does not operate an alternative education program for students in kindergarten through grade six, the local school board at its discretion may permit a student in kindergarten through grade six who has committed an act of physical violence as defined in paragraph (2) of subsection (a) of this Code section to reenroll in the public school system;

(2) Any student who is found by a disciplinary hearing officer, panel, or tribunal to have committed an act of physical violence against a teacher, school bus driver, school official, or school employee as defined in paragraph (2) of subsection (a) of this Code section shall be referred to juvenile court with a request for a petition alleging delinquent behavior; and

(3) Any student who is found by a disciplinary hearing officer, panel, or tribunal to have committed an act of physical violence as defined in paragraph (1) of subsection (a) of this Code section against a teacher, school bus driver, school official, or school employee may be disciplined by expulsion, long-term suspension, or short-term suspension.

(d) The provisions of this Code section shall apply with respect to any local school system which receives state funding pursuant to Code Sections 20-2-161 and 20-2-260.

(e) Nothing in this Code section shall be construed to infringe on any right provided to students with Individualized Education Programs pursuant to the federal Individuals with Disabilities Education Act, Section 504 of the federal Rehabilitation Act of 1973, or the federal Americans with Disabilities Act of 1990.

§ 20-2-751.2: Students Subject to Disciplinary Orders in Other Schools

(a) As used in this Code section, the term "disciplinary order" means any order of a local school system in this state, a private school in this state, or a public school outside of this state which imposes short-term suspension, long-term suspension, or expulsion upon a student in such system or school.

(b) A local board of education which has a student who attempts to enroll or who is enrolled in any school in its school system during the time in which that student is subject to a disciplinary order is authorized to refuse to enroll or subject that student to short-term suspension, long-term suspension, or expulsion for any time remaining in that other school system's or school's disciplinary order upon receiving a certified copy of such order if the offense which led to such suspension or expulsion in the other school system or school was an offense for which suspension or expulsion could be imposed in the enrolling school.

(c) A local school system or school may request of another school system or school whether any disciplinary order has been imposed by the other school system or school upon a student who is seeking to enroll or is enrolled in the requesting system or school. If such an order has been imposed and is still in effect for such student, the requested school system or private school in this state shall so inform the requesting system or school and shall provide a certified copy of the order to the requesting system or school.

(d) If any school administrator determines from the information obtained pursuant to this Code section or from Code Section 15-11-28 or 15-11-80 that a student has been convicted of or has been adjudicated to have committed an offense which is a designated felony act under Code Section 15-11-63, such administrator shall so inform all teachers to whom the student is assigned and other school personnel to whom the student is assigned. Such teachers and other certificated professional personnel as the administrator deems appropriate may review the information in the student's file provided pursuant to this Code section that has been received from other schools or from the juvenile courts or superior courts. Such information shall be kept confidential.

§ 20-2-751: Student Discipline; Weapons

As used in this subpart, the term:

> (1) "Expulsion" means expulsion of a student from a public school beyond the current school quarter or semester.
> (2) "Long-term suspension" means the suspension of a student from a public school for more than ten school days but not beyond the current school quarter or semester.
> (3) "Short-term suspension" means the suspension of a student from a public school for not more than ten school days.
> (4) "Weapon" means a firearm as such term is defined in Section 921 of Title 18 of the United States Code.
>
> **From: 18 U.S.C.A. § 921:**
>
> The term "firearm" means (A) any weapon (including a starter gun) which will or is designed to or may readily be converted to expel a projectile by the action of an explosive; (B) the frame or receiver of any such weapon; (C) any firearm muffler or firearm silencer; or (D) any destructive device. Such term does not include an antique firearm . . .
>
> (4) The term "destructive device" means—
>
> (A) Any explosive, incendiary, or poison gas—
>
>> (i) bomb,
>> (ii) grenade,

(iii) rocket having a propellant charge of more than four ounces,
(iv) missile having an explosive or incendiary charge of more than one-quarter ounce,
(v) mine, or
(vi) device similar to any of the devices described in the preceding clauses;

(B) Any type of weapon (other than a shotgun or a shotgun shell which the Attorney General finds is generally recognized as particularly suitable for sporting purposes) by whatever name known which will, or which may be readily converted to, expel a projectile by the action of an explosive or other propellant, and which has any barrel with a bore of more than one-half inch in diameter; and
(C) Any combination of parts either designed or intended for use in converting any device into any destructive device described in subparagraph (A) or (B) and from which a destructive device may be readily assembled.

The term "destructive device" shall not include any device which is neither designed nor redesigned for use as a weapon; any device, although originally designed for use as a weapon, which is redesigned for use as a signaling, pyrotechnic, line throwing, safety, or similar device; surplus ordnance sold, loaned, or given by the Secretary of the Army pursuant to the provisions of section 4684(2), 4685, or 4686 of title 10; or any other device which the Attorney General finds is not likely to be used as a weapon, is an antique, or is a rifle which the owner intends to use solely for sporting, recreational or cultural purposes.

§ 20-2-751.1: Weapons in School; Expulsion Required

(a) Each local board of education shall establish a policy requiring the expulsion from school for a period of not less than one calendar year of any student who is determined, pursuant to this subpart, to have brought a weapon to school.
(b) The local board of education shall have the authority to modify such expulsion requirement as provided in subsection (a) of this Code section on a case-by-case basis.
(c) A hearing officer, tribunal, panel, superintendent, or local board of education shall be authorized to place a student determined to have brought a weapon to school in an alternative educational setting.
(d) Nothing in this Code section shall infringe on any right provided to students with Individualized Education Programs pursuant to the federal Individuals with Disabilities Education Act, Section 504 of the federal Rehabilitation Act of 1973, or the federal Americans with Disabilities Act.

§ 16-11-127.1: Weapons in School Safety Zones

(a) As used in this Code section, the term:

(1) "School safety zone" means in or on any real property owned by or leased to any public or private elementary school, secondary school, or school board and used for elementary or secondary education and in or on the campus of any public or private technical school, vocational school, college, university, or institution of postsecondary education.

(2) "Weapon" means and includes any pistol, revolver, or any weapon designed or intended to propel a missile of any kind, or any dirk, bowie knife, switchblade knife, ballistic knife, any other knife having a blade of two or more inches, straight-edge razor, razor blade, spring stick, knuckles, whether made from metal, thermoplastic, wood, or other similar material, blackjack, any bat, club, or other bludgeon-type weapon, or any flailing instrument consisting of two or more rigid parts connected in such a manner as to allow them to swing freely, which may be known as a nun chahka, nun chuck, nunchaku, shuriken, or fighting chain, or any disc, of whatever con-figuration, having at least two points or pointed blades which is designed to be thrown or propelled and which may be known as a throwing star or oriental dart, or any weapon of like kind, and any stun gun or taser as defined in subsection (a) of Code Section 16-11-106. This paragraph excludes any of these instruments used for classroom work authorized by the teacher.

(b)(1) Except as otherwise provided in subsection (c) of this Code section, it shall be unlawful for any person to carry to or to possess or have under such person's control while within a school safety zone or at a school building, school function, or school property or on a bus or other transportation furnished by the school any weapon or explosive compound, other than fireworks the possession of which is regulated by Chapter 10 of Title 25.

(2) Any license holder who violates this subsection shall be guilty of a misdemeanor. Any person who is not a license holder who violates this subsection shall be guilty of a felony and, upon conviction thereof, be punished by a fine of not more than $10,000.00, by imprisonment for not less than two nor more than ten years, or both.

(3) Any person convicted of a violation of this subsection involving a dangerous weapon or machine gun, as such terms are defined in Code Section 16-11-121, shall be punished by a fine of not more than $10,000.00 or by imprisonment for a period of not less than five nor more than ten years, or both.

(4) A child who violates this subsection may be subject to the provisions of Code Section 15-11-63.

(c) The provisions of this Code section shall not apply to:

(1) Baseball bats, hockey sticks, or other sports equipment possessed by competitors for legitimate athletic purposes;

(2) Participants in organized sport shooting events or firearm training courses;

(3) Persons participating in military training programs conducted by or on behalf of the armed forces of the United States or the Georgia Department of Defense;

(4) Persons participating in law enforcement training conducted by a police academy certified by the Georgia Peace Officer Standards and Training Council or by a law enforcement agency of the state or the United States or any political subdivision thereof;

(5) The following persons, when acting in the performance of their official duties or when en route to or from their official duties:

> (A) A peace officer as defined by Code Section 35-8-2;
> (B) A law enforcement officer of the United States government;
> (C) A prosecuting attorney of this state or of the United States;
> (D) An employee of the Georgia Department of Corrections or a correctional facility operated by a political subdivision of this state or the United States who is authorized by the head of such correctional agency or facility to carry a firearm;
> (E) A person employed as a campus police officer or school security officer who is authorized to carry a weapon in accordance with Chapter 8 of Title 20; and
> (F) Medical examiners, coroners, and their investigators who are employed by the state or any political subdivision thereof;

(6) A person who has been authorized in writing by a duly authorized official of the school to have in such person's possession or use as part of any activity being conducted at a school building, school property, or school function a weapon which would otherwise be prohibited by this Code section. Such authorization shall specify the weapon or weapons which have been authorized and the time period during which the authorization is valid;

(7) A person who is licensed in accordance with Code Section 16-11-129 or issued a permit pursuant to Code Section 43-38-10, when such person carries or picks up a student at a school building, school function, or school property or on a bus or other transportation furnished by the school or a person who is licensed in accordance with Code Section 16-11-129 or issued a permit pursuant to Code Section 43-38-10 when he or she has any weapon legally kept within a vehicle when such vehicle is parked at such school property or is in transit through a designated school zone;

(8) A weapon possessed by a license holder which is under the possessor's control in a motor vehicle or which is in a locked compartment of a motor vehicle or one which is in a locked container in or a locked firearms rack which is on a motor vehicle which is being used by an adult over 21 years of age to bring to or pick up a student at a school building, school function, or school property or on a bus or other transportation furnished by the school, or when such vehicle is used to transport someone to an activity being conducted on school property which has been authorized by a duly authorized official of the school; provided, however, that this exception shall not apply to a student attending such school;

(9) Persons employed in fulfilling defense contracts with the government of the United States or agencies thereof when possession of the weapon is necessary for manufacture, transport, installation, and testing under the requirements of such contract;

(10) Those employees of the State Board of Pardons and Paroles when specifically designated and authorized in writing by the members of the State Board of Pardons and Paroles to carry a weapon;

(11) The Attorney General and those members of his or her staff whom he or she specifically authorizes in writing to carry a weapon;

(12) Probation supervisors employed by and under the authority of the Department of Corrections pursuant to Article 2 of Chapter 8 of Title 42, known as the "State-wide Probation Act," when specifically designated and authorized in writing by the director of the Division of Probation;

(13) Public safety directors of municipal corporations;

(14) State and federal trial and appellate judges;

(15) United States attorneys and assistant United States attorneys;

(16) Clerks of the superior courts;

(17) Teachers and other school personnel who are otherwise authorized to possess or carry weapons, provided that any such weapon is in a locked compartment of a motor vehicle or one which is in a locked container in or a locked firearms rack which is on a motor vehicle; or

(18) Constables of any county of this state.

(d)(1) This Code section shall not prohibit any person who resides or works in a business or is in the ordinary course transacting lawful business or any person who is a visitor of such resident located within a school safety zone from carrying, possessing, or having under such person's control a weapon within a school safety zone; provided, however, it shall be unlawful for any such person to carry, possess, or have under such person's control while at a school building or school function or on school property, a school bus, or other transportation furnished by the school any weapon or explosive compound, other than fireworks the possession of which is regulated by Chapter 10 of Title 25

(2) Any person who violates this subsection shall be subject to the penalties specified in subsection (b) of this Code section.

(3) This subsection shall not be construed to waive or alter any legal requirement for possession of weapons or firearms otherwise required by law.

(e) It shall be no defense to a prosecution for a violation of this Code section that:

(1) School was or was not in session at the time of the offense;
(2) The real property was being used for other purposes besides school purposes at the time of the offense; or
(3) The offense took place on a school vehicle.

(f) In a prosecution under this Code section, a map produced or reproduced by any municipal or county agency or department for the purpose of depicting the location and boundaries of the area of the real property of a school board or a private or public elementary or secondary school that is used for school purposes or the area of any campus of any public or private technical school, vocational school, college, university, or institution of postsecondary education, or a true copy of the map, shall, if certified as a true copy by the custodian of the record, be admissible and shall constitute prima-facie evidence of the location and boundaries of the area, if the governing body of the municipality or county has approved the map as an official record of the location and boundaries of the area. A map approved under this Code section may be revised from time to time by the governing body of the municipality or county. The original of every map approved or revised under this subsection or a true copy of such original map shall be filed with the municipality or county and shall be maintained as an official record of the municipality or county. This subsection shall not preclude the prosecution from introducing or relying upon any other evidence or testimony to establish any element of this offense. This subsection shall not preclude the use or admissibility of a map or diagram other than the one which has been approved by the municipality or county.

(g) A county school board may adopt regulations requiring the posting of signs designating the areas of school boards and private or public elementary and secondary schools as "Weapon-free and Violence-free School Safety Zones."

§ 20-2-671: Felony Acts Committed by Students

If any school administrator determines from the information obtained pursuant to Code Section 15-11-63 or 20-2-670 or from any other source that a student has committed a designated felony act, such administrator shall so inform all teachers to whom the student is assigned that they may review the information in the student's file provided pursuant to subsection (b) of Code Section 20-2-670 received from other schools or from the juvenile courts. Such information shall be kept confidential.

§ 20-2-1181: Disrupting or Interfering with School Operations

It shall be unlawful for any person to knowingly, intentionally, or recklessly disrupt or interfere with the operation of any public school, public school bus, or public school bus stop as designated by local school boards of education. Any person violating this Code section shall be guilty of a misdemeanor of a high and aggravated nature.

§ 20-2-1182: Upbraiding, Insulting, or Abusing School Personnel Prohibited

Any parent, guardian, or person other than a student at the public school in question who has been advised that minor children are present and who continues to upbraid, insult, or abuse any public school teacher, public school administrator, or public school bus driver in the presence and hearing of a pupil while on the premises of any public school or public school bus may be ordered by any of the above-designated school personnel to leave the school premises or school bus, and upon failure to do so such person shall be guilty of a misdemeanor and, upon conviction thereof, shall be punished by a fine not to exceed $500.00.

§ 20-2-1184: Reporting Designated Student Crimes

(a) Any teacher or other person employed at any public or private elementary or secondary school or any dean or public safety officer employed by a college or university who has reasonable cause to believe that a student at that school has committed any act upon school property or at any school function, which act is prohibited by any of the following:

(1) Code Section 16-5-21, relating to aggravated assault if a firearm is involved;
(2) Code Section 16-5-24, relating to aggravated battery;
(3) Chapter 6 of Title 16, relating to sexual offenses;
(4) Code Section 16-11-127, relating to carrying a weapon or long gun in an unauthorized location;
(5) Code Section 16-11-127.1, relating to carrying weapons at school functions or on school property or within school safety zones;
(6) Code Section 16-11-132, relating to the illegal possession of a handgun by a person under 18 years of age; or
(7) Code Section 16-13-30, relating to possession and other activities regarding marijuana and controlled substances,

shall immediately report the act and the name of the student to the principal or president of that school or the principal's or president's designee.

(b) The principal or designee who receives a report made pursuant to subsection (a) of this Code section who has reasonable cause to believe that the report is valid shall make an oral report thereof immediately by telephone or otherwise to the appropriate school system superintendent and to the appropriate police authority and district attorney.

(c) Any person participating in the making of a report or causing a report to be made as authorized or required pursuant to this Code section or participating in any judicial proceeding or any other proceeding resulting therefrom shall in so doing be immune from any civil or criminal liability that might otherwise be incurred or imposed, providing such participation pursuant to this Code section is made in good faith.

(d) Any person required to make a report pursuant to this Code section who knowingly and willfully fails to do so shall be guilty of a misdemeanor.

Georgia Regulations

160-4-8-.15: Student Discipline

(1) Definitions:
(a) Behavior Support Process: a student support process for identifying and addressing the behavioral needs through providing integrated resources that promote behavioral change.
(b) Disciplinary Order: any public or private school or school system order that imposes short-term suspension, long-term suspension, or expulsion upon a student in such school or system.

(c) Discipline Policies: outlines consequences and punishments that will occur in the response to specify unacceptable behaviors.

(d) Progressive Discipline: the levels of consequences assigned to students who violate codes of conduct based on severity of misbehavior, students discipline history, and other relevant factors.

(2) Requirements:

(a) Each local board of education shall adopt policies designed to improve the student learning environment by improving student behavior and discipline. These policies shall provide for the development of age appropriate student codes of conduct that contain the following, at a minimum:

> (1) Standards for student behavior during school hours, at school-related functions, on school buses, and at school bus stops designed to create the expectation that students will behave themselves in such a way so as to facilitate a learning environment for themselves and other students, respect each other and school district employees, obey student behavior policies adopted by the local board of education, and obey student behavior rules established by individual schools;
>
> (2) Verbal assault, including threatening violence, of teachers, administrators, and other school personnel;
>
> (3) Physical assault or battery of teachers, administrators or other school personnel;
>
> (4) Disrespectful conduct toward teachers, administrators, other school personnel, persons attending school related functions or other students, including use of vulgar or profane language;
>
> (5) Verbal assault of other students, including threatening violence or sexual harassment as defined pursuant to Title IX of the Education Amendments of 1972;
>
> (6) Sexual harassment as defined pursuant to Title IX of the Education Amendments of 1972 or physical assault or battery of other students;
>
> (7) Guidelines and consequences resulting from failure to comply with compulsory attendance as required under O.C.G.A § 20-2-690.1;
>
> (8) Willful or malicious damage to real or personal property of the school or to personal property of any person legitimately at the school;
>
> (9) Inciting, advising, or counseling of others to engage in prohibited acts;
>
> (10) Marking, defacing or destroying school property or the property of another student;
>
> (11) Possession of a weapon, as provided for in O.C.G.A. § 16-11-127.1;
>
> (12) Unlawful use or possession of illegal drugs or alcohol;
>
> (13) Willful and persistent violation of student codes of conduct;
>
> (14) Bullying as defined in O.C.G.A. § 20-2-751.4;
>
> (15) Any off-campus behavior of a student which could result in the student being criminally charged with a felony and which makes the student's continued presence at school a potential danger to persons or property at the school or which disrupts the educational process;

(16) Each local board of education shall adopt policies, applicable to students in grades 6 through 12 that prohibit bullying of a student by another student and shall require such prohibition to be included in the student code of conduct in that school system. Local board policies shall require that, upon a finding that a student in grades 6 through 12 has committed the offense of bullying for the third time in a school year, such student shall be assigned to an alternative school.

(17) Behavior support processes designed to consider, as appropriate in light of the severity of the behavioral problem, support services that may be available through the school, school system, other public entities, or community organizations that may help the student address behavioral problems. This rule neither mandates nor prohibits the use of student support teams as part of the student support process;

(18) Progressive discipline processes designed to create the expectation that the degree of discipline will be in proportion to the severity of the behavior; that the previous discipline history of the student and other relevant factors will be taken into account; and that all due process procedures required by federal and state law will be followed;

(19) Parental involvement processes designed to create the expectation that parents, guardians, teachers and school administrators will work together to improve and enhance student behavior and academic performance and will communicate freely their concerns about, and actions in response to, student behavior that detracts from the learning environment. Local boards of education shall provide opportunities for parental involvement in developing and updating student codes of conduct;

(20) A statement that major offenses including, but not limited to, drug and weapon offenses can lead to schools being named as an Unsafe School according to the provisions of State Board of Education Rule 160-4-8-.16 Unsafe School Choice Option.

(b) Local boards of education shall provide for the distribution of student codes of conduct to each student upon enrollment and to the parents and guardians of each student and may solicit the signatures of students and parents or guardians in acknowledgment of the receipt of such student codes of conduct.

(c) Student codes of conduct shall be available in each school and classroom.

(d) Local boards of education shall provide for disciplinary actions against students who violate student codes of conduct.

(e) Local board policies relating to student codes of conduct shall provide that each local superintendent shall fully support the authority of principals and teachers in the school system to remove a student from the classroom pursuant to O.C.G.A. § 20-2-738, including establishing and disseminating procedures.

(f) It is the preferred policy of the board that disruptive students are placed in alternative education settings in lieu of being suspended or expelled.

(g) Local board policies shall require the filing of a report by a teacher documenting a student's violation of the student code of conduct which repeatedly or substantially interferes with the teacher's ability to communicate effectively with the students in his or her class or with the ability of such student's classmates to learn within one school day of the most recent occurrence of such behavior. The report shall be filed with the principal or principal's designee, shall not exceed one page, and shall describe the behavior. The principal or principal's designee shall, within one day of receiving such report, send to the student's parents or guardians a copy of the report, and information regarding how the principal or principal's designee may be contacted.

(h) The principal or the principal's designee shall send written notification to the teacher and to the student's parents or guardians of the student support services being utilized or the disciplinary action taken within one school day and shall make a reasonable attempt to confirm receipt of such written notification by the student's parents or guardians. Written notification shall include information regarding how student's parents or guardians may contact the principal or principal's designee.

(i) Each local board of education shall observe Georgia law in developing and implementing disciplinary hearings held by a disciplinary hearing officer, disciplinary panel, or disciplinary tribunal pursuant to O.C.G.A. § 20-2-751 through § 20-2-758 including the ability to honor disciplinary orders of private schools and other public schools/school systems pursuant to O.C.G.A. § 20-2-751.2:

> (1) Disciplinary hearings shall be held no later than ten school days after the beginning of the student's suspension unless the school system and parents or guardians mutually agree to an extension;
>
> (2) Any teacher who is called as a witness by the school system shall be given notice no later than three days prior to the hearing.

Authority O.C.G.A §§ 16-11-127.1; 20-2-152; 20-2-240; 20-2-735 to 20-2-738; 20-2-751.1; 20-2-751.2; 20-2-751.4 to 20-2-751.6; 20-2-752 to 20-2-756; 20-2-1181

160-4-8-.16: Unsafe School Choice Option (USCO)

(1) Definitions:

(a) Corrective action plan: a written plan developed by a local school system and adopted by the local board of education for a public school that is identified as a persistently dangerous school for the purpose of remedying the causes that result in this school being identified as persistently dangerous.

(b) Jurisdiction of a public school: events that are sponsored by a public school and that occur away from the property of a public school over which the public school has direct control or authority.

(c) Official action: an official tribunal held by the school system; a hearing conducted by a disciplinary hearing officer of the school system (O.C.G.A. § 20-2-752 through § 20-2-758); through a waiver process; through an action of the local board of education; or for non-felony drug offenses that result in placement in a drug intervention program.

(d) Persistently dangerous school: a public school in which for each of three consecutive years on the property of the public school, or at an event within the jurisdiction of a public school, or at a school sponsored event:

(1) At least one student enrolled in that school is found by official action to have committed an offense in violation of a school rule that involved one or more of the following criminal offenses:

    (i) Aggravated battery (O.C.G.A. § 16-5-24)
    (ii) Aggravated child molestation (O.C.G.A. § 16-6-4)
    (iii) Aggravated sexual battery (O.C.G.A. § 16-6-22.2)
    (iv) Aggravated sodomy (O.C.G.A. § 16-6-2)
    (v) Armed robbery (O.C.G.A. § 16-8-41)
    (vi) Arson – first degree (O.C.G.A. § 16-7-60)
    (vii) Kidnapping (O.C.G.A. § 16-5-40)
    (viii) Murder (O.C.G.A. § 16-5-1)
    (ix) Rape (O.C.G.A. § 16-6-1)
    (x) Voluntary manslaughter (O.C.G.A. § 16-5-2); or

(2) Two percent or more of the student population or ten students, whichever is greater, are found by official action to have committed an offense in violation of a school rule that involved one or more of the following offenses:

    (i) Non-felony drugs (O.C.G.A. § 16-13-2)
    (ii) Felony drugs (O.C.G.A. §§ 16-13-30; 16-13-31; 16-13-32.4)
    (iii) Felony weapons (O.C.G.A. § 16-11-127.1)
    (iv) Terroristic threats (O.C.G.A. § 16-11-37); or

(3) Any combination of paragraphs (1)(d)(1). or (1)(d)(2).

(e) Property of a public school: Any building, land, school bus, or other vehicular equipment owned or leased by the local school system.

(f) Student population: the unduplicated October full-time equivalent (FTE) count.

(g) Unsafe School Choice Option (USCO): the process of allowing students who attend a persistently dangerous public school or students who become victims of a violent criminal offense while on the property of a public school in which they are enrolled to transfer to a safe public school.

(h) Victim: a person against whom a violent criminal offense has been committed and whose perpetrator has been found by official action to be in violation of a school rule related to the violent criminal offense.

(i) Violent criminal offense: for the purposes of this rule, the following felony transgressions of law as defined in state statute, including aggravated battery (O.C.G.A. § 16-5-24), aggravated child molestation (O.C.G.A. § 16-6-4), aggravated sexual battery (O.C.G.A. § 16-6-22.2), aggravated sodomy (O.C.G.A. § 16-6-2), armed robbery (O.C.G.A. § 16-8-41), first degree arson (O.C.G.A. § 16-7-60), felony weapons charge (O.C.G.A. § 16-11-127.1), kidnapping (O.C.G.A. § 16-5-40), murder (O.C.G.A. § 16-5-1), rape (O.C.G.A. § 16-6-1), voluntary manslaughter (O.C.G.A. § 16-5-2), or terroristic threats (O.C.G.A. § 16-11-37).

(2) Requirements:

(a) Local school systems (LSSs) shall annually report to the Georgia Department of Education on a date and in a manner specified by the Department data regarding students found by official action to be in violation of a school rule related to a criminal offense as identified in paragraphs (1)(d)(1) and (1)(d)(2).

(b) The Georgia Department of Education shall identify by July 1 of each year persistently dangerous public schools using the criteria specified in paragraph (1)(d) and shall notify the LSS superintendent of such identification.

(c) The LSS shall within ten school days of notification by the Georgia Department of Education notify the parents/guardians of students enrolled in a school that has been classified as a persistently dangerous school. This parental notification shall be written in English and any other language prevalent in the student population of that school. This notification shall also specify the process adopted by the local board of education to be used for the transfer of a student to a safe public school, including a charter school, either within the school system or to one located in another school system with which the system has an agreement, upon the request of a parent/guardian or by a student if the student has reached the age of 18. Following student transfer guidelines consistent with the No Child Left Behind Act of 2001, LSSs shall allow students to transfer to a school that is making adequate yearly progress and has not been identified as being in school improvement, corrective action, or restructuring. Student transfers to safe schools within the school system or to a safe school within another school system with which the school system has an agreement shall be completed within 30 school days of the request.

(d) Any student who is the victim of a violent criminal offense that occurs on the property of a public school in which the student is enrolled, while attending a school-sponsored event that occurs on the property of a public school, or while attending an event under the jurisdiction of a public school shall be permitted to attend a safe public school, including a charter school. Each local board of education shall adopt a policy that facilitates the transfer of students who are victims of violent criminal offenses. This policy shall provide that the transfer shall occur within ten school days of the commission of the violent criminal offense, and to the extent possible, shall allow victims to transfer to a school that is making adequate yearly progress and has not been identified as being in school improvement, corrective action, or restructuring.

(e) A local board of education with one or more of its schools identified as persistently dangerous is not required to cover the cost of transportation to a safe public school beyond the levels identified by federal legislation.

(f) LSSs shall develop and local boards of education shall adopt a corrective action plan for each school identified by the Georgia Department of Education as a persistently dangerous school. The corrective action plan shall be based on an analysis of the problems faced by the school and address the issues that resulted in the school being identified as persistently dangerous. The LSS shall submit to the Georgia Department of Education for approval the corrective action plan. This plan shall be submitted within 20 school days after the Georgia Department of Education notifies the local school system that a school has been classified as a persistently dangerous school.

> (1) Upon completion of its planned corrective action, a LSS may apply to the Georgia Department of Education to have the school removed from the list of

persistently dangerous schools. After ensuring that all corrective action has been completed, the Georgia Department of Education shall reassess the school using the criteria for persistently dangerous schools as specified in paragraph (1)(d) of this rule.

Authority O.C.G.A. §§ 3-3-23, 16-5-1, 16-5-2, 16-5-24, 16-5-40, 16-6-1, 16-6-2, 16-6-4, 16-6-22.2, 16-7-60, 16-8-41, 16-11-37, 16-11-106, 16-11-127.1, 16-13-2, 16-13-30, 16-13-31, 16-13-32.4, 20-2-240, 20-2-752 to 20-2-758

160-1-3-.04: School Law Tribunals and Appeals

(1) Purpose: The purpose of this rule is to specify the procedures for appeals from local boards of education (LBOE) to the State Board of Education on issues respecting the administration or construction of school law.

(2) Role of the Vice Chairperson:

(a) The vice chairperson for appeals of the state board or a hearing officer contracted with or employed by the state board shall conduct a review of appeals to the state board and shall acquaint state board members with the matters to be considered.

(b) The vice chairperson for appeals or the hearing officer shall draft the ruling of the state board.

(3) Procedures before the Local Board of Education:

(a) LBOEs shall hold hearings when required by law. The LBOE shall adopt, except as otherwise provided for by law, the following hearing procedures:

> (1) The LBOE shall notify the parties of the time and place of the hearing.
>
> (2) The LBOE shall sign and issue subpoenas.
>
> (3) All witnesses shall testify under oath and shall be subject to cross-examination.
>
> (4) The LBOE shall require the testimony and other evidence to be transcribed by a court reporter or recorded by other appropriate means.
>
> (5) The strict rules of evidence prevailing in courts of law shall not be applicable to hearings before LBOEs.
>
> (6) At the conclusion of the hearing, or within 15 days thereafter, the LBOE shall notify the parties of its decision in writing and shall notify the parties of their right to appeal the decision to the State Board of Education.

(4) Appeals to the State Board of Education:

(a) After a hearing by the LBOE when held in accordance with state law and/or state board policies, regulations or rules, any party aggrieved by a decision of the LBOE rendered on an issue respecting the administration or construction of school law may appeal to the state board by filing the appeal in writing with the local school superintendent. The appeal shall set forth:

> (1) The question in dispute;
>
> (2) The decision of the local board; and
>
> (3) A concise statement of the reasons why the decision is being appealed.

(b) The party making the appeal shall file with the appeal the complete record, including a transcript of testimony certified as true and correct by the local school superintendent or a request that the superintendent transcribe and prepare such transcript. The party making the appeal shall assume the costs of such preparation.

(c) When any party is unable to pay the cost of a transcript of the hearing because of indigence, the party shall be relieved from paying the cost if said party provides to the local school superintendent an affidavit to that effect. The party's rights shall be the same as those had the party paid the cost of the transcript. Upon receipt of an affidavit, the local school superintendent may inquire into the ability of the applicant to pay the cost of the transcript. After a hearing, the local school superintendent may order the party to pay the cost of the transcript by a certain date. Such decision of the local school superintendent may be appealed by the party to the State Board of Education in the same manner as other issues. If a party appeals the order of the local board to pay the cost, the local school superintendent shall submit to the State Board of Education a transcript of the hearing on indigence that is certified by the local school superintendent. If no appeal of the issue of indigence is filed and the cost is not paid as ordered by the LBOE, or if an appeal is filed and the State Board of Education affirms the local board decision, the appeal shall not be docketed.

(d) The appeal to the State Board of Education shall be filed with the local school superintendent within 30 days of the decision in question.

(e) Transmission to the State School Superintendent: The local superintendent shall within 10 days after the filing of the appeal, transmit to the state school superintendent a copy of the appeal, together with the transcript of evidence and proceedings, the decision of the local board and other matters in the file relating to the appeal. All materials should be certified as true and correct. The appeal may be amended and a transcript filed any time prior to transmission to the state board.

(f) Notice: After a determination by the state school superintendent or designee that the appeal is in proper form for hearing, the appeal shall be docketed and placed on the calendar for review before the hearing officer of the state board at the earliest practical time.

(g) The party requesting the appeal shall file a brief with the state board discussing the party's position within 20 days of the date of docketing. The opposing party shall have 40 days from the date of docketing to file a brief.

(h) Oral arguments shall not be heard unless requested by a party or requested by the hearing officer. Oral arguments must be requested by a party within 10 days of the date the appeal is docketed.

(i) Procedure at Oral Argument: If oral argument is ordered or granted, the appellant may be represented by counsel. The argument shall be confined to the issues in the record and the evidence transmitted from previous proceedings. No new evidence shall be received. The state board shall not consider any question not specifically raised in the written appeal or the statement of contentions.

(j) Decision of State Board: The state board shall render its decision in a written order within 25 days after it hears the case and shall notify the parties in writing of its decision and of their right to appeal the decision to the Superior Court of the county wherein the LBOE is located.

(k) Dismissal of Appeal: Failure to comply with any of the provisions herein may be grounds for dismissal.

(l) No Supersedeas: No appeal shall act as a stay of a local board's order unless so ordered by the local board or by the vice chairperson for appeals of the state board.

(5) Severability: The provisions of this rule are hereby declared to be severable, and the invalidation of any part hereof shall not affect or invalidate any other part.

Authority O.C.G.A. §§ 20-2-240, 20-2-940, 20-2-1160

Chapter 7: Equal Protection of the Laws

No system of government is perfect. Further, even if a perfect system of government was possible, the individuals responsible for administering the government are imperfect. Like other humans, too many government officials regrettably bring the tragic human imperfections of selfishness, ignorance, and prejudice from their private lives into their public work. And while a democratic form of government has many virtues, democracy also has a serious potential flaw: In a system of governance in which the majority rules, because of selfishness, ignorance, and prejudice the majority may too often fail to respect the equal rights of political minorities.

The Fourteenth Amendment to the U.S. Constitution was adopted to help guard against these dangers by providing equal protection of the laws to all persons. Concerning government actions, equal protection of the laws is guaranteed by the Fourteenth Amendment to the U.S. Constitution, and by similar provisions in state constitutions. The Fourteenth Amendment (1868) states:

> All persons born or naturalized in the United States, and subject to the jurisdiction thereof, are citizens of the United States and of the State wherein they reside. No State shall make or enforce any law which shall abridge the privileges or immunities of citizens of the United States; nor shall any State deprive any person of life, liberty, or property, without due process of law; nor deny to any person within its jurisdiction the equal protection of the laws.

The Fourteenth Amendment specifically prohibits discrimination by state governments, requiring states to provide due process and equal protection of the laws to all persons. Equal protection of the laws prohibits differential treatment based on factors that are legally irrelevant, and are instead the products of irrational prejudice or discrimination (e.g., differential treatment by government based on race, color, national origin, etc.). But principles of equal protection may allow or even require differential treatment when there are legally relevant differences among individuals (e.g., persons with disabilities may be entitled to additional resources as reasonable accommodations to provide them with a fair opportunity to participate in publicly funded activities).

In interpreting the Equal Protection Clause of the Fourteenth Amendment, the U.S. Supreme Court developed a multi-tiered approach for adjudicating allegations of governmental denial of equal protection of the laws. Most state courts have adopted a similar model for reviewing equal protection cases. Where differential treatment by government is established by plaintiffs, the purpose of the court's inquiry is to determine whether the differential treatment is justified by a sufficient governmental interest. The graduated levels of scrutiny reflect the Court's determination that certain categories of government action (i.e., discrimination based on race, national origin, or a fundamental right) are inherently more suspect than others (i.e., general social and economic regulations), and therefore merit heightened levels of judicial scrutiny and require greater levels of proof by government officials seeking to defend the differential treatment.

Basic Framework for Judicial Review of Equal Protection Challenges

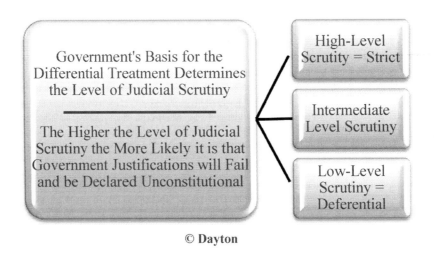

© Dayton

The Court has recognized three basic levels of judicial scrutiny based on judicial suspicion of the government's differential treatment: Low-level; intermediate; and high-level judicial scrutiny. Concerning when low-level scrutiny is appropriate, members of the legislative and administrative braches are elected to make decisions about general social and economic issues. The judicial branch is not a general overseer of all government decisions. Courts should defer to the political branches concerning general social and economic issues, and only intervene where warranted because of irrational governmental discrimination. Therefore differential treatments based on general social and economic regulations (e.g., tax rates, zoning regulations, etc.) are only subjected to the low-level scrutiny of the rational basis test. Under the rational basis test government officials need only establish that their actions are rationally related to a legitimate governmental interest. Whether legislative and administrative decisions on general social and economic issues are unwise is for voters to decide in subsequent elections. It is only when these actions discriminate without any rational basis that judicial intervention is warranted.

Government actions that discriminate based on gender, age, or legitimacy have been viewed as quasi-suspect by the Court and subjected to an intermediate-level of scrutiny. Differential treatment based on these quasi-suspect criteria is deemed unconstitutional under the equal protection clause unless government officials can prove that the differential treatment was substantially related to an important government interest. More recently, however, the Court has applied a further elevated scrutiny to differential treatment based on gender, requiring that differential treatment based on gender be justified by an exceedingly persuasive justification,

Differential treatment based on fundamental rights or suspect classifications such as race and national origin, are subjected to the strictest judicial scrutiny. To qualify as a suspect classification, the Court has held that the government action must be aimed at a "discrete and insular minority" that is: 1) Politically powerless; and 2) Historically discriminated against. To be politically powerless doesn't mean the group has no political power, but instead they have no realistic opportunity to defend their rights against majoritarian power in the common legislative realm. Women, for example, have not been deemed a suspect class because voting age women outnumber voting age men, making it politically possible for women to defend their rights in the legislative realm or to even dominate the political process. Men are not a suspect class, however, because there is no substantial legislative history of discrimination against men. The Court treats gender discrimination as a quasi-suspect class, subject to an elevated standard of review.

Discrimination against racial and ethnic minorities has been so pervasive, however, that the Court subjects any governmental use of race, color, or ethnicity to strict scrutiny. All suspect classifications are subject to strict judicial scrutiny and must be justified by establishing that the differential treatment is necessary to a compelling governmental interest and narrowly tailored to achieving that interest. In practice, governmental actions subjected to strict judicial scrutiny rarely survive this rigorous judicial test. Justice Marshall recognized that strict scrutiny is generally "strict in theory, but fatal in fact." Until the Court's sharply divided 5-4 decision in *Grutter v. Bollinger*, 539 U.S. 306 (2003), the last time a governmental racial classification survived strict scrutiny by the Court was in *Korematsu v. U.S.*, 323 U.S. 214 (1944), the now universally condemned case in which the Court upheld forced relocations and internments of Japanese-Americans in "war relocation camps."

Summary of Judicial Standards of Review under the Equal Protection Clause

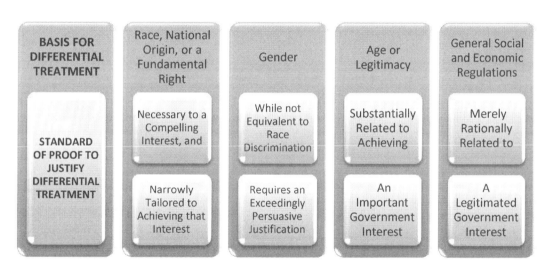

© Dayton

The core teaching of the Court's cases on equal protection is that government officials cannot legally treat individuals differently for irrelevant, discriminatory reasons, such as the person's race, color, religion, sex, national origin, disability, etc., when those factors bear no appropriate relationship to a sufficient governmental justification. Absent a legitimate and sufficient reason for differential treatment, federal, state, and local governments must treat all persons equally under the laws. The Fourteenth Amendment also grants Congress the power to enforce the Fourteenth Amendment through appropriate legislation, legislation which includes, for example, the Civil Rights Act of 1964 and subsequent legislation prohibiting discrimination based on race, color, religion, sex, national origin, and disability. State laws or local policies may provide additional protections for citizens.

In summary, generally government officials must provide equal treatment to individuals in equal circumstances. Differential treatment must be justified by proving an appropriate relationship between the differential treatment and a sufficient governmental justification. Equal protection of the laws prohibits differential treatment based on factors that are legally irrelevant (e.g., race; color; national origin; etc.), and are instead the products of irrational prejudice or discrimination. But differential treatment may be allowed or even required when there are legally relevant differences among individuals.

Discrimination based on gender remains among the most challenging areas of equal protection concerns in schools. Discrimination based on race, color, ethnicity, or national origin are *per se* irrational and strictly prohibited by law. Unlike race, color, ethnicity, or national origin, however, there are sometimes relevant physical differences based on gender that may justify differential treatment. These limited, relevant gender differences cannot, however, be allowed to become a pretext for irrational discrimination based on gender.

Regarding differential treatment based on gender the Court has recognized: "Physical differences between men and women . . . are enduring: The two sexes are not fungible." Nonetheless, gender based classifications by government require an "exceedingly persuasive justification." Government officials must show "at least that the challenged classification serves important governmental objectives and that the discriminatory means employed are substantially related to the achievement of those objectives . . . The justification must be genuine, not hypothesized or invented post hoc in response to litigation. And it must not rely on overbroad generalizations about the different talents, capacities, or preferences of males and females."

Sexual harassment is a particularly invidious and reprehensible form of gender discrimination. For ethical and moral reasons alone, sexual harassment cannot be tolerated in schools. But when sexual harassment of students occurs, at least since *Franklin v. Gwinnett*, 503 U.S. 60 (1992), there is a strong potential for litigation and significant monetary damages under Title IX. Sexual harassment involving employees under Title VII is addressed in Chapter 9. Sexual harassment involving students under Title IX is addressed below.

Sexual Harassment under Title IX

Title IX, 20 U.S.C. § 1681 (2012), governs sexual harassment of students in educational institutions receiving federal funding. To prevail in a sexual harassment suit for monetary damages under Title IX, plaintiffs must generally establish that:

1) School officials had actual notice of the sexual harassment, and;
2) School officials reacted with deliberate indifference.

The Court defined "actual notice" in *Gebser v. Lago Vista*, 524 U.S. 274 (1998), finding that it required "notice to an 'appropriate person'" and that "an 'appropriate person' . . . is, at a minimum, an official of the recipient entity with authority to take corrective action to end the discrimination." The Court defined "deliberate indifference" in *Davis v. Monroe*, 526 U.S. 629 (1999), finding that "school officials will be "deemed 'deliberately indifferent' . . . where the recipient's response to the harassment or lack thereof is clearly unreasonable in light of the known circumstances."

Concerning peer sexual harassment among students under Title IX, in *Davis* the Court found that: "The fact that it was a teacher who engaged in harassment in *Franklin* and *Gebser* is relevant." School officials have greater responsibility for the conduct of employees, and students are more prone to engaging in some gender-based adolescent behavior. To hold school officials liable for peer sexual harassment under Title IX the plaintiff must prove:

Proving Peer Sexual Harassment Under Title IX

 1) Actual Notice
School officials had actual notice of the sexual harassment;

 2) Deliberate Indifference
School officials reacted with deliberate indifference; and

 3) Severe & Pervasive
Harassment was so severe, pervasive, and objectively offensive equal access was denied

© Dayton

The plaintiff must prove school officials had actual notice of the sexual harassment; school officials reacted with deliberate indifference; and the harassment was so severe, pervasive, and objectively offensive, and so undermined and detracted from the educational experience, that the student was effectively denied equal access to an institution's resources and opportunities.

Under Title IX students are not only protected from discrimination, but they are also shielded from being "excluded from participation in" or "denied the benefits of" any "education program or activity receiving Federal financial assistance." It is the tolerance of sexual harassment in the school that is the basis for liability under Title IX. To avoid liability, school officials "must merely respond to known peer harassment in a manner that is not clearly unreasonable."

Together *Franklin*, *Gebser*, and *Davis* teach the following lessons to avoid liability:

1) Have a reasonable policy in place for the prevention and correction of sexual harassment;

2) Promptly and fairly investigate reports of alleged sexual harassment; and

3) Take reasonable remedial actions when appropriate to assure that no one is excluded from educational opportunities because of sexual harassment or other differential treatment based on gender.

© Dayton

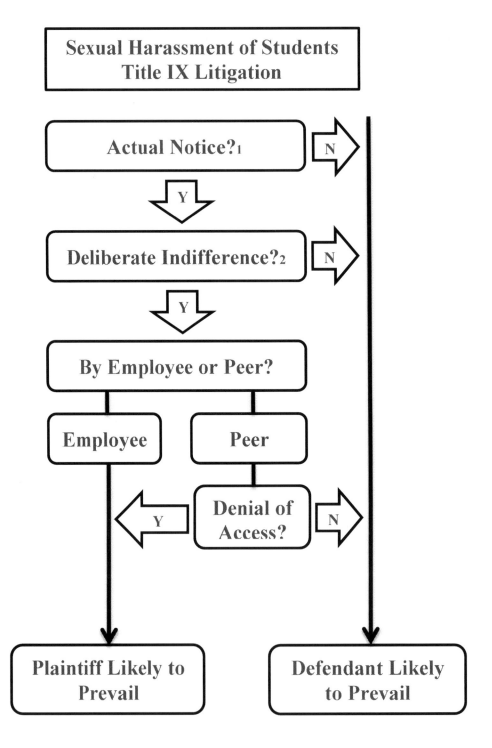

1 "Actual notice": Notice to an official with authority to take corrective action.
2 "Deliberately indifference": Response is clearly unreasonable in light of the known circumstances.

© Dayton

Selected Georgia Laws

Georgia Constitution

Article I, Section I

Article I, Section I, Paragraph II: Protection to person and property; equal protection. Protection to person and property is the paramount duty of government and shall be impartial and complete. No person shall be denied the equal protection of the laws.

Paragraph VII: Citizens, protection of. All citizens of the United States, resident in this state, are hereby declared citizens of this state; and it shall be the duty of the General Assembly to enact such laws as will protect them in the full enjoyment of the rights, privileges, and immunities due to such citizenship.

Georgia Statutes

§ 20-2-133: Public School Instruction to be Free

(a) Admission to the instructional programs funded under this article shall be free to all eligible children and youth who enroll in such programs within the local school system in which they reside and to children as provided in subsection (b) of this Code section. Therefore, a local school system shall not charge resident students tuition or fees, nor shall such students be required to provide materials or equipment except for items specified by the State Board of Education, as a condition of enrollment or full participation in any instructional program. However, a local school system is authorized to charge nonresident students tuition or fees or a combination thereof; provided, however, that such charges to a student shall not exceed the average locally financed per student cost for the preceding year, excluding the local five mill share funds required pursuant to Code Section 20-2-164; provided, further, that no child in a placement operated by the Department of Human Services or the Department of Behavioral Health and Developmental Disabilities or for which payment is made by the Department of Juvenile Justice, the Department of Human Services or any of its divisions, or the Department of Behavioral Health and Developmental Disabilities and no child who is in the physical or legal custody of the Department of Juvenile Justice, under the care or physical or legal custody of the Department of Human Services or any of its divisions, or under the physical custody of the Department of Behavioral Health and Developmental Disabilities shall be charged tuition, fees, or a combination thereof. A local school system is further authorized to contract with a nonresident student's system of residence for payment of tuition. The amount of tuition paid directly by the system of residence shall be limited only by the terms of the contract between systems. Local units of administration shall provide textbooks or any other reading materials to each student enrolled in a class which has a course of study that requires the use of such materials by the students . . .

Georgia Regulations

160-4-5-.02: Language Assistance for English Learners (Els)

(1) Definitions:

(a) English Learners (Els): Students whose primary or home language is other than English and who are eligible for services based on the results of an English language proficiency assessment.

(b) English language proficiency: The level of language competence necessary to participate fully and learn successfully in classrooms where the primary language of instruction is English.

(c) English to Speakers of Other Languages (ESOL): An educational support program provided to help Els overcome language barriers and participate meaningfully in schools' educational programs.

(d) Georgia Department of Education: The state agency charged with the fiscal and administrative management of certain aspects of K-12 public education, including the implementation of federal and state mandates. Such management is subject to supervision and oversight by the State Board of Education.

(e) Home Language Survey: A questionnaire administered upon enrollment to each student's parent or guardian for the purpose of determining whether a language other than English is used by the student or used in the student's home.

(f) Language Assessment Conference (LAC): A meeting held to determine appropriate placement of Els with borderline proficiency scores.

(g) Language assistance services: Supplemental language support programs that promote academic language development for students with limited English proficiency.

(h) Local Educational Agency (LEA): Local school system pursuant to local board of education control and management.

(i) School: Any school or special entity as defined in State Board Rule 160-5-1-.03 Identification and Reporting of Schools.

(j) State-adopted English proficiency measure: An English language proficiency test administered annually to all English learners (Els) in Georgia for the purposes of determining the English language proficiency level of students; providing districts with information that will help them evaluate the effectiveness of their ESOL programs; providing information that enhances instruction and learning in programs for English learners; assessing the annual English language proficiency gains using a standards-based assessment instrument; and providing data for meeting federal and state requirements with respect to student assessment.

(k) State-adopted English proficiency screening measure: A formal measure of social and academic English language proficiency that assesses students' need for initial placement in supplemental language assistance services.

(l) Student Record: The state's required end-of-year student data collection.

(2) Requirements:

(a) Eligibility for entry into and exit from language assistance:

>(1) Prior to entry into a school in Georgia, each student's parent or guardian shall complete a Home Language Survey or an equivalent to determine if a language

other than English is used in the home or is the student's native language or first language. All students whose native language, first language or language of the home includes a language other than English shall be assessed for English language proficiency using the state-adopted English proficiency screening measure.

(2) Initial eligibility for language assistance services shall be determined by the student's score on the state-adopted English proficiency screening measure:

> (i) Students who have an English language proficiency score below proficient on the state-adopted English proficiency screening measure shall be determined to be English learners (Els) and shall be eligible for language assistance services. Coding guidance for Els can be found in the ESOL/Title III Resource Guide.
>
> (ii) Students who have an English language proficiency score at or above proficient on the state adopted English proficiency screening measure shall be considered English proficient and shall not be eligible for language assistance. Coding guidance for non-Els is located in the ESOL/Title III Resource Guide.

(3) All Els shall be assessed annually on the state-adopted English proficiency measure to
determine English language proficiency. Students who score at the developing level or below on the state-adopted English proficiency measure shall continue to be eligible for language assistance services.

(4) Exiting from ESOL services:

> (i) Students who score at the proficient level on both the state-adopted English proficiency measure and on the state reading assessment shall be considered English proficient.
>
> (ii) If the LEA does not administer a state reading assessment for the student, the student shall be considered English proficient if the student scores at the proficient level on both the state-adopted English proficiency measure and on the literacy (reading and writing) sub-score of the state-adopted English proficiency measure.
>
> (iii) Students who score at the proficient level on either the state-adopted English proficiency measure or the state reading assessment but not both shall have their continued eligibility for language assistance determined through a Language Assessment Conference (LAC). The LAC shall be attended by the student's classroom teacher(s), the teacher providing language assistance services, and other relevant parties selected from the following: parent, principal or designee, counselor, school psychologist, or lead teacher. The LAC shall be conducted in accordance with the ESOL/Title III Resource Guide.
>
> (iv) Students who are considered English proficient shall not be eligible for continued language assistance services and shall be exited from language assistance services.

(v) Each LEA shall monitor students that are considered English proficient for two years after exit from language assistance services. These students shall be considered EL Monitored. Coding guidance for Monitored Els is located in the ESOL/Title III Resource Guide. The monitoring process shall consist of a documented review of report card grades, state assessment results, classroom performance and teacher observations for the purpose of ensuring the successful transition to the general classroom. Additional guidance can be found in the ESOL/Title III Resource Guide.

(b) Language assistance service delivery models:
1. LEAs and schools shall provide English language assistance to all Els. Such assistance shall be provided through the state-funded ESOL program or placement in a locally-developed language assistance program approved in advance by the Georgia Department of Education. Approved instructional delivery models include:

(i) Pull-out model: students are taken out of a general education class for the purpose of receiving small group language instruction from the ESOL teacher;
(ii) Push-in model (within reading, language arts, mathematics, science or social studies): students remain in their core academic class where they receive content instruction from their content area teacher along with targeted language instruction from the ESOL teacher;
(iii) A cluster center to which students are transported for instruction: students from two or more schools are grouped in a center designed to provide intensive language assistance;
(iv) A resource center/laboratory: students receive language assistance in a group setting supplemented by multimedia materials;
(v) A scheduled class period: students at the middle and high school levels receive language assistance and/or content instruction in a class composed only of Els;
(vi) An innovative delivery model approved in advance by the Georgia Department of Education through a process described in the ESOL/Title III Resource Guide.

(c) Language assistance curricula and assessment:
(1) Language assistance curricula in the state-funded ESOL program shall consist of plans of instruction which are adapted to the English language proficiency of students and are designed to develop: 1) listening, speaking, reading, writing and American cultural concepts and 2) the language of academic instruction used in language arts, mathematics, science and social studies.
(2) All Els receiving language assistance shall be assessed annually for language proficiency. Els shall also participate in state assessments pursuant to Georgia State Board of Education rule 160-3-1-.07 Testing Programs—Student Assessment.

(d) Funding:
(1) Students identified as eligible for language assistance services who are served by the state-funded ESOL program shall receive at least five segments per week (or yearly equivalent) of English language instruction using ESOL curricula in allowable service

delivery models. For purposes of funding, ESOL-served students in grades K-3 shall be counted for a maximum of one segment at the ESOL weight; grades 4-8 students for a maximum of two segments at the ESOL weight; and grades 9-12 students for a maximum of five segments at the ESOL weight:

    (i) The class is limited to the maximum size specified in State Board of Education Rule 160-5-1-.08 Class Size.
    (ii) The state-funded ESOL program teacher shall hold necessary and appropriate ESOL endorsement or ESOL certification issued by the Georgia Professional Standards Commission.

Authority: O.C.G.A. § 20-2-156

Chapter 8: Disability Law

Humans exhibit a remarkable range of abilities in all physical and intellectual endeavors, and every individual has strengths and weaknesses in different areas. Some individuals though, are challenged in areas affecting major life activities such as seeing, hearing, speaking, walking, learning, and working. Their challenges may be severe enough to constitute a disability in these or other important areas of daily life. But regardless of abilities every person has a fundamental right to equal human dignity and a fair opportunity to participate in and contribute to society.

Tragically, however, there has been a long and painful history of prejudice against persons with disabilities often resulting in intolerance, abuse, and exclusion from the mainstream of society. But as Dr. Martin Luther King, Jr., recognized concerning irrational discrimination, though the arc of history may often be agonizingly long, over time it ultimately does bend toward moral justice. Despite deeply rooted bigotry against persons with disabilities, eventually understanding of human disabilities began to overcome ignorance, and irrational prejudice started to give way to greater acceptance and social justice. Increasingly humanity is coming to understand that disability is a natural part of the human experience occurring world-wide throughout the human population. It is estimated that 10% of humans have a disability, making persons with disabilities the world's largest minority group.

In recognition of the moral imperative to overcome and remedy the ignorance and prejudice that resulted in excluding persons with disabilities from the mainstream of society, protections for the rights of persons with disabilities were enacted into law. Disability law is the means of operationalizing the social and legal obligation of providing reasonable accommodations and support for the integration of persons with disabilities back into the mainstream of human society, and ending the discrimination of irrational exclusion.

With appropriate educational services and reasonable accommodations persons with disabilities, like all other persons, can be prepared to lead productive, independent lives to the maximum extent possible. Educational services and reasonable accommodations help persons with disabilities to develop their personal strengths and talents and become more independent, reducing future costs and improving everyone's quality of life. As persons with disabilities are better integrated into mainstream society, including the work force, they are able to offer their unique skills and contribute to the economy and the common good.

This chapter provides a brief overview of the three major laws governing the rights of persons with disabilities in educational institutions: The Individuals with Disabilities Education Act (IDEA), 20 U.S.C. § 1401 (2012); Section 504 of the Rehabilitation Act (§ 504), 29 U.S.C § 794 (2012); and the Americans with Disabilities Act (ADA), 42 U.S.C. § 12101 (2012). This chapter also provides a summary of discipline options under the IDEA; manifestation determinations in disciplinary proceedings; dealing with a dangerous IDEA eligible student; developing positive parental relationships and cooperation; promoting a culture of respect and inclusion for children with disabilities; helping children receive needed services; and selected state law provisions concerning disability law.

A Brief Overview of the IDEA, § 504, and the ADA

Although case law and state regulations play an important role in the administration of disability laws, as noted above, the law in this area is largely defined by three federal statutes: The IDEA, § 504, and the ADA. The IDEA is a federal conditional funding grant functioning as a contract between the federal and state governments. The federal government provides funding to support special education, the state agrees to the statutory conditions in the IDEA, and the IDEA eligible child is the third-party beneficiary of this federal-state contract. The IDEA requires the state, through local schools, to provide a Free Appropriate Public Education (FAPE) and related services for IDEA eligible students. This is a critically important mission, but also a complex and expensive undertaking with federal funding only covering a relatively small portion of the total costs of providing a FAPE, related services, and mandated due process protections and associated administrative costs.

In contrast § 504 and the ADA generally only require non-discrimination and the provision of reasonable accommodations, usually resulting in relatively lower costs and administrative burdens in the provision of services per eligible individual. Section 504 requires reasonable accommodations necessary to allow persons with disabilities to participate in programs receiving federal funding. The ADA extends § 504 like protections to the private sector in employment, public accommodations, transportation, and telecommunications.

Contrasting the Scope of Who is Covered and What is Provided Under the IDEA, § 504, and the ADA

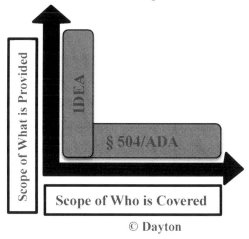

© Dayton

Through § 504 and the ADA Congress intended to cover large numbers of persons, children and adults, potentially including any person with a physical or mental disability that substantially limits a major life activity, including "caring for one's self, performing manual tasks, walking, seeing, hearing, speaking, breathing, learning, and working." Because the scope of who is potentially covered under § 504 and the ADA is so broad, the scope of what is provided is necessarily limited in recognition of finite resources. While § 504 and the ADA cover a broad range of the population, what is provided is fundamentally a right to non-discrimination and to the provision of a reasonable accommodation when necessary for the participation of the otherwise qualified person with a disability.

In contrast, in the IDEA Congress recognized that some children would need vastly more resources to provide for their educational needs due to the severity of their disabilities.

Therefore Congress limited who is covered under the IDEA to only those children who fit within 13 defined categories of eligibility, and who needed special education and related services because of an eligible disability. Under 20 U.S.C. § 1401 (2004) of the IDEA these include:

> Mental retardation, hearing impairments (including deafness), speech or language impairments, visual impairments (including blindness), serious emotional disturbance . . ., orthopedic impairments, autism, traumatic brain injury, other health impairments, or specific learning disabilities.

Congress clearly intended that IDEA eligibility be limited to only students with disabilities in these designated areas, and who need special education and related services because of the qualifying disability. Section 504 and the ADA were intended to serve other persons with disabilities, children and adults, through the more cost-efficient structure of § 504 and the ADA.

In carefully evaluating individual cases, it will be clear that some individuals will be eligible for services under the IDEA, others will be eligible under § 504 and/or the ADA, and others will not qualify as eligible under any of these provisions. But what should school officials do in those close cases that occur at the border of the IDEA and § 504?

In close cases, erring on the side of the IDEA may be prudent if it assures that the child will receive needed services, avoids contentious and expensive battles with parents, and forecloses future claims for compensatory damages. This is not, however, a decision to be made without careful consideration. To legally qualify under the IDEA, the student must be able to meet the minimum statutory requirements (i.e., the child: 1) Has an eligible disability; and 2) Needs special education and related services because of that disability). If declared eligible, however, what is provided for IDEA eligible students may be extensive and expensive for the educational institution to provide. IDEA eligible students are guaranteed the right to a FAPE, required related services, and extensive due process protections, all of which can prove to be very expensive and administratively burdensome in some cases. Further, claiming excessive expense and/or administrative burden as a defense under the IDEA can be very difficult.

In contrast to the IDEA, it is considerably easier to assert excessive expense and/or administrative burden as a defense to a requested accommodation under § 504 or the ADA. It is an affirmative defense to a requested accommodation if the accommodation would result in unreasonable costs, administrative burdens, or health or safety risks. Further, under § 504/ADA individuals are not entitled to their preferred accommodation, only a reasonable accommodation. When there is more than one reasonable accommodation possible, school officials may choose which of these reasonable accommodations to provide. Because the laws concerning individuals with disabilities continue to rapidly evolve, school officials responsible for compliance with the IDEA, § 504, and the ADA should closely monitor new legislation, regulations, and judicial decisions concerning these laws to assure current compliance.

A Summary of Discipline Options under the IDEA

Discipline procedures under the IDEA may be among the most significant and the most confusing provisions for many educators and lawyers. Accordingly, the following summary of incrementally severe disciplinary options under the IDEA is provided:

Incrementally Severe Disciplinary Options under the IDEA

Behavior Management Strategies
- To modify problem behavior school officials may unilaterally use behavior and conflict management strategies including student carrels, time-outs, detention, restrictions in privileges, etc., if IEP services are provided, and there is no change in placement

Obtaining Parental Consent
- If parental consent is obtained for needed changes in placement or for other appropriate behavior management strategies, IDEA due process protections are generally not triggered

Unilateral 10 Day Removal
- If not discriminatory, school officials may unilaterally remove an IDEA eligible student for up to 10 consecutive school days for violating a code of student conduct; no services are required; no manifestation determination is necessary

Subsequent 10 Day Removals
- Subsequent removals are allowed if no single removal exceeds 10 consecutive school days, and there is no pattern of removals; in consultation with at least one of the student's teachers, school officials must provide services necessary to allow progress toward meeting IEP goals and participation in the general curriculum, although in a different setting

Longer Removals
- May long-term suspend or expel for conduct violations that are not manifestations of disability; removals beyond 10 consecutive school days constitute a change in placement triggering IDEA due process protections; must continue to provide a FAPE; IEP team determines what services are necessary

Weapons, Drugs, or Injury
- School officials may unilaterally remove a student to an alternative educational placement for up to 45 school days for possession of weapons, drugs, or inflicting serious bodily injury

Removals for Danger
- May ask a hearing officer to remove a potentially dangerous student to an alternative educational placement for up to 45 school days; additional 45 day extensions may be requested as necessary to prevent a dangerous placement

Court Ordered Remedies
- School officials may obtain a court order for a removal or change of placement of a student that presents a serious danger of harm to self or others in the school

Reporting Crimes
- May report students suspected of crimes to law enforcement agents who are not bound by IDEA limitations; the State must continue to provide a FAPE to eligible incarcerated students

© Dayton

Manifestation Determinations in Disciplinary Proceedings

Another critical consideration in disciplining children with disabilities is determining whether the problem behavior is a manifestation of the student's disability. If a child's behavior is a manifestation of a disability, it would be unfair to punish that child for behavior that was caused by the disability and was not reasonably within the volitional control of the child. For example, children suffering from Tourette's syndrome may exhibit symptoms including involuntary movements or "tics"; vocal sounds; or obscene or inappropriate language, resulting in behaviors that would merit punishment in most children, but may be uncontrollable manifestations for a child suffering from Tourette's syndrome.

Accordingly, the IDEA, 20 U.S.C. § 1415 (2004), requires the IEP Team and other qualified personnel to conduct a review to determine whether an IDEA eligible child's problem behavior is a manifestation of a disability when proposed disciplinary actions constitute a change in placement:

> (E) *Manifestation Determination*:
> (i) In General: Except as provided in subparagraph (B) [10 day or less removal for a violation of a code of student conduct], within 10 school days of any decision to change the placement of a child with a disability because of a violation of a code of student conduct, the local educational agency, the parent, and relevant members of the IEP Team (as determined by the parent and the local educational agency) shall review all relevant information in the student's file, including the child's IEP, any teacher observations, and any relevant information provided by the parents to determine:
>> (I) If the conduct in question was caused by, or had a direct and substantial relationship to, the child's disability; or
>> (II) If the conduct in question was the direct result of the local educational agency's failure to implement the IEP.
>
> (ii) *Manifestation*: If the local educational agency, the parent, and relevant members of the IEP Team determine that either subclause (I) or (II) of clause (i) is applicable for the child, the conduct shall be determined to be a manifestation of the child's disability.

Manifestation Determination

- **Behavior Caused by the Child's Disability?**
  - Yes → **Manifestation of the Child's Disability**
  - No → **Related to a Unit Failure to the Implement IEP?**
    - Yes → **Manifestation of the Child's Disability**
    - No → **Not a Manifestation of the Child's Disability**

© Dayton

If the behavior is a manifestation of the child's disability, the IEP Team must implement a behavioral intervention plan, and except as provided for under the provisions of the IDEA, 20 U.S.C. § 1415 (2004) (allowing for a removal for weapons, drugs, or serious bodily injury) "return the child to the placement from which the child was removed, unless the parent and the local educational agency agree to a change of placement as part of the modification of the behavioral intervention plan."

Under 34 C.F.R. § 300.530(e) (2006) manifestation determinations are only required when a child is subjected to a disciplinary change of placement. A change in placement under 34 C.F.R. § 300.536(a) (2006) occurs when:

(1) The removal is for more than 10 consecutive school days; or
(2) The child has been subjected to a series of removals that constitute a pattern:
    (i) Because the series of removals total more than 10 school days in a school year;
    (ii) Because the child's behavior is substantially similar to the child's behavior in previous incidents that resulted in the series of removals; and
    (iii) Because of such additional factors as the length of each removal, the total amount of time the child has been removed, and the proximity of the removals to one another.

If the result of the review is a determination that the student's behavior was not a manifestation of the disability, school officials may discipline the student in the same manner that other student's would be disciplined, including suspension for up to 10 consecutive school days. No special services are required during this initial 10 school day suspension. Any removal for more than 10 consecutive school days, however, constitutes a change in placement and triggers the procedural protections of the IDEA.

When a student's behavior is not a manifestation of the student's disability school officials may lawfully long-term suspend for more than 10 consecutive school days or expel the student, subject to IDEA procedural protections and state law. School officials cannot, however, terminate special education services for these students.

Dealing with a Dangerous IDEA Eligible Student

In cases where parents refuse to cooperate with an appropriate change of placement and their child poses a genuine danger, safety must remain the first priority. School officials must take prompt, appropriate, and lawful actions to assure the safety of everyone in the school. Allowing a known danger to persist could lead to consequences far more serious than a due process hearing with parents over the Least Restrictive Environment (LRE) appropriate for the child, including tragic injury, death, and resulting tort suits or criminal charges. A truly dangerous student cannot be allowed to cause self-injury or injury to others when the danger was known and the injuries could have reasonably been prevented. The IDEA does not require this result, and tort and criminal laws will not allow it.

When faced with a safety emergency or imminent danger, make safety the first and immediate priority. Immediately take all necessary actions to assure safety. If the threat to safety is emergent, and not immediate, start now in building a compelling case for the changes necessary to assure future safety. Document causes for concern, document expert opinions on appropriate remedies, and when the necessary course of action is clear and well documented, begin taking the essential steps to protect safety as soon as legally possible. Seek parental cooperation and support whenever possible, but never fail to do what is necessary to protect everyone's safety with or without parental cooperation.

Developing Positive Parental Relationships and Cooperation

Although good faith cooperation is likely to yield the best results at the lowest costs for all parties, the IDEA is nonetheless largely structured as an advocacy driven, adversarial system. Parents who are the strongest advocates and who demand the most under the IDEA often get the most from the school. And when a parent-school relationship becomes adversarial, even relatively minor disagreements can become the subjects of bitter disputes between parents and school officials. Further, the system for resolving these disputes under the IDEA is litigation oriented, often aggravating rather than resolving tensions between parents and school officials. Litigation can make ongoing working relationships more difficult; delay the resolution of problems; and consume resources that are needed to support educational services.

Developing positive parent-school relationships and good faith cooperation is in everyone's best interests. Because it is easier to build functional relationships initially, rather than to try to fix broken ones later, developing a relationship of mutual trust and cooperation with parents early in the IDEA process can be invaluable in effectively meeting the needs of IDEA eligible children without undue conflict or expense. Not all relationships will be positive and functional. But with appropriate efforts at building positive working relationships, less of these relationships have to be negative and dysfunctional. To promote positive working relationships:

> *Be sensitive to parents' emotions concerning their child*: Good parents rightly want the very best possible education and future for their child. Accepting the limitations resulting from a child's disability can be emotionally difficult for parents. It often takes time for parents to move through the stages of grief resulting from discovering that the child may be limited now and in the future by mental or physical disabilities. But parents are more likely to resolve these challenges and reach a positive resolution when school officials are appropriately sensitive and supportive of the emotional concerns of parents and the child throughout this process. Although you may be responsible for a large number of special education students, remember that these children are not just names and numbers, but individual, feeling humans with parents and families who love them, want to protect them, and want the best for their future. Parent's emotions concerning their child are understandably strong. Failure to sufficiently recognize and respect this reality is likely to unnecessarily inflame parental anger and impede cooperation.

> *Be certain all of the child's teachers understand applicable laws and regulations; what is required of them under the IDEA and § 504; and know that all teachers are responsible for special education students*: There are many common misconceptions among teachers concerning special education. For example, some teachers assume, wrongly, that special education and special education students are the responsibility of only those teachers certified and designated as special educators. To the contrary, the IDEA and § 504 were clearly intended to prevent unnecessary segregation of persons with disabilities from regular classrooms. Special educators have special expertise concerning disabilities. But

all teachers are responsible for teaching and helping special needs students in their class. And all teachers are equally bound by the law in providing a FAPE for these children. All teachers need to understand that their compliance with the IDEA, § 504, and the ADA is mandated by law, not voluntary. Further, they have a professional responsibility to offer their best efforts in helping special needs students, and in assuring that these students, like all students, are treated fairly and respectfully in their classrooms.

Make sure parents' understand applicable laws and what the laws actually require and provide: There are many common misconceptions among parents concerning disability laws and what these laws do and do not require and provide. Ultimately, however, what is required under the IDEA, § 504 and the ADA is what these laws actually mandate, and not what rumors or common misconceptions may suggest. If you can clearly show parents what the law actually requires or provides they are much more likely to accept the realities of the law, even if they don't like the result, than if they believe that the negative result was simply the product of an arbitrary decision by school officials.

Help parent's to understand not just their child's needs, but to also recognize and respect the legitimate interests of others: IDEA eligible students are entitled to special education and related services necessary to provide a FAPE. Parents need to understand how they can help school officials to provide their child with the best educational experience under the circumstances. But parents must also understand that while their child has a right to a FAPE in the LRE appropriate, school officials must also respect and protect the rights of other students and teachers in the school. Everyone has a right to a safe, orderly, and respectful learning and working environment.

Emphasize your common objective: To provide the best possible education and future for the child under the circumstances: Both parents and teachers want children to have the best possible education available under the circumstances, and an educational experience that prepares them for their best possible future. If school officials can establish a relationship of trust with parents, built on knowledge that school officials are acting in good faith with parents to pursue the best interests of the child, school officials are far more likely to succeed in developing positive parental relationships and cooperation.

Promoting a Culture of Respect and Inclusion for Children with Disabilities

Despite significant progress in recent years, persons with disabilities continue to experience discrimination. Ignorance and fear are at the core of this discrimination. So to reduce this discrimination, you must address its core causes. Too many people still misunderstand and dehumanize persons with disabilities based on highly irrational beliefs and unfounded fears. They may, for example, wrongly assume that a person with a severe disability is somehow not as capable of intelligence, understanding, and feeling as others; that the person may be dangerous; that the disability may be contagious, etc. In schools this ignorance and fear increases the chances that persons with disabilities will be ignored, avoided, and excluded, and become the victims of neglect, bullying, and abuse.

Promoting a positive culture of mutual respect, kindness, understanding, and inclusion in the school can help to reduce the frequency and severity of bullying and abuse and other harmful treatment of children with disabilities. Through leadership and educational efforts, school officials can help everyone in the school to see special education students as valued members of the school community, and to understand that disabilities are a natural part of the human experience. With the development of mutual understanding and respect, special education students can become valued friends and not the targets of misguided bullying and abuse. Everyone has an important role to play in making these positive cultural changes:

School administrators: As school leaders, school administrators are responsible for creating a respectful and inclusive school culture. School leaders must make it absolutely clear to everyone, students, teachers, staff, and community members, that the school is a place of mutual respect, and that all persons have a right to be included whenever possible and to be treated with equal respect at all times.

Teachers: Teachers are on the fronts lines in creating an inclusive and respectful classroom. The teacher sets the tone for the classroom climate, and the teacher has a responsibility for supervising student behavior in the classroom. For educational, legal, ethical, and moral reasons, it is imperative that teachers never tolerate disrespect, bullying, and abuse in the classroom.

Parents: Parents play a central role under the IDEA system, serving as the child's chief advocate and protector. It is essential that parents of children with disabilities educate themselves concerning the IDEA and other laws governing special education. Further, they must take a lead role in helping their child to become a well-adjusted and strong student and advocate for themselves and other children with disabilities.

Children: Children with disabilities must learn to become their own best advocates, actively reaching out to make new friends; communicating their needs to others; and standing up for themselves and their peers when necessary. Student leaders must also set a positive example for all students by respecting and including children with disabilities.

Helping Children Receive Needed Services

Children generally do not understand the physical, mental, or emotional challenges they may be facing, and they do not know what services may be available to help them. Children must rely on adults to help identify the underlying causes of their challenges, and to help them receive appropriate services. Concerning children with eligible disabilities, the IDEA's "child find" provision creates an affirmative duty for school officials to identify children with disabilities. IDEA 20 U.S.C. § 1412 (2004) mandates: "All children with disabilities residing in the State, including children with disabilities who are homeless children or are wards of the State and children with disabilities attending private schools, regardless of the severity of their disabilities, and who are in need of special education and related services, are identified."

Some of these children are identified through mass screening tests including vision tests, hearing tests, and other basic tests administered to all school children. Parents, school personnel, medical personnel, or other persons that suspect a child needs IDEA services may also refer the child for an individual evaluation to determine whether the child is eligible for these services. Indicators that a child may need IDEA or other services may include challenges in these areas:

Example Indicators that a Child May Need IDEA or Other Disability Services

The behavioral, academic, motor, emotional, and social indicators below may be cause for further investigation into whether a child needs IDEA or other disability services.*

Behavioral:
- Frequently distracted
- Unable to stay on task
- Highly disorganized or messy
- Hyperactive or unusually inactive
- Covering eyes, squinting, or straining to see
- Loud speech or imperfect pronunciation
- Chronic illness
- Hypersensitive to touch, sound, light, etc.
- Frequently disrupts class
- Poor judgment and impulse control
- Persistently repeats the same pattern of misconduct
- Aggressive or violent
- Engages in self-injury

Academic:
- Expresses frequent confusion and frustration re: assignments
- Does well in some areas but performs poorly in others
- Unable to follow clear directions in assignments
- Difficulty reading, writing, or speaking
- Limited reasoning ability
- Impaired memory

Motor:
- Poor hand-writing
- Eye-hand coordination problems
- Lacking in age appropriate muscle development
- Trouble walking, running, jumping, etc.
- Unusual clumsiness
- Frequent accidents
- Unusual lack of physical stamina

Emotional:
- Emotionally volatile
- Situationally inappropriate emotional behavior
- Over or under reacts to stress
- Persistent depression
- Frequent headaches or stomach problems

Social:
- Socially isolated
- Lacks interest in playing with other children
- Has great difficulty playing or working with others
- Extremely awkward or inappropriate social interactions
- Inability to read common social cues

* *Nota bene*: This is an illustrative list only, and not an exhaustive list. This list is intended to stimulate academic discussions and raise awareness in helping children receive needed services. It is in no way intended as a substitute for IDEA child find obligations or professional evaluations of individual children.

© **Dayton**

Selected Georgia Laws

Georgia Regulations

160-4-7-.02: Free Appropriate Public Education (FAPE)

(1) *General*:
(a) A free appropriate public education (FAPE) must be available to all children residing in the State between the ages of 3 and 21, inclusive, including children with disabilities who have been suspended or expelled from school, as provided for in 160-4-7-.18 Discipline. [34 C.F.R. § 300.101(a); 34 C.F.R. § 300.530(d)]
(b) If a student is receiving services upon reaching age 22, the LEA shall have a written procedure that identifies a process for completing services to which the adult student has been previously entitled. LEAs shall state in writing that the goal is to secure the successful transition of students to their desired post-school outcomes and will collaborate to complete that transition by age 22. If a student is still attending school at age 22, the LEA shall state whether services will cease on the student's 22nd birthday, or will continue until the end of the semester or until the end of the current school year. If an adult student remains after their 22nd birthday, the LEA shall notify the adult student and the parent(s) that although services will continue, no individual entitlement to FAPE or other rights under IDEA are afforded the adult student.
(c) FAPE for children beginning at age 3: Each LEA must ensure that:

> (1) The obligation to make FAPE available to each eligible child residing in the LEA begins no later than the child's third birthday; and
> (2) An IEP or an IFSP is in effect for the child by that date. [34 C.F.R. § 300.101(b)(1)(i)(ii)]
> (3) If a child's third birthday occurs during the summer, the child's IEP Team shall determine the date when services under the IEP or IFSP will begin. [34 C.F.R. § 300.101(b)(2)]

(d) Children advancing from grade to grade:

> (1) Each LEA must ensure that FAPE is available to any individual child with a disability who needs special education and related services, even though the child has not failed or been retained in a course or grade, and is advancing from grade to grade. [34 C.F.R. § 300.101(c)(1)]
> (2) The determination that a child described above is eligible under this part, must be made on an individual basis by the group responsible within the child's LEA for making eligibility determinations. [34 C.F.R. § 300.101(c)(2)]

(2) *Limitation*: Exception to FAPE for certain ages:
(a) General: The obligation to make FAPE available to all children with disabilities does not apply with respect to the following:

(1) Adult students aged 18 through 21, who, in the last educational placement, prior to their incarceration in an adult correctional facility:

(i) Were not actually identified as being a child with a disability;
(ii) Did not have an IEP in effect; and [34 C.F.R. § 300.102(a)(2)(i)(A)(B)]
(iii) Graduates from high school with a regular high school diploma. This constitutes a change in placement, requiring written prior notice. [34 C.F.R. § 300.102(a)(3)(iii)]

(2) The exception does not apply to adult students with disabilities, aged 18 through 21, who:

(i) Had been identified as a child with a disability and had received services in accordance with an IEP but who left school prior to their incarceration in an adult correctional facility or local jail;
(ii) Did not have an IEP in their last educational setting, but who had actually been identified as a child with a disability; or [34 C.F.R. § 300.102(a)(2)(ii)(A)(B)]
(iii) Have graduated from high school but have not been awarded a regular high school diploma. [34 C.F.R. § 300.102(a)(3)(ii)]
(iv) The term regular high school diploma does not include an alternative degree that is not aligned with the State's academic standards such as a special education diploma, certificate of attendance or a general educational development credential (GED). [34 C.F.R. § 300.102(a)(3)(iv)]

(b) Documents relating to exceptions: The LEA must assure that the information it has provided is current and accurate. [34 C.F.R. § 300.102(b)]

(3) *FAPE*: Methods and Payments:

(a) Georgia may use whatever State, local, Federal, and private sources of support that are available in the State to meet the requirements of this Rule. For example, if it is necessary to place a child with a disability in a residential facility, Georgia could use joint agreements between the agencies involved for sharing the cost of that placement. [34 C.F.R. § 300.103(a)]

(b) Nothing relieves an insurer or similar third party from an otherwise valid obligation to provide or to pay for services provided to a child with a disability. [34 C.F.R. § 300.103(b)]

(c) The LEA must ensure that there is no delay in implementing a child's IEP, including any case in which the payment source for providing or paying for special education and related services to the child is being determined. [34 C.F.R. § 300.103(c)]

(d) Children with disabilities who are covered by public benefits or insurance:

(1) A LEA may use the Medicaid or other public benefits or insurance programs in which a child participates to provide or pay for services required under IDEA, as permitted by the public benefits or insurance [34 C.F.R. § 300.154(d)(1)] except:

(i) With regard to services required to provide FAPE, the LEA may not require the parents to sign up for or enroll in public benefits or insurance programs in order for their child to receive FAPE; [34 C.F.R. § 300.154(d)(2)(i)]

(ii) The LEA may not require the parents to incur any out-of-pocket expenses such as the payment of a deductible or co-pay amount incurred in filing a claim for services provided, but may pay the cost the parents would otherwise be required to pay; [34 C.F.R. § 300.154(d)(2)(ii)]

(iii) The LEA may not use a child's benefits under a public benefits or insurance program if that use would:

> (I) Decrease available lifetime coverage or any other insured benefit;
> (II) Result in the family paying for services that would otherwise be covered by the public benefits or insurance program and are required for the child outside of the time the child is in school;
> (III) Increase premiums or lead to the discontinuation of benefits or insurance; or
> (IV) Risk loss of eligibility for home and community-based waivers, based on aggregate health-related expenses; and [34 C.F.R. § 300.154(d)(2)(iii)]

(iv) Must obtain parental consent each time that access to public benefits or insurance is sought; and

(v) Notify parents that the parents' refusal to allow access to their benefits does not relieve the LEA of its responsibility to ensure that all required services are provided at no cost to the parents. [34 C.F.R. § 300.154(d)(2)(iv)]

(e) Children with disabilities who are covered by private insurance:

(1) With regard to services required to provide FAPE to an eligible child, a LEA may access the parents private insurance proceeds only if the parents provide consent. [34 C.F.R. § 300.154(e)]

(2) Each time the LEA proposes to access the parents' private insurance proceeds, the LEA must:

> (i) Obtain parental consent; and
> (ii) Inform the parents that their refusal to permit the LEA to access their private insurance does not relieve the LEA of its responsibility to ensure that all required services are provided at no cost to the parents. [34 C.F.R. § 300.154(e)(2)(i)–(ii)]

(4) **Residential Placement**: If placement in a public or private residential program is necessary to provide special education and related services to a child with a disability, the program, including non-medical care and room and board, must be at no cost to the parents of the child. [34 C.F.R. § 300.104]

(5) *Accessible Instructional Materials*:

(a) LEAs will provide print instructional materials in specialized, accessible formats (*i.e.* Braille, audio, digital, large-print, etc.) to children who are blind or other print disabled in a timely manner. LEAs will take all reasonable steps to ensure that children with print disabilities have access to their accessible format instructional materials at the same time as students without print disabilities: [*See* 34 C.F.R. § 300.172(a); § 300.172(b)(4)]

(1) Print instructional materials include textbooks and related core materials that are required by the LEA for use by children in the classroom.

(2) Specialized formats refer to Braille, audio, or digital text which is exclusively for use by children who are blind or other persons with print disabilities. Large print formats are also included when the materials are distributed exclusively for use by children who are blind or other persons with disabilities: [17 U.S.C. § 121(d)(4)]

> (i) Specialized formats do not include altering the content (*e.g.* breadth, depth, or complexity) of the print instructional material in the production of accessible instructional materials.

(3) Children who are blind or print disabled include:

> (i) Children whose visual acuity, as determined by a competent authority, is 20/200 or less in the better eye with correcting glasses, or whose widest diameter if visual field subtends an angular distance no greater than 20 degrees.
>
> (ii) Children whose visual disability, with correction and regardless of optical measurement, is certified by competent authority as preventing the reading of standard printed material.
>
> (iii) Children certified by competent authority as unable to read or unable to use standard printed material as a result of physical limitations.
>
> (iv) Children certified by competent authority as having a reading disability resulting from organic dysfunction and of sufficient severity to prevent their reading printed material in a normal manner. [36 C.F.R. § 701.6(b)(1)]

[Editor's Note: There is no section 4 in the official state regulation]

(5) The following groups of individuals are eligible to certify children who are blind or other print disabled for specialized format instructional materials:

> (i) In cases of blindness, visual disability, or physical limitations "competent authority" is defined to include doctors of medicine, doctors of osteopathy, ophthalmologists, optometrists, registered nurses, therapists, professional staff of hospitals, institutions, and public or welfare agencies (e.g., social workers, case workers, counselors, rehabilitation teachers, and superintendents).
>
> (ii) In the case of a reading disability from organic dysfunction, competent authority is defined as doctors of medicine who may consult with colleagues in associated disciplines. [36 C.F.R. § 701.6(b)(2)]

(b) In order to insure the timely provision of high quality, accessible instructional materials to children who are blind and other print disabled, the LEA must adopt the National Instructional Materials Accessibility Standard (NIMAS):

(1) The NIMAS refers to a standard for source files created by textbook publishers for the purpose of producing accessible instructional materials. NIMAS files are not child ready files and will be used by authorized users and entities to produce accessible materials for children who are blind and visually impaired.

(2) Children who are certified as blind or other print disabled are eligible to receive accessible instructional materials produced with NIMAS files.

(c) The LEA may coordinate with the National Instructional Materials Access Center (NIMAC) to facilitate the production and delivery of accessible materials to children who are blind or other print disabled:

(1) The NIMAC refers to the central repository which is responsible for processing, storing, and distributing NIMAS files of textbooks and core instructional materials.

(2) LEAs must provide written assurances to the GaDOE regarding their intention to coordinate with the NIMAC.

(3) LEAs coordinating with the NIMAC will require textbook publishers to deliver the contents of the print instructional materials to the NIMAC in a NIMAS format file on or before delivery of the print instructional materials. The files will be used in the production of accessible instructional materials.

(4) LEAs coordinating with the NIMAC may also purchase instructional materials from the textbook publishers that are produced in or may be rendered in a specialized format.

(d) If the LEA chooses not to coordinate with the NIMAC, assurances must be made to the GaDOE that the LEA will provide accessible instructional materials to children who are blind or other print disabled in a timely manner. LEAs will take all reasonable steps to ensure that students with print disabilities have access to their accessible format instructional materials at the same time as students without print disabilities. [34 C.F.R. § 300.210(b)(2)]

(1) LEAs that do not coordinate with the NIMAC will be responsible for purchasing, producing or otherwise providing high-quality, accessible instructional materials in specialized formats in a timely manner for children who are blind or print disabled. LEAs will take all reasonable steps to ensure that students with print disabilities have access to their accessible format instructional materials at the same time as students without print disabilities.

(e) The LEA is also responsible for providing accessible materials to children who require instructional materials in accessible formats, but who do not qualify for the materials under the definition of blind and other print disabled or who need materials that cannot be produced from NIMAS. [20 U.S.C. § 1413(a)(6)]

(f) Some children who require accessible instructional materials will need assistive technology to access the materials (e.g. text reader to read digital file, screen magnification program to read digital file).

(6) *Assistive Technology*:

(a) Children with disabilities who require assistive technology in order to receive a free appropriate public education (FAPE) are eligible for assistive technology devices or services, or both, as a part of the child's special education, related services, or supplemental aids and services.

(b) Each IEP Team will consider whether or not a child requires assistive technology devices and services in order to receive a free appropriate public education (FAPE). Minimal compliance will be indicating the appropriate response in the Consideration of Special Factors section of the IEP. Assistive technology can also be addressed when considering other factors such as communication needs and instruction in the use of Braille. [34 C.F.R. § 300.324]

(c) An assistive technology evaluation may be required if appropriate assistive technology solutions are not known to the child's IEP Team through the consideration process. This evaluation shall be conducted by a multidisciplinary team of professionals knowledgeable about assistive technology devices in the technology areas being assessed. The child and family should also be included in this evaluation process. The evaluation should result in recommendations for assistive technology devices and services, if required.

(d) If the child's IEP Team determines that assistive technology devices or services are required for the child to receive a FAPE, a statement to that effect must be included in the child's IEP.

(1) If assistive technology is required for the child to participate in district-wide or State-wide testing, the need for technology should be documented in the appropriate section of the IEP and provided to the child.

(2) If assistive technology devices or services, or both, are required for a child who is blind or other print disabled to access alternative format instructional materials, the assistive technology should be documented in the IEP and provided to the child.

(e) If the IEP Team determines that the child with a disability requires school-purchased assistive technology at home or in other settings to receive a FAPE, the assistive technology must be provided to the child at no cost to the parent. The need for assistive technology in the non-school settings should be documented in the child's IEP. [34 C.F.R. § 300.105]

*(7) **Extended School Year Services**:*

(a) Each LEA must ensure that extended school year services are available as necessary to provide a FAPE. [34 C.F.R. § 300.106(a)(1)]

(1) Extended school year services must be provided only if a child's IEP Team determines, on an individual basis, that the services are necessary for the provision of FAPE to the child. [34 C.F.R. § 300.106(a)(2)]

(2) In implementing the requirements of this section, the LEA may not:

> (i) Limit extended school year services to particular categories of disability; or
> (ii) Unilaterally limit the type, amount, or duration of those services. [34 C.F.R. § 300.106(a)(3)(i)–(ii)]

(b) Definition: As used in this Rule, the term extended school year services means special education and related services that:

> (1) Are provided to a child with a disability:

(i) Beyond the normal school year of the LEA;
(ii) In accordance with the child's IEP;
(iii) At no cost to the parents of the child; and
(iv) Meet the standards of the State. [34 C.F.R. § 300.106(b)(1)–(2)]

(8) *Nonacademic Services*:
(a) Each LEA must take steps, including the provision of supplementary aids and services determined appropriate and necessary by the child's IEP Team, to provide nonacademic and extracurricular services and activities in the manner necessary to afford children with disabilities equal opportunity for participation in those services and activities. [34 C.F.R. § 300.107(a)]
(b) Nonacademic and extracurricular services and activities may include counseling services, athletics, transportation, health services, recreational activities, special interest groups or clubs sponsored by the LEA, referrals to agencies that provide assistance to individuals with disabilities, and employment of students, including both employment by the LEA and assistance in making outside employment available. [34 C.F.R. § 300.107(b)]

(9) *Physical Education*: The LEA must ensure that its public schools comply with the following:
(a) General: Physical education services, specially designed if necessary, must be made available to every child with a disability receiving FAPE, unless the LEA enrolls children without disabilities and does not provide physical education to children without disabilities in the same grades. [34 C.F.R. § 300.108(a)]
(b) Regular physical education: Each child with a disability must be afforded the opportunity to participate in the regular physical education program available to nondisabled children unless:

(1) The child is enrolled full time in a separate facility; or
(2) The child needs specially designed physical education, as prescribed in the child's IEP. [34 C.F.R. § 300.108(b)]

(c) Special physical education: If specially designed physical education is prescribed in a child's IEP, the LEA responsible for the education of that child must provide the services directly or make arrangements for those services to be provided through other public or private programs. [34 C.F.R. § 300.108(c)]
(d) Education in separate facilities: The LEA responsible for the education of a child with a disability who is enrolled in a separate facility must ensure that the child receives appropriate physical education services in compliance with this Rule. [34 C.F.R. § 300.108(d)]

(10) *Full Educational Opportunity Goal* **(FEOG)**: Each LEA must have in effect policies and procedures to demonstrate that the LEA has established a goal of providing full educational opportunity to all children with disabilities, aged birth through 21, and a detailed timetable for accomplishing that goal. [34 C.F.R. § 300.109]

(11) *Charter Schools*:
(a) Children with disabilities who attend public charter schools and their parents retain all rights to a FAPE as described in this Rule. [34 C.F.R. § 300.209(a)]

(b) Charter schools that are public schools of an LEA: Each LEA must ensure that charter schools that are public schools of the LEA must:

(1) Serve children with disabilities attending those charter schools in the same manner as the LEA serves children with disabilities in its other schools, including providing supplementary and related services on site at the charter school to the same extent to which the LEA has a policy or practice of providing such services on the site to its other public schools; and

(2) Provide funds to those charter schools at the same time and on the same basis as the LEA provides funds to the LEA's other public schools, including proportional distribution based on relative enrollment of children with disabilities. [34 C.F.R. § 300.209(b)]

(c) Public charter schools that are LEAs: If the public charter school is an LEA, that charter school is responsible for ensuring that all of these requirements are met. [34 C.F.R. § 300.209(c)]

(12) *Program Options*: Each LEA shall take steps to ensure that children with disabilities have available to them the variety of educational programs and services available to nondisabled children in the area served by the LEA, including art, music, and Career, Technical and Agricultural Education. [34 C.F.R. § 300.110]

(13) *Routine Checking of Hearing Aids/Other Components*:

(a) Hearing aids: Each LEA must ensure that hearing aids worn in school by children with hearing impairments, including deafness, are functioning properly. [34 C.F.R. § 300.113(a)]

(b) External components of surgically implanted medical devices: Each LEA must ensure that the external components of surgically implanted medical devices are functioning properly. The LEA is not responsible for the post-surgical maintenance, programming or replacement of the medical device that has been surgically implanted (or of an external component of the surgically implanted medical device). [34 C.F.R. § 300.113(b)]

(14) *Prohibition on Mandatory Medication*:

(a) Each LEA must prohibit personnel from requiring parents to obtain a prescription for substances identified under schedules I, II, III, IV, or V in section 202(c) of the Controlled Substances Act (21 U.S.C. 812(c)) for a child as a condition of attending school, receiving an evaluation or receiving services. [34 C.F.R. § 300.174(a)]

(b) Nothing under paragraph (14)(a) above shall be construed to create a prohibition against teachers and other school personnel consulting or sharing classroom-based observations with parents or guardians regarding a child's academic and functional performance, or behavior in the classroom or school, or regarding the need for evaluation for special education or related services as it relates to child find. [34 C.F.R. § 300.174(b)]

(15) This rule shall become effective July 1, 2007.

Authority O.C.G.A. §§ 20-2-133; 20-2-150; 20-2-152; 20-2-160; 20-2-161; 20-2-168; 20-2-240; 20-2-1160

160-4-7-.03: Child Find Procedures

(1) *General*:
(a) Each LEA must have in effect policies and procedures to ensure that all suspected children with disabilities, including those who are homeless, are wards of the State or are attending private schools, regardless of the severity of their disability, and who are in need of special education and related services, are identified, located and evaluated. [34 C.F.R. § 300.111]
(b) Each LEA shall ensure that before conducting any significant activity that is designed to identify, locate or evaluate children, annual notice must be published or announced in newspapers or other media, or both, to notify parents of this activity. [34 C.F.R. § 300.612 (b)]
(c) These policies and procedures shall provide for the screening and evaluation of all children with suspected disabilities birth through age 21 to include:

> (1) Children birth through age three. An LEA may fulfill its child find responsibility through referral to the Babies Can't Wait early intervention program operated by the Department of Community Health.
> (2) Preschool children, ages 3-5, not yet eligible for state-funded kindergarten.
> (3) Children enrolled in the LEA schools including public charter schools:
>
>> (i) Children who are suspected of being children with disabilities and in need of special education, even though they are progressing from grade to grade. [34 C.F.R. § 300.111(c)(1)]
>> (ii) Highly mobile children, including migrant children. [34 C.F.R. 300.111(c)(2)]
>
> (4) Children who are detained or incarcerated in city/county operated jails or correctional facilities.
> (5) Children who reside in the LEA and are enrolled in home school/study programs.
> (6) Parentally-placed private school children: [34 C.F.R. § 300.131(a)]
>
>> (i) Children enrolled by their parents in private, including religious, elementary and secondary schools located in the LEA's jurisdiction. [34 C.F.R. § 300.130]

(d) A practical method is developed and implemented to determine which children are currently receiving needed special education and related services: [34 C.F.R. § 300.111(a)(ii)]

> (1) Each LEA shall submit to the Georgia Department of Education (GaDOE), in an electronic format specified by GaDOE, data requested by the GaDOE on all children ages three through twenty-one who have been found eligible for special education and related services.
> (2) All data shall be accurate and timely. [34 C.F.R. § 300.645]

(2) *Interventions Prior to Referral*:
(a) The screening of children by a teacher or specialist to determine appropriate instructional strategies for curriculum implementation shall not be considered to be an evaluation for eligibility for special education and related services. [34 C.F.R. § 300.302]
(b) Prior to referring a student for consideration for eligibility for special education and related services, a student must have received scientific, research or evidence based interventions selected to correct or reduce the academic, social or behavioral problem(s) the student is having:

> (1) Student referrals must be accompanied by documentation of scientific, research or evidence based academic and/or behavioral interventions that have been implemented as designed for the appropriate period of time to show effect or lack of effect that demonstrates the child is not making sufficient rate of progress to meet age or State approved grade-level standards within a reasonable time frame.
> (2) Exceptions may be made in circumstances where immediate evaluation and/or placement is required due to a significant disability that precludes access to instruction.
> (3) The exception noted in (2)(b)(2) should be an infrequent and rare occurrence, and the circumstances evidencing the need for the LEA's use of the exception must be clearly documented in the eligibility decision.

Authority O.C.G.A. §§ 20-2-133; 20-2-152; 20-2-168; 20-2-240; 20-2-1160

160-4-7-.04: Evaluations and Reevaluations

(1) *Initial Evaluations*:
(a) Each LEA must conduct a full and individual initial evaluation before the initial provision of special education and related services to a child with a disability: [34 C.F.R. § 300.301(a)]

> (1) Each LEA shall ensure that evaluation procedures are established and implemented that meet the requirements of this Rule.

(b) Once a child is referred for an evaluation by a parent or Student Support Team (SST) to determine if the child is a child with a disability, the initial evaluation:

> (1) Must be completed within 60 calendar days of receiving parental consent for evaluation: [34 C.F.R. § 300.301(c)(1)(i)]
>
>> (i) Holiday periods and other circumstances when children are not in attendance for five consecutive school days shall not be counted toward the 60 calendar day timeline, including the weekend days before and after such holiday periods, if contiguous to the holidays except:

(ii) Any summer vacation period in which the majority of an LEA's teachers are not under contract shall not be included in the 60 day timeline for evaluation. However an LEA is not prohibited from conducting evaluations over a summer vacation period.

> (I) Consent received 30 days or more prior to the end of the school year must be completed within the 60 calendar day evaluation timeframe.
> (II) Students who turn three during the summer period or other holiday periods must have an eligibility decision and IEP (if appropriate) in place by the third birthday.

(2) Must consist of procedures which determine if the child is a child with a disability and to determine the educational needs of the child. [34 C.F.R. § 300.301(c)(2)(i)–(ii)]

(c) The timeframe described above does not apply to a LEA if:

1. The parent of a child repeatedly fails or refuses to produce the child for the evaluation; or
2. A child enrolls in a school of another LEA after the relevant timeline in this Rule has begun and prior to a determination by the child's previous LEA as to whether the child is a child with a disability; [34 C.F.R. § 300.301(d)(1)–(2)]
3. The exception in (c)(2) above applies only if the subsequent LEA is making sufficient progress to ensure a prompt completion of the evaluation and the parent and subsequent LEA have agreed to a specific time when the evaluation will be completed. [34 C.F.R. § 300.301(e)]
4. If extenuating circumstances, e.g., illness, unusual evaluation needs, or revocation of parent's consent for evaluation affect this time line, the LEA shall document the exceptions.

(2) *Parental Consent for Evaluation*:
(a) The LEA proposing to conduct an initial evaluation to determine if the child qualifies as a child with a disability shall, after providing notice, obtain an informed consent from the parents of such child before the evaluation is conducted. The LEA must make reasonable efforts to obtain the informed consent from the parents. To meet the reasonable efforts requirement, the LEA must document its attempts to obtain parental consent using procedures that may include detailed records of telephone calls made or attempted and the results of those calls, copies of correspondence sent to the parents and any responses received, and detailed records of visits made to the parent's home or place of employment and the results of those visits. [34 C.F.R. § 300.300(a)(1)(i); § 300.300(a)(1)(iii); § 300.300(d)(5); § 300.322(d)(1)–(3)]
(b) If the parents of a child refuses consent for the evaluation or the parents fail to respond to a request to provide consent, the LEA may, but is not required to, pursue the initial evaluation of the child by utilizing the mediation and impartial due process hearing procedures provided for in the procedural safeguards. However, if a parent of a child

who is home schooled or placed in a private school by the parents at their own expense does not provide consent for the initial evaluation or the reevaluation, or such parent fails to respond to a request to provide consent, the LEA may not use the consent override procedures, and the LEA is not required to consider the child as eligible for services. [34 C.F.R. § 300.300(a)(3)(i); § 300.300(d)(4)(i)–(ii)]

(c) For initial evaluations only, if the child is a ward of the State and is not residing with the child's parent, the LEA is not required to obtain informed consent from the parent for initial evaluation to determine whether the child is a child with a disability if:

(1) Despite reasonable efforts to do so, the LEA cannot discover the whereabouts of the parent of the child;
(2) The rights of the parents of the child have been terminated in accordance with State law; or
(3) The rights of the parents to make educational decisions have been subrogated by a judge in accordance with State law and consent for an initial evaluation has been given by an individual appointed by the judge to represent the child. [34 C.F.R. § 300.300(a)(2)(i)–(iii)]

(d) Other consent requirements:
(1) Parental consent is not required before:

(i) Reviewing existing data as part of an evaluation or a reevaluation; or
(ii) Administering a test or other evaluation that is administered to all children unless, before administration of that test or evaluation, consent is required of parents of all children. [34 C.F.R. § 300.300(d)(1)(i)–(ii)]
(iii) The screening of a child by a teacher or specialist to determine appropriate instructional strategies for curriculum implementation. This shall not be considered to be an evaluation for eligibility for special education and related services. [34 C.F.R. § 300.302]

(3) *Reevaluation*:
(a) Each LEA must ensure that a reevaluation of each child with a disability is conducted at least once every 3 years, unless the parent and the LEA agree that a reevaluation is unnecessary:
(1) If the LEA determines that the educational or related services needs, including improved academic achievement and functional performance, of the child warrants a reevaluation; or
(2) If the child's parent or teacher requests a reevaluation. [34 C.F.R. § 300.303(a)(1)–(2); § 300.303(b)(2)]
(b) Limitation: A reevaluation may not occur more than once a year, unless the parent and the LEA agree otherwise; and must occur at least once every 3 years, unless the parent and the LEA agree that a reevaluation is unnecessary. [34 C.F.R. § 300.303(b)]
(c) Each LEA shall obtain informed parental consent prior to conducting any reevaluation of a child with a disability, except that such informed parental consent need not be obtained if the LEA can demonstrate that it has taken reasonable measures to obtain such consent and the child's parents failed to respond. [34 C.F.R. § 300.300 (c)(1)–(2)]

(4) ***Evaluation Procedures***:
(a) Notice: The LEA shall provide notice to the parents of a child suspected with a disability, in accordance with all notice requirements as described in Rule 160-4-7-.09 Procedural Safeguards/Parent Rights. [34 C.F.R. § 300.304(a)]
(b) Conduct of evaluation. In conducting an evaluation, the LEA must:
(1) Use a variety of evaluation tools and strategies to gather relevant academic, functional and developmental information about the child, including information provided by the parents that may assist in determining:

> (i) Whether the child is a child with a disability; and
> (ii) The content of the child's individualized education program including information related to enabling the child to be involved in and progress in the general curriculum (or for a preschool child to participate in appropriate activities);

(2) Not use any single procedure as the sole criterion for determining whether a child is a child with a disability and for determining an appropriate educational program for the child;
(3) Use technically sound instruments that may assess the relative contribution of cognitive and behavioral factors, in addition to physical or developmental factors. [34 C.F.R. § 300.304(b)(1)–(3)]
(c) Other evaluation procedures: Each LEA shall ensure that:
(1) Assessments and other evaluation materials used to assess a child under this section:

> (i) Are selected and administered so as not to be discriminatory on a racial or cultural basis;
> (ii) Are provided and administered in the child's native language or other mode of communication and in the form most likely to yield accurate information on what the child knows and can do academically, developmentally, and functionally, unless it is clearly not feasible to so provide or administer;
> (iii) Are used for the purposes for which the evaluations or measures are valid and reliable;
> (iv) Are administered by trained and knowledgeable personnel; and
> (v) Are administered in accordance with any instructions provided by the producer of the assessments. [34 C.F.R. § 300.304(c)(1)(i)–(v)]

(2) The child is assessed in all areas related to the suspected disability, including, if appropriate, health, vision, hearing, social and emotional status, general intelligence, academic performance, communicative status, and motor abilities. [34 C.F.R. § 300.304(c)(4)]
(3) Evaluation tools and strategies are used which provide relevant information that directly assists persons in determining the educational needs of the child. [34 C.F.R. § 300.304(c)(7)]
(4) Assessments and other evaluation materials include those tailored to assess specific areas of educational need and not merely those which are designed to provide a single general intelligence quotient. [34 C.F.R. § 300.304(c)(2)]

(5) Assessment selection and administration is such that, when administered to a child with impaired sensory, manual or speaking skills, the results accurately reflect the child's aptitude or achievement level, or whatever other factors the assessment purports to measure, rather than reflecting the child's impaired sensory, manual or speaking skills, except where those skills are the factors which the assessment purports to measure. [34 C.F.R. § 300.304(c)(3)]

(6) If an evaluation is not conducted under standard conditions, a description of the extent to which it varied from standard conditions, *i.e.*, the qualifications of the person administering the test or the method of test administration must be included in the evaluation report.

(7) In evaluating each child with a disability under this rule, the evaluation shall be sufficiently comprehensive to identify all of the child's special education and related services needs, whether or not commonly linked to the disability category in which the child has been classified. [34 C.F.R. § 300.304(c)(6)]

(8) Evaluations of children with disabilities who transfer from one LEA to another LEA in the same school year are coordinated with those children's prior and subsequent schools, as necessary and expeditiously as possible, to ensure prompt completion of full evaluations. [34 C.F.R. § 300.304(c)(5)]

(9) The evaluation of children referred because of learning and/or behavior problems is the responsibility of a multidisciplinary evaluation team. For children who require a psychological and clinical evaluation, it must be conducted by a qualified psychological examiner:

> (i) Qualified Psychological Examiner Requirements.
> (ii) Initial evaluation results used for consideration of eligibility for special education, if not provided by a school psychologist with a valid S-5 (or higher) certificate in school psychology, shall be from one of the following:
>
>> (I) A psychologist licensed by the Georgia Board of Examiners of Psychologists and having training and experience in school psychology or child clinical psychology.
>> (II) A full-time graduate student in an approved, properly supervised school psychology or child clinical psychology training program internship/practicum, who has completed a minimum of one year of approved appropriate graduate training.
>> (III) A Georgia Merit System employee who has a classification rating of psychologist, senior psychologist, or psychology program specialist.

(5) ***Additional Requirements***:

(a) Review of existing evaluation data: As part of an initial evaluation (if appropriate) and as part of any re-evaluation, the parent and other qualified professionals, as appropriate, must review existing evaluation data on the child, including:

(1) Evaluations and information provided by the parents of the child;

(2) Current classroom-based, local, or State assessments and classroom-based observations; and

(3) Observations by teachers and related services providers. [34 C.F.R. § 300.305(a)(1)(i)–(iii)]

(b) On the basis of that review and input from the child's parents, identify what additional data, if any, are needed to determine:

(1) Whether the child is a child with a disability and the educational needs of the child, or in case of a reevaluation of a child, whether the child continues to have such a disability and the educational needs of the child; [34 C.F.R. § 300.305(a)(2)(i)(A)–(B)]

(2) The present levels of academic achievement and related developmental needs of the child; [34 C.F.R. § 300.305(a)(2)(ii)]

(3) Whether the child needs special education and related services, or in the case of a reevaluation of a child, whether the child continues to need special education and related services; and [34 C.F.R. § 300.305(a)(2)(iii)(A)–(B)]

(4) Whether any additions or modifications to the special education and related services are needed to enable the child to meet the measurable annual goals set out in the IEP of the child and to participate, as appropriate, in the general curriculum. [34 C.F.R. § 300.305(a)(2)(iv)]

(c) The parent and other qualified professionals may conduct its review without a meeting. [34 C.F.R. § 300.305(b)]

(d) The LEA must administer such assessments and other evaluation measures as may be needed to produce the data identified. [34 C.F.R. § 300.305(c)]

(e) Requirements if additional data are not needed:

(1) If the IEP Team and other qualified professionals, as appropriate, determine that no additional data are needed to determine whether the child continues to be a child with a disability and to determine the child's educational needs, the LEA:

> (i) Must notify the child's parents of that determination and the reasons for it and notify the parents of the right to request an evaluation to determine whether the child continues to be a child with a disability and to determine the child's educational needs; [34 C.F.R. § 300.305(d)(1)(i)–(ii)]
>
> (ii) Is not required to conduct such an evaluation to determine whether the child continues to be a child with a disability unless requested by the child's parents. [34 C.F.R. § 300.305(d)(2)]

(f) Evaluations before change in eligibility: The LEA must evaluate a child with a disability before determining that the child is no longer a child with a disability. [34 C.F.R. § 300.305(e)(1)]

(1) The evaluation is not required before termination of a child's disability due to graduation from high school with a regular education diploma, or due to exceeding the age eligibility for FAPE. [34 C.F.R. § 300.305(e)(2)]

(2) However, the LEA must provide the child with a summary of the child's academic achievement and functional performance, which shall include recommendations on how to assist the child in meeting the child's post-secondary goals. [34 C.F.R. § 300.305(e)(3)]

(6) *Determination of Eligibility*:

(a) Upon completion of the administration of tests and other evaluation measures:

(1) A group of qualified professionals and the parents of the child (Eligibility Team) determines whether the child is a child with a disability and the educational needs of the child; and

(2) The LEA provides a copy of the evaluation report and the documentation of determination of eligibility at no cost to the parents. [34 C.F.R. § 300.306(a)(1)-(2)]

(b) In making a determination of eligibility, a child must not be determined to be a child with a disability: if the determinant factor for that eligibility is lack of appropriate instruction in reading, including the essential components of reading instruction (as defined in section 1208(3) of ESEA); lack of appropriate instruction in math; or limited English proficiency; and if the child does not otherwise meet the program area eligibility criteria for a child with a disability. [34 C.F.R. § 300.306(b)(1)–(2)]

(c) Procedures for determining eligibility and educational need:

(1) In interpreting evaluation data for the purpose of determining if a child is a child with a disability and the educational needs of the child, each LEA must:

(i) Draw upon information from a variety of sources, including aptitude and achievement tests, parent input, and teacher recommendations, as well as information about the child's physical condition, social or cultural background and adaptive behavior;

(ii) Ensure that information obtained from all of these sources is documented and carefully considered. [34 C.F.R. § 300.306(c)(1)(i)–(ii)]

(2) If a determination is made that:

(i) A child has a disability,
(ii) And the disability affects educational performance (academic, functional and/or developmental) and
(iii) The child needs special education and related services, an eligibility document and IEP must be developed for the child. [34 C.F.R. § 300.306(c)(2)]

Authority O.C.G.A. §§ 20-2-133; 20-2-150; 20-2-152; 20-2-168; 20-2-240; 20-2-302; 20-2-1160

* For additional regulations please see the Georgia Department of Education regulations online.

http://rules.sos.state.ga.us/pages/GEORGIA_DEPARTMENT_OF_EDUCATION/SPECIAL_EDUCATION/index.html

Chapter 9: Contracts and Employment Law

All professionals need a working knowledge of contract law, and the laws governing employment, in order to protect their own rights and to promote personal and institutional compliance with the law. Entering into contracts for goods and services is a necessary part of every adult's personal life, and an important job duty for professionals involved in institutional procurement and employment decisions.

Disputes over employment are among the most common and contentious areas of litigation in educational institutions. Many employment problems can be avoided, however, by simply complying with the law and making wise decisions in the hiring and retention of personnel. Like a bad marriage, bad personnel situations are far easier to get into than out of. And the pains caused by bad hiring and retention decisions generally don't go away until the people do. Instead, personnel problems tend to worsen and increasingly haunt and harm the institution, often resulting in significant damage to the institution and everyone in it. The injuries resulting from bad hiring and retention decisions are, however, generally self-inflicted and avoidable.

> ***If you don't want Bad Apples in your Institution, then Stop Hiring and Retaining them.***
> ***Further, when it is Necessary for the Good of the Institution and its People,***
> ***Do Not Hesitate to Lawfully Non-Renew or Dismiss them.***

Hiring and retention decisions are the most important decisions any institution makes. Institutions are defined by the people in them. People create the institutional culture and generate an institutional reputation that either helps or hurts the institution's present and future efforts to achieve its mission. For institutional success, it is essential that you hire and retain highly qualified and ethical persons. Just as surely as good hires help to guarantee the future success of the institution, bad hires sow the seeds for future institutional failures. One "bad apple" can do enormous damage to the culture and reputation of the institution. Bad employees drive off good people and give the institution a bad reputation. And your institutional reputation can be either your greatest asset or liability.

For these reasons, it is essential that all persons involved in the hiring and retention process fully understand the importance of making wise employment decisions. Further, they must be sufficiently versed in the law and good employment practices to assure that the institutional employment process is fair and open; that no form of invidious employment discrimination is ever tolerated in the institution; and that institutional personnel decisions are fair-minded, prudent, and lawful.

To promote these important goals, this chapter reviews the law and employment practices related to equal opportunity employment; job announcements and recruitment; pre-employment screening of applicants; pre-employment interviews; reference and background checks; employee supervision; performance evaluations; dismissals; tenure and due process; defenses in dismissal proceedings; and applicable state laws.

Equal Opportunity Employment

Equal opportunity employment is not just good institutional practice: It is the law. The U.S. Equal Employment Opportunity Commission (EEOC) has lawful authority to address prohibited employment policies and practices. As the EEOC stated in its *Prohibited Employment Policies/Practices* (2012) rules, under the laws enforced by the EEOC:

> [I]t is illegal to discriminate against someone (applicant or employee) because of that person's race, color, religion, sex (including pregnancy), national origin, age (40 or older), disability or genetic information. It is also illegal to retaliate against a person because he or she complained about discrimination, filed a charge of discrimination, or participated in an employment discrimination investigation or lawsuit.

Discrimination violating the laws enforced by the EEOC could result in significant legal sanctions, including an order for substantial monetary damages. But even beyond those areas of discrimination now enforced by the EEOC, invidious employment discrimination should never be tolerated in any form. Even if not in a form that is currently expressly unlawful, irrational and invidious employment discrimination (e.g., discrimination based on sexual orientation; personal appearance; or other personal attributes that may not yet be unlawful under federal law but are irrelevant to individual merit and qualifications for employment) is professionally unethical and an unwise business practice harmful to the institution.

The goal of the institution must always be to hire and retain the most highly qualified and best performing individuals regardless of irrelevant personal attributes. To assure legal compliance, however, great care must be taken throughout the employment process to assure that there is no invidious discrimination based on factors prohibited under applicable federal or state laws.

Consistent with these goals, the purpose of any legitimate and lawful job announcement is to communicate the position opening to a large and diverse pool of highly qualified potential job applicants. Once applications for the position are received, the process of lawfully screening applications involves an objective search for the most highly qualified applicants in order to narrow the pool of applicants to a reasonable number of top candidates (based on legitimate job qualifications) for job interviews. An aggressive, open, and lawful job announcement and recruitment process is essential to hiring the top candidates for job openings.

Job Announcements and Recruitment

EEOC rules prohibit any job announcement that suggests preferential treatment or discourages applications based on prohibited factors such as race, color, religion, sex, etc. In addition to having a lawful announcement, all other recruitment efforts must also be non-discriminatory. Required and preferred qualifications communicated through job announcements or other means should be based on anticipated duties.

Avoid any terms or phrases that could reasonably be misunderstood as implying an unlawful preference (e.g., phrases such as "Adams County residents preferred" when location is associated with racial or ethnic demographics; "must be available weekends" when this is not a necessary duty and it is likely to discourage applications from persons observing a weekend religious Sabbath; "salesman" implying a gender preference; "excellent communication skills" if not an actual job requirement and may appear to discriminate based on national origin or disability; "seeking energetic recent graduate" implying an age preference; etc.).

Pre-employment Screening of Applicants

Concerning the pre-employment screening of applicants (i.e., reviews of applications; checking references; conducting interviews; etc.), EEOC *Prohibited Employment Policies/Practices* (2012) rules state:

> As a general rule, the information obtained and requested through the pre-employment process should be limited to those essential for determining if a person is qualified for the job; whereas, information regarding race, sex, national origin, age, and religion are irrelevant in such determinations. Employers are explicitly prohibited from making pre-employment inquiries about disability. Although state and federal equal opportunity laws do not clearly forbid employers from making pre-employment inquiries that relate to, or disproportionately screen out members based on race, color, sex, national origin, religion, or age, such inquiries may be used as evidence of an employer's intent to discriminate unless the questions asked can be justified by some business purpose. Therefore, inquiries about organizations, clubs, societies, and lodges of which an applicant may be a member or any other questions, which may indicate the applicant's race, sex, national origin, disability status, age, religion, color or ancestry if answered, should generally be avoided. Similarly, employers should not ask for a photograph of an applicant. If needed for identification purposes, a photograph may be obtained after an offer of employment is made and accepted.

If the job announcement was properly drafted to include a complete and accurate description of essential job qualifications and duties, it is a relatively easy matter to extract from the job announcement a valid list of job qualifications and duties to use as objective criteria in the pre-employment screening of applicants. It is also good practice to assure that each identified job qualification and duty can be justified by a legitimate business purpose (e.g., "must be able to lift 100 pounds" was included because heavy lifting is a necessary part of the job and not intended to screen out women or persons with disabilities; "must hold a doctoral degree" was included because licensing, certification, accreditation, etc., rules require a doctoral degree for the position and not to screen out members of minority groups holding fewer doctoral degrees; "must be available for work on Saturday" was included because the employee will be supervising the Saturday School Program and not to exclude persons who observe a Saturday Sabbath; etc.).

Pre-employment Interviews

Pre-employment interviews can be stressful and socially awkward for both applicants and interviewers. When faced with social stress, an awkward silence, etc., even a well-intentioned interviewer may be tempted to try to fill the silence with a question that is not well thought out. Unplanned questions can, however, potentially stray into impermissible areas of inquiry or otherwise be misperceived as involving employment discrimination. To avoid potentially falling into the abyss of suspected employment discrimination, avoid irrelevant personal questions.

Avoid Irrelevant Personal Questions in Job Interviews

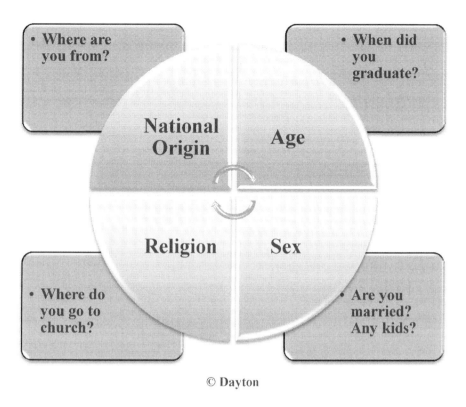

© Dayton

To survive a legal challenge, interview questions should be related to actual job requirements, *i.e.*, employment inquiries should be logically connected to Bona Fide Occupational Qualifications (BFOQs). A useful test for determining the legal relevancy of an interview questions is: Can you clearly explain what your question has to do with a BFOQ if challenged? If not, do not ask the question.

Relevancy Test for Potential Interview Questions

© Dayton

All applicants should be asked the same general questions and given the same fair opportunity to respond and demonstrate qualifications. Be certain to inquire of all applicants whether any reasonable accommodations (i.e., under § 504 or the ADA) are needed for the interview, along with an express assurance of non-discrimination for all persons consistent with applicable federal and state laws.

Reference and Background Checks

Employers have a duty to reasonably inquire into the relevant qualifications, conduct, and character of potential employees. If employers fail in this duty, and third parties are injured because of the new employee's discoverable lack of qualifications, a violent criminal history, sexual offenses, etc., the employer has negligently introduced an avoidable danger into the institution and may be held liable for resulting damages.

Employer inquiries may include reference checks, verification of educational and work history, criminal background checks, etc., to verify information received through the application and interview, and to assure that the individual is qualified and presents no danger to others in the workplace. It is good practice to generally inform applicants that references and background checks will be conducted, and to request that job candidates sign a waiver form authorizing necessary background checks. Criminal background checks may be required by state law. In making an initial contact with a previous employer or other reference person:

1) Identify who you are, your title, and the institution you are with;
2) Generally explain the nature of your inquiry;
3) Confirm the identity of the person you are contacting, their title, and institution; and
4) Verify the identity of the person you are inquiring about (i.e., you want to make sure you are both discussing the same individual).

In questioning prior employers about potential employees for your institution, as with employment interviews, questions should be related to BFOQs for the new position and relevant job performance in the prior position. Questions may include, for example: The applicant's prior job title; dates of employment; duties; work performance; attendance; the quality of working relationships with supervisors, subordinates, colleagues, and students; and other legitimate job related questions.

As an employer, you will also likely receive similar calls from other potential employers concerning your current or former employees. In responding to inquiries about current or former employees, responses should be based on employment related facts and good faith efforts to respond to BFOQs. Do not respond to discriminatory, unethical, or otherwise improper questions from potential employers. Do not say anything to the potential employer that you would not say to the employee or others. Do not defame the employee or others, breach their privacy, or make malicious statements intended to interfere with contract or employment. Keep all communications factual and professional. Remember that depending on state law, it is possible that phone conversations may be lawfully recorded even without your knowledge.

State law or professional ethics may require you to disclose certain material facts that may make a job candidate unfit for employment. Public policy should certainly prohibit what was known among personnel directors as "passing the trash" (e.g., agreeing to give a known child molester a positive recommendation in exchange for a resignation, thereby quietly solving one institution's problem, but allowing the abuser to find unsuspecting new targets in the new institution). You must warn others about known dangers. When doing so, however, only communicate facts sufficient to satisfy your legal and professional duty (e.g., "that teacher, Mr. Jones, resigned from our school district in March of this year after being arrested for child abuse. We have no further comment"). You must provide a sufficient warning. But you do not want to open the door to a defamation suit by going beyond provable facts to rumor and speculation.

If you discover clear evidence that a potential employee is unfit for the position or presents a significant risk to students or others, this person cannot be hired. Applicants will often omit negative but relevant information from their applications. Evidence of dishonesty alone, however, may make the individual unfit for employment. It is possible for anyone to make a good faith misstatement, omission, or harmless error. But clear evidence that an employee intentionally misrepresented a material fact on an employment application, or lied during a job interview, may be grounds for termination of employment even after hiring.

In the age of the Internet and extensive public records it is very difficult to keep a secret. If an employee has a negative event in his or her employment history, it is better for the employee to be honest about the event; to provide an explanation for the event; evidence of remediation or rehabilitation; and to explain why it does not make him or her unfit for the current position.

Employee Supervision

As noted above, employers are required to exercise due diligence in assuring that employees have adequate skills, certification, and character prior to assuming their duties. Employers must conduct all necessary reference and background checks to assure that they are protecting others in the institution from reasonably discoverable dangers. Further, employers are required to provide adequate post-employment training and supervision to assure that employees continue to safely perform their duties and do not engage in unlawful work-related activities.

Under the legal doctrine of *respondeat superior* (i.e., the superior must answer) employers may be held liable for wrongful acts of employees when those acts occur within the scope of employment. To protect the interests of the institution and to assure work place safety, employers have the right and responsibility to supervise work performed by employees.

Performance Evaluations

An effective system of performance evaluations is essential to any successful institution. The quality of individual work performance collectively defines the quality of the institution. To support institutional success, evaluations must effectively document work performance for recognition, reward, remediation, or dismissal of employees as appropriate.

Work performance evaluations are very significant events for employers and employees. Evaluations affect retention, promotion, and tenure decisions, and may also be used as the basis for performance pay, reassignments, or reduction in force decisions by the institution.

Most states have enacted statutes addressing teacher evaluations. But many of these statutes simply require an evaluation system; authorize local school officials to require evaluations; or otherwise leave considerable discretion to local school officials. Depending on state law, performance evaluations of school employees may be governed more or less by state law or local policy. Union agreements may also affect aspects of the evaluation process in many states.

What is consistent among all U.S. public educational institutions, however, is that because an evaluation may significantly affect the individual's employment rights and professional reputation, evaluation policies must be in accordance with the requirements of the Due Process Clause. Evaluation systems must provide adequate notice, an opportunity to be heard, and policies and practices that are fundamentally fair.

Where lawful state or local evaluation policies have been established, school officials should strictly comply with established policies or risk charges of arbitrariness and violations of due process in the evaluation process. Generally, judges tend to be highly deferential to professional judgments by school officials. But judges have been firm in enforcing requirements of established policy and procedures in the evaluation process where non-compliance significantly affected an employee's protected rights. When there is less prejudice to the rights of the employee, judges may accept substantial compliance with established procedures as minimally sufficient in deference to school officials, and decline assessing damages against school officials.

Nonetheless, there is really no excuse for failure to follow current state laws and your own established institutional policies. Further, if an administrator makes a procedural error serious enough to result in litigation, even if the educational institution does not lose the case or incur significant monetary damages, this level of negligence and incompetence will likely be remembered by the administrator's supervisors in future decisions concerning retention and promotion. A clear message emerges from the case law and experiences in practice: Read your State's statutes and your local policies governing employment and evaluations and comply with established procedures.

Administrators and other supervisors are hired in part for their ability to be fair and exercise good judgment, in realization that a certain degree of subjectivity is inevitable in the evaluation process. Human behavior and the totality of the employment circumstance cannot be accurately and fairly distilled to only simple, objective measures without missing important individual factors and the genuine context of the employee's work and performance. To maximize objectivity and fairness in the evaluation process, however, evaluations should generally focus on criteria that are: 1) Related to essential job duties; and 2) Observable or measurable.

Persons being evaluated should have advance notice of the criteria for the evaluation, and a fair opportunity to demonstrate successful job performance under the established criteria (i.e., fair notice and opportunity to be heard consistent with due process). Following the evaluation, the employee should receive timely notification of the results of the evaluation, including any noted deficiencies.

When remediation is still possible, it is good practice to start with positive observations (so that the employee knows that the evaluator is attempting to be fair and supportive) and then move to the areas needing improvement. In addressing deficiencies the supervisor should:

1) Clearly identify deficiencies, providing a summary of the criteria and evidence;
2) Precisely explain what is necessary to correct deficiencies;
3) Give the employee a fair opportunity to be heard in response; and
4) Allow a fair opportunity to remedy deficiencies prior to the next evaluation.

A failure to remedy identified deficiencies after sufficient notice and a fair opportunity to do so may constitute neglect of duties or incompetency. A willful refusal to correct identified deficiencies may constitute insubordination.

The evaluation process must be an open and honest process, with good faith efforts by the supervisor to help the employee improve performance, and good faith efforts by the employee to comply with the lawful orders of the supervisor. The evaluating supervisor is responsible for both coaching for success when possible and documenting failure when necessary. But there should be no pretenses or duplicity about the evaluator's true role, and all aspects of the process should be fair and open. Honesty is essential to building trust between the supervisor and the employee. Secrecy or duplicity in the process may unfairly blind-side the employee, and also jeopardize employment actions based on any unfair evaluation practices.

When necessary, negative employment actions should be proportional and progressive. Consequences should be proportional to the employee's conduct and employment status. If necessary changes do not occur, however, the consequences should appropriately escalate in seriousness toward dismissal when necessary. For example, if employee conduct is serious enough to warrant sanctions but does not constituent an immediate peril to anyone, the employee may first be given a verbal warning; then a written notice and warning for a subsequent occurrence; followed by a suspension or other appropriate employment sanction as warned in the prior written notice; and then final dismissal if the problem is not remedied.

Progressive Employment Consequences

© Dayton

Very serious misconduct or actions that pose a present danger in the workplace may require immediate removal and the initiation of formal dismissal proceedings.

The employer should thoroughly document the process of proportional and progressive sanctions, proving that the employee had clear notice and an opportunity to conform conduct to acceptable standards but did not do so. This proportional and progressive approach, and the resulting paper trail, helps to document that any impacts on protected liberty or property rights were consistent with requirements of procedural and substantive due process, and that the process was fair and proportional even when the final result was dismissal.

Dismissals

Dismissal proceedings succeed or fail based on the fundamental fairness of the process and the quality of the documentation. No amount of documentation, however, could or should cover up an unfair dismissal rooted in retaliation, discrimination, or other improper motives. But a fair evaluation process and thorough documentation are the keys to success in necessary dismissals where the employee is being properly removed from the institution for good and sufficient cause.

Hourly staff, non-certificated support personnel, and other at-will employees generally have no long-term contract or any reasonable expectation of continued employment. They can generally be dismissed at any time. Untenured teachers are offered year-to-year contracts until they acquire tenure. They can be let go simply by not renewing their contracts. Only tenured educators have a right to continued employment beyond the current contract term. They can only be dismissed based on a valid cause, and they are entitled to due process of law.

Tenure and Due Process

To claim a right to due process of law, a plaintiff must establish that there has been a sufficient impingement on a protected life, liberty, or property interest. Only liberty or property interests are relevant in the educational context. Untenured and tenured teachers hold very different types of property rights in employment. Untenured teachers are granted year-to-year contracts. The property right of an untenured teacher runs only from the start of the contract period to the end. In contrast, tenured teachers have a property right that extends indefinitely. The property right of a tenured teacher extends until the teacher leaves employment or school officials can show a valid cause for termination.

Untenured Teacher's Property Right to Employment

Tenured Teacher's Property Right to Employment

© Dayton

In *Board of Regents v. Roth*, 408 U.S. 564 (1972) the Court decided that when an untenured teacher has been paid the amount due under the contract, then no property right has been taken away simply by not renewing the contract. The contract promised one academic year's pay. After the teacher received what was promised under the contract, there were no further promises and no further property rights. Accordingly, there is no property right to due process based on not renewing the contract for another academic year.

Untenured teachers are also generally not entitled to an explanation for the non-renewal and a knowledgeable administrator is unlikely to volunteer one. Providing an explanation for the non-renewal may arguably create a right to due process. In *Roth* the Court recognized that: "Where a person's good name, reputation, honor, or integrity is at stake because of what the government is doing to him, notice and an opportunity to be heard are essential." If school officials give a negative reason for the non-renewal, the non-renewed teacher could argue that the statement impinged on the teacher's "good name, reputation, honor, or integrity" requiring due process.

Statements from school officials that call into question the good name, reputation, honor or integrity of the teacher related to the non-renewal could raise a liberty interest entitling the teacher to due process. But is non-renewal itself sufficiently stigmatizing? In *Roth*, the Court stated "there is no suggestion that the State, in declining to re-employ the respondent, imposed on him a stigma or other disability that foreclosed his freedom to take advantage of other employment opportunities." The lesson from *Roth* is that because untenured teachers are only promised a year-to-year contract, an untenured teacher can simply be non-renewed at the end of the contract term, without any notification of cause or other explanation. Further, no explanation should be given to avoid claims of infringement on a protected liberty interest.

It should be noted that if a non-renewed teacher has evidence that the non-renewal was based on an improper motivation, such as discrimination related to race, gender, religion, national origin, age, disability, etc., the teacher has a right to contest the alleged discriminatory non-renewal. But the burden of proof is with the teacher challenging the non-renewal. Unless the teacher has credible evidence of unlawful actions by school officials the suit is likely to be dismissed. In contrast, in a termination of a tenured teacher the burden of proof lies with school officials. All other things being equal, the party who bears the burden of proof is less likely to prevail. Because tenure status places the burden on school officials, tenure clearly provides an advantageous employment status, but only if school officials cannot meet the burden of proof.

After acquiring tenure, tenured educators can only be terminated for a valid cause proven by school officials. The permissible reasons for termination are specified in state statutes, and may include, for example: incompetency; insubordination; willful neglect of duties; immorality; violation of school policy, state, or federal law; or other good and sufficient causes. These statutes may also include non-punitive reasons for termination, including a reduction in force (RIF) due to loss of students or canceled programs. In general, any involuntary termination of a tenured educator requires extensive due process, as the right to continued employment is a substantial property interest.

Assuming that the charges are true, however, proving a charge of insubordination is a relatively simple two-step process: 1) The employee was given a lawful order; and 2) The employee refused to comply with the lawful order. Willful neglect of duties involves a similar pattern of proof. In contrast, incompetency and immorality are more subjective in nature, and while easy to prove in extreme cases, may be difficult to prove in closer cases. Conduct that some may view as immoral, others may see as an exercise of poor judgment but not immoral.

Common Defenses in Dismissal Proceedings

Common employee defenses in dismissal proceeding may include allegations of violations of due process; failure to comply with institutional policies; insufficient evidence; discrimination; evaluator bias; and retaliation. In responding to all of these defenses, due process and solid documentation are the keys to a successful dismissal hearing and prevailing in any subsequent appeals. Strong documentation can help prove that it was the employee that failed, not the institution. But documentation only counts if it has been entered into the record in the hearing.

Thoroughly Document the Evidence Necessary to Support the Dismissal and be certain the Necessary Evidence is entered into the Official Record of the Hearing

To guard against charges of bias, when possible use multiple sources of evidence from multiple persons (e.g., consistent evaluations by different evaluators; corroborating evidence and testimony; peer evaluations; documented complaints from parents and students; etc.). To guard against charges of retaliation, be certain the claims are not true. Never be a party to institutional retaliation and assure that dismissals are the product of good faith, lawful efforts to protect the legitimate interests of students and the institution.

Selected Georgia Laws

Georgia Statutes

§ 20-2-940: Due Process in Terminations or Suspensions

(a) *Grounds for termination or suspension.* Except as otherwise provided in this subsection, the contract of employment of a teacher, principal, or other employee having a contract for a definite term may be terminated or suspended for the following reasons:

> (1) Incompetency;
> (2) Insubordination;
> (3) Willful neglect of duties;
> (4) Immorality;
> (5) Inciting, encouraging, or counseling students to violate any valid state law, municipal ordinance, or policy or rule of the local board of education;
> (6) To reduce staff due to loss of students or cancellation of programs;
> (7) Failure to secure and maintain necessary educational training; or
> (8) Any other good and sufficient cause.

A teacher, principal, or other employee having a contract of employment for a definite term shall not have such contract terminated or suspended for refusal to alter a grade or grade report if the request to alter a grade or grade report was made without good and sufficient cause.

(b) *Notice.* Before the discharge or suspension of a teacher, principal, or other employee having a contract of employment for a definite term, written notice of the charges shall be given at least ten days before the date set for hearing and shall state:

> (1) The cause or causes for his discharge, suspension, or demotion in sufficient detail to enable him fairly to show any error that may exist therein;
> (2) The names of the known witnesses and a concise summary of the evidence to be used against him. The names of new witnesses shall be given as soon as practicable;
> (3) The time and place where the hearing thereon will be held; and
> (4) That the charged teacher or other person, upon request, shall be furnished with compulsory process or subpoena legally requiring the attendance of witnesses and the production of documents and other papers as provided by law.

(c) *Service.* All notices required by this part relating to suspension from duty shall be served either personally or by certified mail or statutory overnight delivery. All notices required by this part relating to demotion, termination, nonrenewal of contract, or reprimand shall be served by certified mail or statutory overnight delivery. Service shall be deemed to be perfected when the notice is deposited in the United States mail addressed to the last known address of the addressee with sufficient postage affixed to the envelope.

(d) *Counsel; testimony.* Any teacher, principal, or other person against whom such charges listed in subsection (a) of this Code section have been brought shall be entitled to be represented by counsel and, upon request, shall be entitled to have subpoenas or other compulsory process issued for attendance of witnesses and the production of documents and other evidence. Such subpoenas and compulsory process shall be issued in the name of the local board and shall be signed by the chairperson or vice chairperson of the local board. In all other respects, such subpoenas and other compulsory process shall be subject to Article 2 of Chapter 13 of Title 24.

(e) *Hearing.* (1) The hearing shall be conducted before the local board, or the local board may designate a tribunal to consist of not less than three nor more than five impartial persons possessing academic expertise to conduct the hearing and submit its findings and recommendations to the local board for its decision thereon.

(2) The hearing shall be reported at the local board's expense. If the matter is heard by a tribunal, the transcript shall be prepared at the expense of the local board and an original and two copies shall be filed in the office of the superintendent. If the hearing is before the local board, the transcript need not be typed unless an appeal is taken to the State Board of Education, in which event typing of the transcript shall be paid for by the appellant. In the event of an appeal to the state board, the original shall be transmitted to the state board as required by its rules.

(3) Oath or affirmation shall be administered to all witnesses by the chairman, any member of the local board, or by the local board attorney. Such oath shall be as follows:

> "You do solemnly swear (or affirm) that the evidence shall be the truth, the whole truth, and nothing but the truth. So help you God."

(4) All questions relating to admissibility of evidence or other legal matters shall be decided by the chairman or presiding officer, subject to the right of either party to appeal to the full local board or hearing tribunal, as the case may be; provided, however, the parties by agreement may stipulate that some disinterested member of the State Bar of Georgia shall decide all questions of evidence and other legal issues arising before the local board or tribunal. In all hearings, the burden of proof shall be on the school system, and it shall have the right to open and to conclude. Except as otherwise provided in this subsection, the same rules governing nonjury trials in the superior court shall prevail.

(f) *Decision; appeals.* The local board shall render its decision at the hearing or within five days thereafter. Where the hearing is before a tribunal, the tribunal shall file its findings and recommendations with the local board within five days of the conclusion of the hearing, and the local board shall render its decision thereon within ten days after the receipt of the transcript. Appeals may be taken to the state board in accordance with Code Section 20-2-1160, as now or hereafter amended, and the rules and regulations of the state board governing appeals.

(g) *Superintendent's power to relieve from duty temporarily.* The superintendent of a local school system may temporarily relieve from duty any teacher, principal, or other employee having a contract for a definite term for any reason specified in subsection (a) of this Code section, pending hearing by the local board in those cases where the charges are of such seriousness or other circumstances exist which indicate that such teacher or employee could not be permitted to continue to perform his duties pending hearing without danger of disruption or other serious harm to the school, its mission, pupils, or personnel. In any such case, the superintendent shall notify the teacher or employee in writing of such action, which notice shall state the grounds thereof and shall otherwise comply with the requirements of the notice set forth in subsection (b) of this Code section. Such action by the superintendent shall not extend for a period in excess of ten working days, and during such period it shall be the duty of the local board to conduct a hearing on the charges in the same manner provided for in subsections (e) and (f) of this Code section, except that notice of the time and place of hearing shall be given at least three days prior to the hearing. During the period that the teacher or other employee is relieved from duty prior to the decision of the local board, the teacher or employee shall be paid all sums to which he is otherwise entitled. If the hearing is delayed after the ten-day period as set out in this subsection at the request of the teacher or employee, then the teacher or employee shall not be paid beyond the ten-day period unless he is reinstated by the local board, in which case he shall receive all compensation to which he is otherwise entitled.

§ 20-2-942: Tenure, Nonrenewal, or Demotion

(a) As used in this Code section, the term:

> (1) "Local board of education" or "local board" means a county or independent board of education, a board of education of an area school system, or any agent with the authority to act on behalf of any such board.
> (1.1) "School administrator" means any professional school employee certificated by the Professional Standards Commission who is required to hold a leadership certificate and is assigned to a leadership position pursuant to rules of the State Board of Education, Department of Education, Professional Standards Commission, or requirements of local policy or job description.
> (2) "School year" means a period of at least 180 school days, or the equivalent thereof as determined in accordance with State Board of Education guidelines, beginning in or about September and ending in or about June.
> (3) "School year contract" means a contract of full-time employment between a teacher and a local board of education covering a full school year. A contract of employment for a portion of a school year shall not be counted as a school year contract, nor shall contracts of employment for portions of a school year be cumulated and treated as a school year contract. A contract of employment for any time outside a school year shall not be counted as a school year contract, nor shall contracts of employment for time outside a school year be cumulated and treated as a school year contract. A school year contract is deemed included within a contract of full-time employment between a teacher and a local board of education covering a full calendar or fiscal year.
> (4) "Teacher" means any professional school employee certificated by the Professional Standards Commission, but not including school administrators.

(b)(1) A teacher who accepts a school year contract for the fourth consecutive school year from the same local board of education may be demoted or the teacher's contract may not be renewed only for those reasons set forth in subsection (a) of Code Section 20-2-940.
(2) In order to demote or fail to renew the contract of a teacher who accepts a school year contract for the fourth or subsequent consecutive school year from the same local board of education, the teacher must be given written notice of the intention to demote or not renew the contract of the teacher. Such notice shall be given by certified mail or statutory overnight delivery as provided in subsection (c) of Code Section 20-2-940. Such notice shall contain a conspicuous statement in substantially the following form:

> You have the right to certain procedural safeguards before you can be demoted or dismissed. These safeguards include the right to notice of the reasons for the action against you and the right to a hearing. If you desire these rights you must send to the school superintendent by certified mail or statutory overnight delivery a statement that you wish to have a hearing; and such statement must be mailed to the school superintendent within 20 days after this notice was mailed to you. Your rights are governed by subsection (b) of Code Section 20-2-211, Code Section 20-2-940, and Code Sections 20-2-942 through 20-2-947, and a copy of this law is enclosed.

A copy of subsection (b) of Code Section 20-2-211, Code Section 20-2-940, this Code section, and Code Sections 20-2-943 through 20-2-947 shall be enclosed with the notice. A teacher who is so notified that he or she is to be demoted or that his or her contract will not be renewed has the right to the procedures set forth in subsections (b) through (f) of Code Section 20-2-940 before the intended action is taken. A teacher who has the right to these procedures must serve written notice on the superintendent of the local board employing the teacher within 20 days of the day the notice of the intended action is served that he or she requests a hearing. In order to be effective, such written notice that the teacher requests implementation of such procedures must be served by certified mail or statutory overnight delivery as provided in subsection (c) of Code Section 20-2-940. Within 14 days of service of the request to implement the procedures, the local board must furnish the teacher a notice that complies with the requirements of subsection (b) of Code Section 20-2-940.
(3) A teacher is deemed to have accepted a fourth consecutive school year contract if, while the teacher is serving under the third consecutive school year contract, the local board does not serve notice on the teacher by April 15 that it intends not to renew the teacher's contract for the ensuing school year, and the teacher does not serve notice in writing on the local board of education by May 1 of the third consecutive school year that he or she does not accept the fourth consecutive school year contract.
(4) A teacher who has satisfied the conditions set forth in paragraph (1) of this subsection who is subsequently employed by another local board of education and who accepts a second consecutive school year contract from the local board at which the teacher is subsequently employed may be demoted or the teacher's contract may not be renewed only for those reasons set forth in subsection (a) of Code Section 20-2-940. The provisions set forth in paragraph (2) of this subsection shall likewise apply to such a teacher.

(5) A teacher is deemed to have accepted a second consecutive school year contract if, while the teacher is serving under the first school year contract, the local board does not serve notice on the teacher by April 15 that it intends not to renew the teacher's contract for the ensuing school year, and the teacher does not serve notice in writing on the local board of education by May 1 of the first school year that he or she does not accept the second consecutive school year contract.

(6) Local boards shall make contract offers available to teachers for a minimum ten-day review period. A teacher accepts the contract by signing and returning it any time during the ten-day period.

(7)(A) Professional certificated personnel employed by a county or independent local school system that becomes consolidated with or merged into another county or independent local school system as provided in Article 8 of this chapter or otherwise shall retain their employment, except as provided in subparagraph (B) of this paragraph, in the newly created, or surviving, school system. Said professional certificated personnel shall retain and carry over all the rights already accrued and earned in the professional certificated personnel's prior school system and as set forth in this paragraph.

(B) Any reductions in staff due to loss of students or cancellation of programs in the newly created, or surviving, school system necessitated by the consolidation or merger shall be made first in preference of retaining professional certificated personnel on the basis of uniformly applied criteria set forth in local school board policies of the newly created, or surviving, school system.

(c)(1) A person who first becomes a school administrator on or after April 7, 1995, shall not acquire any rights under this Code section to continued employment with respect to any position of school administrator. A school administrator who had acquired any rights to continued employment under this Code section prior to April 7, 1995, shall retain such rights:

> (A) In that administrative position which such administrator held immediately prior to such date; and
>
> (B) In any other administrative position to which such administrator has been involuntarily transferred or assigned, and only in such positions shall such administrator be deemed to be a teacher for the purpose of retaining those rights to continued employment in such administrative positions.

(2) A teacher who had acquired any rights to continued employment under this Code section prior to April 7, 1995, and who is or becomes a school administrator without any break in employment with the local board for which the person had been a teacher shall retain those rights under this Code section to continued employment in the position as teacher with such local board.

(2.1) A local board of education may enter into an employment contract with a school administrator for a term not to exceed three years. During the term of any such contract, that school administrator may not be demoted except as provided in the other subsections of this Code section and may not be terminated or suspended except as provided in Code Section 20-2-940, but the school administrator shall have no right to renewal of such contract. The rights provided under such contracts by this paragraph shall be in addition to any rights which a school administrator may otherwise have under the other provisions of this subsection.

(3) Nothing in this subsection shall affect positions which, prior to April 7, 1995, had no rights to continued employment under this Code section, including coach, athletic director, finance officer, comptroller, business manager, nurse, department head or chairperson, and similar positions. Nothing in this subsection shall impair the rights of teachers or school administrators with respect to their employment under annual contracts, including but not limited to those rights under Code Section 20-2-940.

(4) Notwithstanding the other provisions of this subsection, a local board of education may, as part of its personnel policies, adopt or modify a tenure policy which may include the same policies and procedures for the nonrenewal of contracts for any class or category of school administrators that exist for the nonrenewal of contracts for teachers as set forth in this Code section. Before any adoption or modification of a tenure policy, the local board shall hold a public hearing after at least 30 days' notice published in the local legal organ.

(d) A person who first became a teacher on or after July 1, 2000, shall acquire rights under this Code section to continued employment as a teacher. A teacher who had acquired any rights to continued employment under this Code section prior to July 1, 2000, shall retain such rights.

§ 20-2-943. Powers of Board; Due Process

(a) In exercising its powers in the enforcement of due process under this part, a local board of education shall be authorized:

(1) Under Code Section 20-2-940 to:

(A) Terminate the contract of the teacher or other school employee;
(B) Suspend a teacher or other school employee without pay for a period of time not to exceed 60 days. In such event, the teacher or employee shall provide no services for the school system and shall receive no compensation but shall be considered an employee on suspended status; or
(C) Reinstate a teacher or other school employee in the event the teacher or school employee has been temporarily relieved from duty in accordance with this part;

(2) Under Code Section 20-2-942 to:

(A) Nonrenew a teacher's or other school employee's contract;
(B) Renew a teacher's or other school employee's contract; or
(C) Demote a teacher's other school employee from one position in the school system to another position in the school system having less responsibility, prestige, and salary.

(b) Nothing in this part shall be construed as depriving local boards of education and other school officials from assigning and reassigning teachers and other certificated professional employees from one school to another or from assigning and reassigning teachers to teach different classes or subjects.

§ 20-2-944. Letter of Reprimand; Due Process

A local school superintendent may write a letter of reprimand to a teacher or other school employee for any valid reason. A copy of the letter of reprimand is to remain in the teacher's or employee's permanent personnel file, and the teacher or employee receiving such a letter of reprimand shall have the right to appeal the decision of the superintendent to the local board of education, the hearing to be conducted according to this part. The local board shall have the right either to affirm the decision of the superintendent or to reverse it. If the decision of the local board is to reverse it, the letter of reprimand shall be removed from the teacher's or employee's permanent personnel file.

§ 20-2-989.5: Complaints Policy; Due Process

(a) It is the intent of this part to resolve problems at the lowest possible organizational level with a minimum of conflict and formal proceedings so that good morale may be maintained, effective job performance may be enhanced, and the citizens of the community may be better served. These procedures require local units of administration to implement a simple, expeditious, and fair process for resolving problems at the lowest administrative level.

(b) It shall be the duty of all local units of administration to adopt a complaints policy for certified personnel that shall contain the definitions and standards provided in this part. As used in this part, the term:

> (1) "Administrator" means the individual at each level designated by the local unit of administration to preside over and make decisions with respect to complaints.
> (2) "Central office administrator" means the local school system superintendent or the director of a Regional Education Service Agency (RESA).
> (3) "Complaint" means any claim by a certified employee of any local unit of administration who is affected in his or her employment relationship by an alleged violation, misinterpretation, or misapplication of statutes, policies, rules, regulations, or written agreements of the local unit of administration with which the local unit of administration is required to comply.
> (4) "Local unit of administration" means the local board of education or the local board of control of a RESA.

§ 20-2-989.7: Issues Subject to Compliant Policy

(a) The performance ratings contained in personnel evaluations and professional development plans pursuant to Code Section 20-2-210 and job performance shall not be subject to complaint under the provisions of this part. The termination, nonrenewal, demotion, suspension, or reprimand of any employee, as set forth in Code Section 20-2-940, and the revocation, suspension, or denial of certificates of any employee, as set forth in Code Section 20-2-984.5, shall not be subject to complaint under the provisions of this part.

(b) A certified employee who chooses to appeal under Code Section 20-2-1160 shall be barred from pursuing the same complaint under this part.

§ 20-2-989.8: Complaint Policy; Procedures

Local units of administration shall establish a complaint policy that shall include the following:

(1) A statement that a complaint by the certified employee at the initial level shall be in writing and shall clearly state the intent of the employee to access the complaints policy. All certified employees shall request in writing successive levels of review;

(2) A method and time frame for filing complaints and appeals, including successive levels of appeal from the complainant's immediate supervisor to the central office administrator to the local unit of administration, provided that the complainant shall be entitled to file a complaint within ten days from the most recent incident upon which the complaint is based, and provided that the complainant shall have a minimum of ten days to file an appeal at any level up to and including the local unit of administration, and provided that the total time frame shall not exceed 60 days from the initiation of the complaint until notification to the complainant of the decision rendered by the local unit of administration;

(3) A statement setting forth the manner in which notice of the initial hearing and appeals shall be given;

(4) A statement that the complainant shall be entitled to an opportunity to be heard, to present relevant evidence, and to examine witnesses at each level;

(5) A provision whereby the complainant is entitled to the presence of an individual of his or her choice to assist in the presentation of the complaint to the central office administrator and at the local unit of administration level. The policy shall also include a provision whereby the presence of any individual other than the complainant and the administrator at any lower level is specifically prohibited. At the local unit of administration level nothing shall prevent the local unit from having an attorney present to serve as the law officer who shall rule on issues of law and who shall not participate in the presentation of the case for the administrator or the complainant;

(6) Provisions for keeping an accurate record of the proceedings at each level, requiring the proceedings to be recorded by mechanical means, preserving all evidence, and requiring that these be made available at all times to the parties involved but which provisions do not permit the presence of a third person at any level below the central office administrator or local unit of administration level;

(7) A statement that the complainant cannot present additional evidence at each level of the complaint process unless it is submitted in writing by the complainant five days prior to the set date for the Level II and Level III hearing to the administrator presiding over the complaint. The board of the local unit of administration, when hearing an appeal from a prior complaint level, shall hear the complaint de novo;

(8) A statement that each decision be made in writing and dated. Each decision shall contain findings of fact and reasons for the particular resolution reached. The decision reached at each complaint level shall be sent to the complainant by certified mail or statutory overnight delivery or hand delivered by a person designated by the central office administrator within 20 days of the decision;

(9) A statement that any complaint not processed by the administrator or the local unit of administration within the time frames required by the local complaint procedure and this part shall be forwarded to the next level of the complaint procedure;

(10) A provision that all costs and fees shall be borne by the party incurring them unless otherwise agreed upon by the parties involved, except that the cost of preparing and preserving the record of the proceedings shall be borne by the local board of education; and

(11) A statement that a complainant shall not be the subject of any reprisal as a result of filing a complaint under this part. Should any reprisal occur, the complainant may refer the matter to the Professional Standards Commission.

§ 20-2-989.9: Local Supplemental Rules and Policies

Nothing in this part shall be construed to prevent a local unit of administration from adopting supplemental rules and policies not inconsistent with this part that grant additional substantive and procedural rights to the complainant with respect to this part.

§ 20-2-989.10: Collective Bargaining Not Permitted

Nothing in this part shall be construed to permit or foster collective bargaining as part of the state rules or local unit of administration policies.

20-2-989.11: Appeals

Appeals from the decision of the local unit of administration to the Georgia Board of Education shall be governed by state board policy and Code Section 20-2-1160.

§ 20-2-989.20: Grade Changes; Coercion Prohibited

(a) No classroom teacher shall be required, coerced, intimidated, or disciplined in any manner by the local board of education, superintendent, or any local school administrator to change the grade of a student. This subsection shall not apply when a teacher has failed to comply with grading policies or rules adopted by the local board of education or written procedures established by an individual school that are applicable to the grading process, unless such policy, rule, or procedure would require a student be given a grade different than the actual grade achieved. A violation of this Code section shall constitute an ethics violation reportable to the Professional Standards Commission pursuant to Part 10 of this article.

(b) Nothing in this Code section shall be construed to prevent a principal or other local school administrator from discussing the grade of a student with a classroom teacher.

(c) Nothing in this Code section shall be construed to prevent a central office administrator, superintendent, or local school administrator from changing a student's grade. Any grade change made by a person other than the classroom teacher must be clearly indicated in the student's school records and must indicate the person responsible for making such grade change.

§ 50-14-1: Open Meetings

(a) As used in this chapter, the term:

(1) "Agency" means:
(A) Every state department, agency, board, bureau, office, commission, public corporation, and authority;
(B) Every county, municipal corporation, school district, or other political subdivision of this state;
(C) Every department, agency, board, bureau, office, commission, authority, or similar body of each such county, municipal corporation, or other political subdivision of the state;
(D) Every city, county, regional, or other authority established pursuant to the laws of this state; and
(E) Any nonprofit organization to which there is a direct allocation of tax funds made by the governing body of any agency as defined in this paragraph which constitutes more than 33 1/3 percent of the funds from all sources of such organization; provided, however, that this subparagraph shall not include hospitals, nursing homes, dispensers of pharmaceutical products, or any other type organization, person, or firm furnishing medical or health services to a citizen for which they receive reimbursement from the state whether directly or indirectly; nor shall this term include a sub-agency or affiliate of such a nonprofit organization from or through which the allocation of tax funds is made.
(2) "Executive session" means a portion of a meeting lawfully closed to the public.
(3)(A) "Meeting" means:

> (i) The gathering of a quorum of the members of the governing body of an agency at which any official business, policy, or public matter of the agency is formulated, presented, discussed, or voted upon; or
> (ii) The gathering of a quorum of any committee of the members of the governing body of an agency or a quorum of any committee created by the governing body, at which any official business, policy, or public matter of the committee is formulated, presented, discussed, or voted upon.

(B) "Meeting" shall not include:

> (i) The gathering of a quorum of the members of a governing body or committee for the purpose of making inspections of physical facilities or property under the jurisdiction of such agency at which no other official business of the agency is to be discussed or official action is to be taken;
> (ii) The gathering of a quorum of the members of a governing body or committee for the purpose of attending state-wide, multijurisdictional, or regional meetings to participate in seminars or courses of training on matters related to the purpose of the agency or to receive or discuss information on matters related to the purpose of the agency at which no official action is to be taken by the members;
> (iii) The gathering of a quorum of the members of a governing body or committee for the purpose of meeting with officials of the legislative or executive branches of the state or federal government at state or federal of-fices and at which no official action is to be taken by the members;
> (iv) The gathering of a quorum of the members of a governing body of an agency for the purpose of traveling to a meeting or gathering as otherwise authorized by

this subsection so long as no official business, policy, or public matter is formulated, presented, discussed, or voted upon by the quorum; or

(v) The gathering of a quorum of the members of a governing body of an agency at social, ceremonial, civic, or religious events so long as no official business, policy, or public matter is formulated, presented, discussed, or voted upon by the quorum.

This subparagraph's exclusions from the definition of the term meeting shall not apply if it is shown that the primary purpose of the gathering or gatherings is to evade or avoid the requirements for conducting a meeting while discussing or conducting official business.

(b)(1) Except as otherwise provided by law, all meetings shall be open to the public. All votes at any meeting shall be taken in public after due notice of the meeting and compliance with the posting and agenda requirements of this chapter.

(2) Any resolution, rule, regulation, ordinance, or other official action of an agency adopted, taken, or made at a meeting which is not open to the public as required by this chapter shall not be binding. Any action contesting a resolution, rule, regulation, ordinance, or other formal action of an agency based on an alleged violation of this provision shall be commenced within 90 days of the date such contested action was taken or, if the meeting was held in a manner not permitted by law, within 90 days from the date the party alleging the violation knew or should have known about the alleged violation so long as such date is not more than six months after the date the contested action was taken.

(3) Notwithstanding the provisions of paragraph (2) of this subsection, any action under this chapter contesting a zoning decision of a local governing authority shall be commenced within the time allowed by law for appeal of such zoning decision.

(c) The public at all times shall be afforded access to meetings declared open to the public pursuant to subsection (b) of this Code section. Visual and sound recording during open meetings shall be permitted.

(d)(1) Every agency subject to this chapter shall prescribe the time, place, and dates of regular meetings of the agency. Such information shall be available to the general public and a notice containing such information shall be posted at least one week in advance and maintained in a conspicuous place available to the public at the regular place of an agency or committee meeting subject to this chapter as well as on the agency's website, if any. Meetings shall be held in accordance with a regular schedule, but nothing in this subsection shall preclude an agency from canceling or postponing any regularly scheduled meeting.

(2) For any meeting, other than a regularly scheduled meeting of the agency for which notice has already been provided pursuant to this chapter, written or oral notice shall be given at least 24 hours in advance of the meeting to the legal organ in which notices of sheriff's sales are published in the county where regular meetings are held or at the option of the agency to a newspaper having a general circulation in such county at least equal to that of the legal organ; provided, however, that, in counties where the legal organ is published less often than four times weekly, sufficient notice shall be the posting of a written notice for at least 24 hours at the place of regular meetings and, upon written

request from any local broadcast or print media outlet whose place of business and physical facilities are located in the county, notice by telephone, facsimile, or e-mail to that requesting media outlet at least 24 hours in advance of the called meeting. Whenever notice is given to a legal organ or other newspaper, that publication shall immediately or as soon as practicable make the information available upon inquiry to any member of the public. Upon written request from any local broadcast or print media outlet, a copy of the meeting's agenda shall be provided by facsimile, e-mail, or mail through a self-addressed, stamped envelope provided by the requestor.

(3) When special circumstances occur and are so declared by an agency, that agency may hold a meeting with less than 24 hours' notice upon giving such notice of the meeting and subjects expected to be considered at the meeting as is reasonable under the circumstances, including notice to the county legal organ or a newspaper having a general circulation in the county at least equal to that of the legal organ, in which event the reason for holding the meeting within 24 hours and the nature of the notice shall be recorded in the minutes. Such reasonable notice shall also include, upon written request within the previous calendar year from any local broadcast or print media outlet whose place of business and physical facilities are located in the county, notice by telephone, facsimile, or e-mail to that requesting media outlet.

(e)(1) Prior to any meeting, the agency or committee holding such meeting shall make available an agenda of all matters expected to come before the agency or committee at such meeting. The agenda shall be available upon request and shall be posted at the meeting site, as far in advance of the meeting as reasonably possible, but shall not be required to be available more than two weeks prior to the meeting and shall be posted, at a minimum, at some time during the two-week period immediately prior to the meeting. Failure to include on the agenda an item which becomes necessary to address during the course of a meeting shall not preclude considering and acting upon such item.

(2)(A) A summary of the subjects acted on and those members present at a meeting of any agency shall be written and made available to the public for inspection within two business days of the adjournment of a meeting.

(B) The regular minutes of a meeting subject to this chapter shall be promptly recorded and such records shall be open to public inspection once approved as official by the agency or its committee, but in no case later than immediately following its next regular meeting; provided, however, that nothing contained in this chapter shall prohibit the earlier release of minutes, whether approved by the agency or not. Such minutes shall, at a minimum, include the names of the members present at the meeting, a description of each motion or other proposal made, the identity of the persons making and seconding the motion or other proposal, and a record of all votes. The name of each person voting for or against a proposal shall be recorded. It shall be presumed that the action taken was approved by each person in attendance unless the minutes reflect the name of the persons voting against the proposal or abstaining.

(C) Minutes of executive sessions shall also be recorded but shall not be open to the public. Such minutes shall specify each issue discussed in executive session by the agency or committee. In the case of executive sessions where matters subject to the attorney-client privilege are discussed, the fact that an attorney-client discussion occurred and its subject shall be identified, but the substance of the discussion need not be recorded and shall not be identified in the minutes. Such minutes shall be kept and preserved for in camera inspection by an appropriate court should a dispute arise as to the propriety of any executive session.

(f) An agency with state-wide jurisdiction or committee of such an agency shall be authorized to conduct meetings by teleconference, provided that any such meeting is conducted in compliance with this chapter.

(g) Under circumstances necessitated by emergency conditions involving public safety or the preservation of property or public services, agencies or committees thereof not otherwise permitted by subsection (f) of this Code section to conduct meetings by teleconference may meet by means of teleconference so long as the notice required by this chapter is provided and means are afforded for the public to have simultaneous access to the teleconference meeting. On any other occasion of the meeting of an agency or committee thereof, and so long as a quorum is present in person, a member may participate by teleconference if necessary due to reasons of health or absence from the jurisdiction so long as the other requirements of this chapter are met. Absent emergency conditions or the written opinion of a physician or other health professional that reasons of health prevent a member's physical presence, no member shall participate by teleconference pursuant to this subsection more than twice in one calendar year.

§ 50-18-70: Open Records; Findings and Definitions

(a) The General Assembly finds and declares that the strong public policy of this state is in favor of open government; that open government is essential to a free, open, and democratic society; and that public access to public records should be encouraged to foster confidence in government and so that the public can evaluate the expenditure of public funds and the efficient and proper functioning of its institutions. The General Assembly further finds and declares that there is a strong presumption that public records should be made available for public inspection without delay. This article shall be broadly construed to allow the inspection of governmental records. The exceptions set forth in this article, together with any other exception located elsewhere in the Code, shall be interpreted narrowly to exclude only those portions of records addressed by such exception.

(b) As used in this article, the term:

(1) "Agency" shall have the same meaning as in Code Section 50-14-1 and shall additionally include any association, corporation, or other similar organization that has a membership or ownership body composed primarily of counties, municipal corporations, or school districts of this state, their officers, or any combination thereof and derives more than 33 1/3 percent of its general operating budget from payments from such political subdivisions.

(2) "Public record" means all documents, papers, letters, maps, books, tapes, photographs, computer based or generated information, data, data fields, or similar material prepared and maintained or received by an agency or by a private person or entity in the performance of a service or function for or on behalf of an agency or when such documents have been transferred to a private person or entity by an agency for storage or future governmental use.

§ 50-18-71: Inspecting Public Records

(a) All public records shall be open for personal inspection and copying, except those which by order of a court of this state or by law are specifically exempted from disclosure. Records shall be maintained by agencies to the extent and in the manner required by Article 5 of this chapter.

(b)(1)(A) Agencies shall produce for inspection all records responsive to a request within a reasonable amount of time not to exceed three business days of receipt of a request; provided, however, that nothing in this chapter shall require agencies to produce records in response to a request if such records did not exist at the time of the request. In those instances where some, but not all, records are available within three business days, an agency shall make available within that period those records that can be located and produced. In any instance where records are unavailable within three business days of receipt of the request, and responsive records exist, the agency shall, within such time period, provide the requester with a description of such records and a timeline for when the records will be available for inspection or copying and provide the responsive records or access thereto as soon as practicable.

(B) A request made pursuant to this article may be made to the custodian of a public record orally or in writing. An agency may, but shall not be obligated to, require that all written requests be made upon the responder's choice of one of the following: the agency's director, chairperson, or chief executive officer, however denominated; the senior official at any satellite office of an agency; a clerk specifically designated by an agency as the custodian of agency records; or a duly designated open records officer of an agency; provided, however, that the absence or unavailability of the designated agency officer or employee shall not be permitted to delay the agency's response. At the time of inspection, any person may make photographic copies or other electronic reproductions of the records using suitable portable devices brought to the place of inspection. Notwithstanding any other provision of this chapter, an agency may, in its discretion, provide copies of a record in lieu of providing access to the record when portions of the record contain confidential information that must be redacted.

(2) Any agency that designates one or more open records officers upon whom requests for inspection or copying of records may be delivered shall make such designation in writing and shall immediately provide notice to any person upon request, orally or in writing, of those open records officers. If the agency has elected to designate an open records officer, the agency shall so notify the legal organ of the county in which the agency's principal offices reside and, if the agency has a website, shall also prominently display such designation on the agency's website. In the event an agency requires that requests be made upon the individuals identified in subparagraph (B) of paragraph (1) of this subsection, the three-day period for response to a written request shall not begin to run until the request is made in writing upon such individuals. An agency shall permit receipt of written requests by e-mail or facsimile transmission in addition to any other methods of transmission approved by the agency, provided such agency uses e-mail or facsimile in the normal course of its business.

(3) The enforcement provisions of Code Sections 50-18-73 and 50-18-74 shall be available only to enforce compliance and punish noncompliance when a written request is

made consistent with this subsection and shall not be available when such request is made orally.

(c)(1) An agency may impose a reasonable charge for the search, retrieval, redaction, and production or copying costs for the production of records pursuant to this article. An agency shall utilize the most economical means reasonably calculated to identify and produce responsive, non-excluded documents. Where fees for certified copies or other copies or records are specifically authorized or otherwise prescribed by law, such specific fee shall apply when certified copies or other records to which a specific fee may apply are sought. In all other instances, the charge for the search, retrieval, or redaction of records shall not exceed the prorated hourly salary of the lowest paid full-time employee who, in the reasonable discretion of the custodian of the records, has the necessary skill and training to perform the request; provided, however, that no charge shall be made for the first quarter hour.

(2) In addition to a charge for the search, retrieval, or redaction of records, an agency may charge a fee for the copying of records or data, not to exceed 10¢ per page for letter or legal size documents or, in the case of other documents, the actual cost of producing the copy. In the case of electronic records, the agency may charge the actual cost of the media on which the records or data are produced.

(3) Whenever any person has requested to inspect or copy a public record and does not pay the cost for search, retrieval, redaction, or copying of such records when such charges have been lawfully estimated and agreed to pursuant to this article, and the agency has incurred the agreed-upon costs to make the records available, regardless of whether the requester inspects or accepts copies of the records, the agency shall be authorized to collect such charges in any manner authorized by law for the collection of taxes, fees, or assessments by such agency.

(d) In any instance in which an agency is required to or has decided to withhold all or part of a requested record, the agency shall notify the requester of the specific legal authority exempting the requested record or records from disclosure by Code section, subsection, and paragraph within a reasonable amount of time not to exceed three business days or in the event the search and retrieval of records is delayed pursuant to this paragraph or pursuant to subparagraph (b)(1)(A) of this Code section, then no later than three business days after the records have been retrieved. In any instance in which an agency will seek costs in excess of $25.00 for responding to a request, the agency shall notify the requester within a reasonable amount of time not to exceed three business days and inform the requester of the estimate of the costs, and the agency may defer search and retrieval of the records until the requester agrees to pay the estimated costs unless the requester has stated in his or her request a willingness to pay an amount that exceeds the search and retrieval costs. In any instance in which the estimated costs for production of the records exceeds $500.00, an agency may insist on prepayment of the costs prior to beginning search, retrieval, review, or production of the records. Whenever any person who has requested to inspect or copy a public record has not paid the cost for search, retrieval, redaction, or copying of such records when such charges have been lawfully incurred, an agency may require prepayment for compliance with all future requests for production of records from that person until the costs for the prior production of records have been paid or the dispute regarding payment resolved.

(e) Requests by civil litigants for records that are sought as part of or for use in any ongoing civil or administrative litigation against an agency shall be made in writing and copied to counsel of record for that agency contemporaneously with their submission to that agency. The agency shall provide, at no cost, duplicate sets of all records produced in response to the request to counsel of record for that agency unless the counsel of record for that agency elects not to receive the records.

(f) As provided in this subsection, an agency's use of electronic record-keeping systems must not erode the public's right of access to records under this article. Agencies shall produce electronic copies of or, if the requester prefers, printouts of electronic records or data from data base fields that the agency maintains using the computer programs that the agency has in its possession. An agency shall not refuse to produce such electronic records, data, or data fields on the grounds that exporting data or redaction of exempted information will require inputting range, search, filter, report parameters, or similar commands or instructions into an agency's computer system so long as such commands or instructions can be executed using existing computer programs that the agency uses in the ordinary course of business to access, support, or otherwise manage the records or data. A requester may request that electronic records, data, or data fields be produced in the format in which such data or electronic records are kept by the agency, or in a standard export format such as a flat file electronic American Standard Code for Information Interchange (ASCII) format, if the agency's existing computer programs support such an export format. In such instance, the data or electronic records shall be downloaded in such format onto suitable electronic media by the agency.

(g) Requests to inspect or copy electronic messages, whether in the form of e-mail, text message, or other format, should contain information about the messages that is reasonably calculated to allow the recipient of the request to locate the messages sought, including, if known, the name, title, or office of the specific person or persons whose electronic messages are sought and, to the extent possible, the specific data bases to be searched for such messages.

(h) In lieu of providing separate printouts or copies of records or data, an agency may provide access to records through a website accessible by the public. However, if an agency receives a request for data fields, an agency shall not refuse to provide the responsive data on the grounds that the data is available in whole or in its constituent parts through a website if the requester seeks the data in the electronic format in which it is kept. Additionally, if an agency contracts with a private vendor to collect or maintain public records, the agency shall ensure that the arrangement does not limit public access to those records and that the vendor does not impede public record access and method of delivery as established by the agency or as otherwise provided for in this Code section.

(i) Any computerized index of county real estate deed records shall be printed for purposes of public inspection no less than every 30 days, and any correction made on such index shall be made a part of the printout and shall reflect the time and date that such index was corrected.

(j) No public officer or agency shall be required to prepare new reports, summaries, or compilations not in existence at the time of the request.

§ 50-18-72: Records not Subject to Disclosure

(a) Public disclosure shall not be required for records that are:

(1) Specifically required by federal statute or regulation to be kept confidential;

(2) Medical or veterinary records and similar files, the disclosure of which would be an invasion of personal privacy;

(3) Except as otherwise provided by law, records compiled for law enforcement or prosecution purposes to the extent that production of such records is reasonably likely to disclose the identity of a confidential source, disclose confidential investigative or prosecution material which would endanger the life or physical safety of any person or persons, or disclose the existence of a confidential surveillance or investigation;

(4) Records of law enforcement, prosecution, or regulatory agencies in any pending investigation or prosecution of criminal or unlawful activity, other than initial police arrest reports and initial incident reports; provided, however, that an investigation or prosecution shall no longer be deemed to be pending when all direct litigation involving such investigation and prosecution has become final or otherwise terminated; and provided, further, that this paragraph shall not apply to records in the possession of an agency that is the subject of the pending investigation or prosecution;

(5) Individual Georgia Uniform Motor Vehicle Accident Reports, except upon the submission of a written statement of need by the requesting party to be provided to the custodian of records and to set forth the need for the report pursuant to this Code section; provided, however, that any person or entity whose name or identifying information is contained in a Georgia Uniform Motor Vehicle Accident Report shall be entitled, either personally or through a lawyer or other representative, to receive a copy of such report; and provided, further, that Georgia Uniform Motor Vehicle Accident Reports shall not be available in bulk for inspection or copying by any person absent a written statement showing the need for each such report pursuant to the requirements of this Code section. For the purposes of this subsection, the term "need" means that the natural person or legal entity who is requesting in person or by representative to inspect or copy the Georgia Uniform Motor Vehicle Accident Report:

> (A) Has a personal, professional, or business connection with a party to the accident;
> (B) Owns or leases an interest in property allegedly or actually damaged in the accident;
> (C) Was allegedly or actually injured by the accident;
> (D) Was a witness to the accident;
> (E) Is the actual or alleged insurer of a party to the accident or of property actually or allegedly damaged by the accident;
> (F) Is a prosecutor or a publicly employed law enforcement officer;
> (G) Is alleged to be liable to another party as a result of the accident;
> (H) Is an attorney stating that he or she needs the requested reports as part of a criminal case, or an investigation of a potential claim involving contentions that a roadway, railroad crossing, or intersection is unsafe;
> (I) Is gathering information as a representative of a news media organization;

(J) Is conducting research in the public interest for such purposes as accident prevention, prevention of injuries or damages in accidents, determination of fault in an accident or accidents, or other similar purposes; provided, however, that this subparagraph shall apply only to accident reports on accidents that occurred more than 30 days prior to the request and which shall have the name, street address, telephone number, and driver's license number redacted; or

(K) Is a governmental official, entity, or agency, or an authorized agent thereof, requesting reports for the purpose of carrying out governmental functions or legitimate governmental duties;

(6) Jury list data, including, but not limited to, persons' names, dates of birth, addresses, ages, race, gender, telephone numbers, social security numbers, and when it is available, the person's ethnicity, and other confidential identifying information that is collected and used by the Council of Superior Court Clerks of Georgia for creating, compiling, and maintaining state-wide master jury lists and county master jury lists for the purpose of establishing and maintaining county jury source lists pursuant to the provisions of Chapter 12 of Title 15; provided, however, that when ordered by the judge of a court having jurisdiction over a case in which a challenge to the array of the grand or trial jury has been filed, the Council of Superior Court Clerks of Georgia or the clerk of the county board of jury commissioners of any county shall provide data within the time limit established by the court for the limited purpose of such challenge. Neither the Council of Superior Court Clerks of Georgia nor the clerk of a county board of jury commissioners shall be liable for any use or misuse of such data;

(7) Records consisting of confidential evaluations submitted to, or examinations prepared by, a governmental agency and prepared in connection with the appointment or hiring of a public officer or employee;

(8) Records consisting of material obtained in investigations related to the suspension, firing, or investigation of complaints against public officers or employees until ten days after the same has been presented to the agency or an officer for action or the investigation is otherwise concluded or terminated, provided that this paragraph shall not be interpreted to make such investigatory records privileged;

(9) Real estate appraisals, engineering or feasibility estimates, or other records made for or by the state or a local agency relative to the acquisition of real property until such time as the property has been acquired or the proposed transaction has been terminated or abandoned;

(10) Pending, rejected, or deferred sealed bids or sealed proposals and detailed cost estimates related thereto until such time as the final award of the contract is made, the project is terminated or abandoned, or the agency in possession of the records takes a public vote regarding the sealed bid or sealed proposal, whichever comes first;

(11) Records which identify persons applying for or under consideration for employment or appointment as executive head of an agency or of a unit of the University System of Georgia; provided, however, that at least 14 calendar days prior to the meeting at which final action or vote is to be taken on the position of executive head of an agency or five business days prior to the meeting at which final action or vote is to be taken on the position of president of a unit of the University System of Georgia, all documents concerning as many as three persons under consideration whom the agency has

determined to be the best qualified for the position shall be subject to inspection and copying. Prior to the release of these documents, an agency may allow such a person to decline being considered further for the position rather than have documents pertaining to such person released. In that event, the agency shall release the documents of the next most qualified person under consideration who does not decline the position. If an agency has conducted its hiring or appointment process without conducting interviews or discussing or deliberating in executive session in a manner otherwise consistent with Chapter 14 of this title, it shall not be required to delay final action on the position. The agency shall not be required to release such records of other applicants or persons under consideration, except at the request of any such person. Upon request, the hiring agency shall furnish the number of applicants and the composition of the list by such factors as race and sex. The agency shall not be allowed to avoid the provisions of this paragraph by the employment of a private person or agency to assist with the search or application process;

(12) Related to the provision of staff services to individual members of the General Assembly by the Legislative and Congressional Reapportionment Office, the Senate Research Office, or the House Budget and Research Office, provided that this exception shall not have any application to records related to the provision of staff services to any committee or subcommittee or to any records which are or have been previously publicly disclosed by or pursuant to the direction of an individual member of the General Assembly;

(13) Records that are of historical research value which are given or sold to public archival institutions, public libraries, or libraries of a unit of the Board of Regents of the University System of Georgia when the owner or donor of such records wishes to place restrictions on access to the records. No restriction on access, however, may extend more than 75 years from the date of donation or sale. This exemption shall not apply to any records prepared in the course of the operation of state or local governments of the State of Georgia;

(14) Records that contain information from the Department of Natural Resources inventory and register relating to the location and character of a historic property or of historic properties as those terms are defined in Code Sections 12-3-50.1 and 12-3-50.2 if the Department of Natural Resources through its Division of Historic Preservation determines that disclosure will create a substantial risk of harm, theft, or destruction to the property or properties or the area or place where the property or properties are located;

(15) Records of farm water use by individual farms as determined by water-measuring devices installed pursuant to Code Section 12-5-31 or 12-5- 105; provided, however, that compilations of such records for the 52 large watershed basins as identified by the eight-digit United States Geologic Survey hydrologic code or an aquifer that do not reveal farm water use by individual farms shall be subject to disclosure under this article;

(16) Agricultural or food system records, data, or information that are considered by the Department of Agriculture to be a part of the critical infrastructure, provided that nothing in this paragraph shall prevent the release of such records, data, or information to another state or federal agency if the release of such records, data, or information is necessary to prevent or control disease or to protect public health, safety, or welfare. As used in this paragraph, the term "critical infrastructure" shall have the same meaning as in 42 U.S.C.

§ 5195(c)(e). Such records, data, or information shall be subject to disclosure only upon the order of a court of competent jurisdiction;

(17) Records, data, or information collected, recorded, or otherwise obtained that is deemed confidential by the Department of Agriculture for the purposes of the national animal identification system, provided that nothing in this paragraph shall prevent the release of such records, data, or information to another state or federal agency if the release of such records, data, or information is necessary to prevent or control disease or to protect public health, safety, or welfare. As used in this paragraph, the term "national animal identification program" means a national program intended to identify animals and track them as they come into contact with or commingle with animals other than herdmates from their premises of origin. Such records, data, or information shall be subject to disclosure only upon the order of a court of competent jurisdiction;

(18) Records that contain site-specific information regarding the occurrence of rare species of plants or animals or the location of sensitive natural habitats on public or private property if the Department of Natural Resources determines that disclosure will create a substantial risk of harm, theft, or destruction to the species or habitats or the area or place where the species or habitats are located; provided, however, that the owner or owners of private property upon which rare species of plants or animals occur or upon which sensitive natural habitats are located shall be entitled to such information pursuant to this article;

(19) Records that reveal the names, home addresses, telephone numbers, security codes, e-mail addresses, or any other data or information developed, collected, or received by counties or municipalities in connection with neighborhood watch or public safety notification programs or with the installation, servicing, maintaining, operating, selling, or leasing of burglar alarm systems, fire alarm systems, or other electronic security systems; provided, however, that initial police reports and initial incident reports shall remain subject to disclosure pursuant to paragraph (4) of this subsection;

(20)(A) Records that reveal an individual's social security number, mother's birth name, credit card information, debit card information, bank account information, account number, utility account number, password used to access his or her account, financial data or information, insurance or medical information in all records, unlisted telephone number if so designated in a public record, personal e-mail address or cellular telephone number, day and month of birth, and information regarding public utility, television, Internet, or telephone accounts held by private customers, provided that non-itemized bills showing amounts owed and amounts paid shall be available. Items exempted by this subparagraph shall be redacted prior to disclosure of any record requested pursuant to this article; provided, however, that such information shall not be redacted from such records if the person or entity requesting such records requests such information in a writing signed under oath by such person or a person legally authorized to represent such entity which states that such person or entity is gathering information as a representative of a news media organization for use in connection with news gathering and reporting; and provided, further, that such access shall be limited to social security numbers and day and month of birth; and provided, further, that the news media organization exception in this subparagraph shall not apply to paragraph (21) of this subsection.

(B) This paragraph shall have no application to:

(i) The disclosure of information contained in the records or papers of any court or derived therefrom including without limitation records maintained pursuant to Article 9 of Title 11;

(ii) The disclosure of information to a court, prosecutor, or publicly employed law enforcement officer, or authorized agent thereof, seeking records in an official capacity;

(iii) The disclosure of information to a public employee of this state, its political subdivisions, or the United States who is obtaining such information for administrative purposes, in which case, subject to applicable laws of the United States, further access to such information shall continue to be subject to the provisions of this paragraph;

(iv) The disclosure of information as authorized by the order of a court of competent jurisdiction upon good cause shown to have access to any or all of such information upon such conditions as may be set forth in such order;

(v) The disclosure of information to the individual in respect of whom such information is maintained, with the authorization thereof, or to an authorized agent thereof; provided, however, that the agency maintaining such information shall require proper identification of such individual or such individual's agent, or proof of authorization, as determined by such agency;

(vi) The disclosure of the day and month of birth and mother's birth name of a deceased individual;

(vii) The disclosure by an agency of credit or payment information in connection with a request by a consumer reporting agency as that term is defined under the federal Fair Credit Reporting Act (15 U.S.C. Section 1681, et seq.);

(viii) The disclosure by an agency of information in its records in connection with the agency's discharging or fulfilling of its duties and responsibilities, including, but not limited to, the collection of debts owed to the agency or individuals or entities whom the agency assists in the collection of debts owed to the individual or entity;

(ix) The disclosure of information necessary to comply with legal or regulatory requirements or for legitimate law enforcement purposes; or

(x) The disclosure of the date of birth within criminal records.

(C) Records and information disseminated pursuant to this paragraph may be used only by the authorized recipient and only for the authorized purpose. Any person who obtains records or information pursuant to the provisions of this paragraph and knowingly and willfully discloses, distributes, or sells such records or information to an unauthorized recipient or for an unauthorized purpose shall be guilty of a misdemeanor of a high and aggravated nature and upon conviction thereof shall be punished as provided in Code Section 17-10- 4. Any person injured thereby shall have a cause of action for invasion of privacy.

(D) In the event that the custodian of public records protected by this paragraph has good faith reason to believe that a pending request for such records has been made fraudulently, under false pretenses, or by means of false swearing, such custodian shall apply to the superior court of the county in which such records are maintained for a protective order limiting or prohibiting access to such records.

(E) This paragraph shall supplement and shall not supplant, overrule, replace, or otherwise modify or supersede any provision of statute, regulation, or law of the federal government or of this state as now or hereafter amended or enacted requiring, restricting, or prohibiting access to the information identified in subparagraph (A) of this paragraph and shall constitute only a regulation of the methods of such access where not otherwise provided for, restricted, or prohibited;

(21) Records concerning public employees that reveal the public employee's home address, home telephone number, day and month of birth, social security number, insurance or medical information, mother's birth name, credit card information, debit card information, bank account information, account number, utility account number, password used to access his or her account, financial data or information other than compensation by a government agency, unlisted telephone number if so designated in a public record, and the identity of the public employee's immediate family members or dependents. This paragraph shall not apply to public records that do not specifically identify public employees or their jobs, titles, or offices. For the purposes of this paragraph, the term "public employee" means any officer, employee, or former employee of:

(A) The State of Georgia or its agencies, departments, or commissions;
(B) Any county or municipality or its agencies, departments, or commissions;
(C) Other political subdivisions of this state;
(D) Teachers in public and charter schools and nonpublic schools; or
(E) Early care and education programs administered through the Department of Early Care and Learning;

(22) Records of the Department of Early Care and Learning that contain the:

(A) Names of children and day and month of each child's birth;
(B) Names, addresses, telephone numbers, or e-mail addresses of parents, immediate family members, and emergency contact persons; or
(C) Names or other identifying information of individuals who report violations to the department;

(23) Public records containing information that would disclose or might lead to the disclosure of any component in the process used to execute or adopt an electronic signature, if such disclosure would or might cause the electronic signature to cease being under the sole control of the person using it. For purposes of this paragraph, the term "electronic signature" has the same meaning as that term is defined in Code Section 10-12-2;

(24) Records acquired by an agency for the purpose of establishing or implementing, or assisting in the establishment or implementation of, a carpooling or ridesharing program, including, but not limited to, the formation of carpools, vanpools, or buspools, the provision of transit routes, rideshare research, and the development of other demand management strategies such as variable working hours and telecommuting;

(25)(A) Records, the disclosure of which would compromise security against sabotage or criminal or terrorist acts and the nondisclosure of which is necessary for the protection of life, safety, or public property, which shall be limited to the following:

    (i) Security plans and vulnerability assessments for any public utility, technology infrastructure, building, facility, function, or activity in effect at the time of the request for disclosure or pertaining to a plan or assessment in effect at such time;
    (ii) Any plan for protection against terrorist or other attacks that depends for its effectiveness in whole or in part upon a lack of general public knowledge of its details;
    (iii) Any document relating to the existence, nature, location, or function of security devices designed to protect against terrorist or other attacks that depend for their effectiveness in whole or in part upon a lack of general public knowledge;
    (iv) Any plan, blueprint, or other material which if made public could compromise security against sabotage, criminal, or terroristic acts; and
    (v) Records of any government sponsored programs concerning training relative to governmental security measures which would identify persons being trained or instructors or would reveal information described in divisions (i) through (iv) of this subparagraph.

(B) In the event of litigation challenging nondisclosure pursuant to this paragraph by an agency of a document covered by this paragraph, the court may review the documents in question in camera and may condition, in writing, any disclosure upon such measures as the court may find to be necessary to protect against endangerment of life, safety, or public property.
(C) As used in division (i) of subparagraph (A) of this paragraph, the term "activity" means deployment or surveillance strategies, actions mandated by changes in the federal threat level, motorcades, contingency plans, proposed or alternative motorcade routes, executive and dignitary protection, planned responses to criminal or terrorist actions, after-action reports still in use, proposed or actual plans and responses to bioterrorism, and proposed or actual plans and responses to requesting and receiving the National Pharmacy Stockpile;
(26) Unless the request is made by the accused in a criminal case or by his or her attorney, public records of an emergency 9-1-1 system, as defined in paragraph (3) of Code Section 46-5-122, containing information which would reveal the name, address, or telephone number of a person placing a call to a public safety answering point. Such information may be redacted from such records if necessary to prevent the disclosure of the identity of a confidential source, to prevent disclosure of material which would endanger the life or physical safety of any person or persons, or to prevent the disclosure of the existence of a confidential surveillance or investigation;
(27) Records of athletic or recreational programs, available through the state or a political subdivision of the state, that include information identifying a child or children 12 years of age or under by name, address, telephone number, or emergency contact, unless such identifying information has been redacted;

(28) Records of the State Road and Tollway Authority which would reveal the financial accounts or travel history of any individual who is a motorist upon any toll project;

(29) Records maintained by public postsecondary educational institutions in this state and associated foundations of such institutions that contain personal information concerning donors or potential donors to such institutions or foundations; provided, however, that the name of any donor and the amount of donation made by such donor shall be subject to disclosure if such donor or any entity in which such donor has a substantial interest transacts business with the public postsecondary educational institution to which the donation is made within three years of the date of such donation. As used in this paragraph, the term "transact business" means to sell or lease any personal property, real property, or services on behalf of oneself or on behalf of any third party as an agent, broker, dealer, or representative in an amount in excess of $10,000.00 in the aggregate in a calendar year; and the term "substantial interest" means the direct or indirect ownership of more than 25 percent of the assets or stock of an entity;

(30) Records of the Metropolitan Atlanta Rapid Transit Authority or of any other transit system that is connected to that system's TransCard, SmartCard, or successor or similar system which would reveal the financial records or travel history of any individual who is a purchaser of a TransCard, SmartCard, or successor or similar fare medium. Such financial records shall include, but not be limited to, social security number, home address, home telephone number, e-mail address, credit or debit card information, and bank account information but shall not include the user's name;

(31) Building mapping information produced and maintained pursuant to Article 10 of Chapter 3 of Title 38;

(32) Notwithstanding the provisions of paragraph (4) of this subsection, any physical evidence or investigatory materials that are evidence of an alleged violation of Part 2 of Article 3 of Chapter 12 of Title 16 and are in the possession, custody, or control of law enforcement, prosecution, or regulatory agencies;

(33) Records that are expressly exempt from public inspection pursuant to Code Sections 47-1-14 and 47-7-127;

(34) Any trade secrets obtained from a person or business entity that are required by law, regulation, bid, or request for proposal to be submitted to an agency. An entity submitting records containing trade secrets that wishes to keep such records confidential under this paragraph shall submit and attach to the records an affidavit affirmatively declaring that specific information in the records constitute trade secrets pursuant to Article 27 of Chapter 1 of Title 10. If such entity attaches such an affidavit, before producing such records in response to a request under this article, the agency shall notify the entity of its intention to produce such records as set forth in this paragraph. If the agency makes a determination that the specifically identified information does not in fact constitute a trade secret, it shall notify the entity submitting the affidavit of its intent to disclose the information within ten days unless prohibited from doing so by an appropriate court order. In the event the entity wishes to prevent disclosure of the requested records, the entity may file an action in superior court to obtain an order that the requested records are trade secrets exempt from disclosure. The entity filing such action shall serve the requestor with a copy of its court filing. If the agency makes a determination that the specifically identified information does constitute a trade secret, the agency shall withhold the records, and the requester may file an action in superior

court to obtain an order that the requested records are not trade secrets and are subject to disclosure;

(35) Data, records, or information of a proprietary nature, produced or collected by or for faculty or staff of state institutions of higher learning, or other governmental agencies, in the conduct of, or as a result of, study or research on commercial, scientific, technical, or scholarly issues, whether sponsored by the institution alone or in conjunction with a governmental body or private concern, where such data, records, or information has not been publicly released, published, copyrighted, or patented;

(36) Any data, records, or information developed, collected, or received by or on behalf of faculty, staff, employees, or students of an institution of higher education or any public or private entity supporting or participating in the activities of an institution of higher education in the conduct of, or as a result of, study or research on medical, scientific, technical, scholarly, or artistic issues, whether sponsored by the institution alone or in conjunction with a governmental body or private entity, until such information is published, patented, otherwise publicly disseminated, or released to an agency whereupon the request must be made to the agency. This paragraph shall apply to, but shall not be limited to, information provided by participants in research, research notes and data, discoveries, research projects, methodologies, protocols, and creative works;

(37) Any record that would not be subject to disclosure, or the disclosure of which would jeopardize the receipt of federal funds, under 20 U.S.C. Section 1232g or its implementing regulations;

(38) Unless otherwise provided by law, records consisting of questions, scoring keys, and other materials constituting a test that derives value from being unknown to the test taker prior to administration which is to be administered by an agency, including, but not limited to, any public school, any unit of the Board of Regents of the University System of Georgia, any public technical school, the State Board of Education, the Office of Student Achievement, the Professional Standards Commission, or a local school system, if reasonable measures are taken by the owner of the test to protect security and confidentiality; provided, however, that the State Board of Education may establish procedures whereby a person may view, but not copy, such records if viewing will not, in the judgment of the board, affect the result of administration of such test. These limitations shall not be interpreted by any court of law to include or otherwise exempt from inspection the records of any athletic association or other nonprofit entity promoting intercollegiate athletics;

(39) Records disclosing the identity or personally identifiable information of any person participating in research on commercial, scientific, technical, medical, scholarly, or artistic issues conducted by the Department of Community Health, the Department of Public Health, the Department of Behavioral Health and Developmental Disabilities, or a state institution of higher education whether sponsored by the institution alone or in conjunction with a governmental body or private entity;

(40) Any permanent records maintained by a judge of the probate court pursuant to Code Section 16-11-129, relating to weapons carry licenses, or pursuant to any other requirement for maintaining records relative to the possession of firearms, except to the extent that such records relating to licensing and possession of firearms are sought by law enforcement agencies as provided by law;

(41) Records containing communications subject to the attorney-client privilege recognized by state law; provided, however, that this paragraph shall not apply to the factual findings, but shall apply to the legal conclusions, of an attorney conducting an investigation on behalf of an agency so long as such investigation does not pertain to pending or potential litigation, settlement, claims, administrative proceedings, or other judicial actions brought or to be brought by or against the agency or any officer or employee; and provided, further, that such investigations conducted by hospital authorities to ensure compliance with federal or state law, regulations, or reimbursement policies shall be exempt from disclosure if such investigations are otherwise subject to the attorney-client privilege. Attorney-client communications, however, may be obtained in a proceeding under Code Section 50-18-73 to prove justification or lack thereof in refusing disclosure of documents under this Code section provided the judge of the court in which such proceeding is pending shall first determine by an in camera examination that such disclosure would be relevant on that issue. In addition, when an agency withholds information subject to this paragraph, any party authorized to bring a proceeding under Code Section 50-18-73 may request that the judge of the court in which such proceeding is pending determine by an in camera examination whether such information was properly withheld;

(42) Confidential attorney work product; provided, however, that this paragraph shall not apply to the factual findings, but shall apply to the legal conclusions, of an attorney conducting an investigation on behalf of an agency so long as such investigation does not pertain to pending or potential litigation, settlement, claims, administrative proceedings, or other judicial actions brought or to be brought by or against the agency or any officer or employee; and provided, further, that such investigations conducted by hospital authorities to ensure compliance with federal or state law, regulations, or reimbursement policies shall be exempt from disclosure if such investigations are otherwise subject to confidentiality as attorney work product. In addition, when an agency withholds information subject to this paragraph, any party authorized to bring a proceeding under Code Section 50-18-73 may request that the judge of the court in which such proceeding is pending determine by an in camera examination whether such information was properly withheld;

(43) Records containing tax matters or tax information that is confidential under state or federal law;

(44) Records consisting of any computer program or computer software used or maintained in the course of operation of a public office or agency; provided, however, that data generated, kept, or received by an agency shall be subject to inspection and copying as provided in this article;

(45) Records pertaining to the rating plans, rating systems, underwriting rules, surveys, inspections, statistical plans, or similar proprietary information used to provide or administer liability insurance or self-insurance coverage to any agency;

(46) Documents maintained by the Department of Economic Development pertaining to an economic development project until the economic development project is secured by binding commitment, provided that any such documents shall be disclosed upon proper request after a binding commitment has been secured or the project has been terminated. No later than five business days after the Department of Economic Development secures a binding commitment and the department has committed the use of state funds from the

OneGeorgia Authority or funds from Regional Economic Business Assistance for the project pursuant to Code Section 50-8-8, or other provisions of law, the Department of Economic Development shall give notice that a binding commitment has been reached by posting on its website notice of the project in conjunction with a copy of the Department of Economic Development's records documenting the bidding commitment made in connection with the project and the negotiation relating thereto and by publishing notice of the project and participating parties in the legal organ of each county in which the economic development project is to be located. As used in this paragraph, the term "economic development project" means a plan or proposal to locate a business, or to expand a business, that would involve an expenditure of more than $25 million by the business or the hiring of more than 50 employees by the business;

(47) Records related to a training program operated under the authority of Article 3 of Chapter 4 of Title 20 disclosing an economic development project prior to a binding commitment having been secured, relating to job applicants, or identifying proprietary hiring practices, training, skills, or other business methods and practices of a private entity. As used in this paragraph, the term "economic development project" means a plan or proposal to locate a business, or to expand a business, that would involve an expenditure of more than $25 million by the business or the hiring of more than 50 employees by the business; or

(48) Records that are expressly exempt from public inspection pursuant to Code Section 47-20-87.

(b) This Code section shall be interpreted narrowly so as to exclude from disclosure only that portion of a public record to which an exclusion is directly applicable. It shall be the duty of the agency having custody of a record to provide all other portions of a record for public inspection or copying.

(c)(1) Notwithstanding any other provision of this article, an exhibit tendered to the court as evidence in a criminal or civil trial shall not be open to public inspection without approval of the judge assigned to the case.

(2) Except as provided in subsection (d) of this Code section, in the event inspection is not approved by the court, in lieu of inspection of such an exhibit, the custodian of such an exhibit shall, upon request, provide one or more of the following:

    (A) A photograph;
    (B) A photocopy;
    (C) A facsimile; or
    (D) Another reproduction.

(3) The provisions of this article regarding fees for production of a record, including, but not limited to, subsections (c) and (d) of Code Section 50- 18-71, shall apply to exhibits produced according to this subsection.

(d) Any physical evidence that is used as an exhibit in a criminal or civil trial to show or support an alleged violation of Part 2 of Article 3 of Chapter 12 of Title 16 shall not be open to public inspection except by court order. If the judge approves inspection of such physical evidence, the judge shall designate, in writing, the facility owned or operated by an agency of the state or local government where such physical evidence may be inspected. If the judge permits inspection, such property or material shall not be photographed, copied, or reproduced by any means. Any person who violates the provisions of this subsection shall be guilty of a felony and, upon conviction thereof, shall be punished by imprisonment for not less than one nor more than 20 years, a fine of not more than $100,000.00, or both.

§ 50-18-73: Enforcement of the Provisions

(a) The superior courts of this state shall have jurisdiction in law and in equity to entertain actions against persons or agencies having custody of records open to the public under this article to enforce compliance with the provisions of this article. Such actions may be brought by any person, firm, corporation, or other entity. In addition, the Attorney General shall have authority to bring such actions in his or her discretion as may be appropriate to enforce compliance with this article and to seek either civil or criminal penalties or both.

(b) In any action brought to enforce the provisions of this chapter in which the court determines that either party acted without substantial justification either in not complying with this chapter or in instituting the litigation, the court shall, unless it finds that special circumstances exist, assess in favor of the complaining party reasonable attorney's fees and other litigation costs reasonably incurred. Whether the position of the complaining party was substantially justified shall be determined on the basis of the record as a whole which is made in the proceeding for which fees and other expenses are sought.

(c) Any agency or person who provides access to information in good faith reliance on the requirements of this chapter shall not be liable in any action on account of such decision.

§ 50-18-74: Penalties for Violating the Provisions

(a) Any person or entity knowingly and willfully violating the provisions of this article by failing or refusing to provide access to records not subject to exemption from this article, by knowingly and willingly failing or refusing to provide access to such records within the time limits set forth in this article, or by knowingly and willingly frustrating or attempting to frustrate the access to records by intentionally making records difficult to obtain or review shall be guilty of a misdemeanor and upon conviction shall be punished by a fine not to exceed $1,000.00 for the first violation. Alternatively, a civil penalty may be imposed by the court in any civil action brought pursuant to this article against any person who negligently violates the terms of this article in an amount not to exceed $1,000.00 for the first violation. A civil penalty or criminal fine not to exceed $2,500.00 per violation may be imposed for each additional violation that the violator commits within a 12 month period from the date the first penalty or fine was imposed. It shall be a defense to any criminal action under this Code section that a person has acted in good faith in his or her actions. In addition, persons or entities that destroy records for the purpose of preventing their disclosure under this article may be subject to prosecution under Code Section 45-11-1.

(b) A prosecution under this Code section may only be commenced by issuance of a citation in the same manner as an arrest warrant for a peace officer pursuant to Code Section 17-4-40; such citation shall be personally served upon the accused. The defendant shall not be arrested prior to the time of trial, except that a defendant who fails to appear for arraignment or trial may thereafter be arrested pursuant to a bench warrant and required to post a bond for his or her future appearance.

Georgia Regulations

505-6-.01: Code of Ethics for Educators

(1) ***Introduction***: The Code of Ethics for Educators defines the professional behavior of educators in Georgia and serves as a guide to ethical conduct. The Professional Standards Commission has adopted standards that represent the conduct generally accepted by the education profession. The code defines unethical conduct justifying disciplinary sanction and provides guidance for protecting the health, safety and general welfare of students and educators, and assuring the citizens of Georgia a degree of accountability within the education profession.

(2) ***Definitions***:

(a) "Certificate" refers to any teaching, service, or leadership certificate, license, or permit issued by authority of the Professional Standards Commission.

(b) "Educator" is a teacher, school or school system administrator, or other education personnel who holds a certificate issued by the Professional Standards Commission and persons who have applied for but have not yet received a certificate. For the purposes of the Code of Ethics for Educators, "educator" also refers to paraprofessionals, aides, and substitute teachers.

(c) "Student" is any individual enrolled in the state's public or private schools from preschool through grade 12 or any individual under the age of 18. For the purposes of the Code of Ethics and Standards of Professional Conduct for Educators, the enrollment period for a graduating student ends on August 31 of the year of graduation.

(d) "Complaint" is any written and signed statement from a local board, the state board, or one or more individual residents of this state filed with the Professional Standards Commission alleging that an educator has breached one or more of the standards in the Code of Ethics for Educators. A "complaint" will be deemed a request to investigate.

(e) "Revocation" is the invalidation of any certificate held by the educator.

(f) "Denial" is the refusal to grant initial certification to an applicant for a certificate.

(g) "Suspension" is the temporary invalidation of any certificate for a period of time specified by the Professional Standards Commission.

(h) "Reprimand" admonishes the certificate holder for his or her conduct. The reprimand cautions that further unethical conduct will lead to a more severe action.

(i) "Warning" warns the certificate holder that his or her conduct is unethical. The warning cautions that further unethical conduct will lead to a more severe action.

(j) "Monitoring" is the quarterly appraisal of the educator's conduct by the Professional Standards Commission through contact with the educator and his or her employer. As a condition of monitoring, an educator may be required to submit a criminal background check (GCIC). The Commission specifies the length of the monitoring period.

(k) "No Probable Cause" is a determination by the Professional Standards Commission that, after a preliminary investigation, either no further action need be taken or no cause exists to recommend disciplinary action.

(3) ***Standards***:

(a) *Standard 1: Legal Compliance*: An educator shall abide by federal, state, and local laws and statutes. Unethical conduct includes but is not limited to the commission or conviction of a felony or of any crime involving moral turpitude; of any other criminal offense involving the manufacture, distribution, trafficking, sale, or possession of a controlled substance or marijuana as provided for in Chapter 13 of Title 16; or of any other sexual offense as provided for in Code Section 16-6-1 through 16-6-17, 16-6-20, 16-6-22.2, or 16-12-100; or any other laws applicable to the profession. As used herein, conviction includes a finding or verdict of guilty, or a plea of nolo contendere, regardless of whether an appeal of the conviction has been sought; a situation where first offender treatment without adjudication of guilt pursuant to the charge was granted; and a situation where an adjudication of guilt or sentence was otherwise withheld or not entered on the charge or the charge was otherwise disposed of in a similar manner in any jurisdiction.

(b) *Standard 2: Conduct with Students*: An educator shall always maintain a professional relationship with all students, both in and outside the classroom. Unethical conduct includes but is not limited to:

>(1) Committing any act of child abuse, including physical and verbal abuse;
>(2) Committing any act of cruelty to children or any act of child endangerment;
>(3) Committing any sexual act with a student or soliciting such from a student;
>(4) Engaging in or permitting harassment of or misconduct toward a student that would violate a state or federal law;
>(5) Soliciting, encouraging, or consummating an inappropriate written, verbal, electronic, or physical relationship with a student;
>(6) Furnishing tobacco, alcohol, or illegal/unauthorized drugs to any student; or
>(7) Failing to prevent the use of alcohol or illegal or unauthorized drugs by students who are under the educator's supervision (including but not limited to at the educator's residence or any other private setting).

(c) *Standard 3: Alcohol or Drugs*: An educator shall refrain from the use of alcohol or illegal or unauthorized drugs during the course of professional practice. Unethical conduct includes but is not limited to:

>(1) Being on school premises or at a school-related activity while under the influence of, possessing, using, or consuming illegal or unauthorized drugs; and
>(2) Being on school premises or at a school-related activity involving students while under the influence of, possessing, or consuming alcohol. A school-related activity includes, but is not limited to, any activity sponsored by the school or school system (booster clubs, parent-teacher organizations, or any activity designed to enhance the school curriculum *i.e.* Foreign Language trips, etc.).

(d) *Standard 4: Honesty*: An educator shall exemplify honesty and integrity in the course of professional practice. Unethical conduct includes but is not limited to, falsifying, misrepresenting or omitting:

(1) Professional qualifications, criminal history, college or staff development credit and/or degrees, academic award, and employment history;
(2) Information submitted to federal, state, local school districts and other governmental agencies;
(3) Information regarding the evaluation of students and/or personnel;
(4) Reasons for absences or leaves;
(5) Information submitted in the course of an official inquiry/investigation; and
(6) Information submitted in the course of professional practice.

(e) *Standard 5: Public Funds and Property*: An educator entrusted with public funds and property shall honor that trust with a high level of honesty, accuracy, and responsibility. Unethical conduct includes but is not limited to:

(1) Misusing public or school-related funds;
(2) Failing to account for funds collected from students or parents;
(3) Submitting fraudulent requests or documentation for reimbursement of expenses or for pay (including fraudulent or purchased degrees, documents, or coursework);
(4) Co-mingling public or school-related funds with personal funds or checking accounts; and
(5) Using school property without the approval of the local board of education/governing board or authorized designee.

(f) *Standard 6: Remunerative Conduct*: An educator shall maintain integrity with students, colleagues, parents, patrons, or businesses when accepting gifts, gratuities, favors, and additional compensation. Unethical conduct includes but is not limited to:

(1) Soliciting students or parents of students to purchase equipment, supplies, or services from the educator or to participate in activities that financially benefit the educator unless approved by the local board of education/governing board or authorized designee;
(2) Accepting gifts from vendors or potential vendors for personal use or gain where there may be the appearance of a conflict of interest;
(3) Tutoring students assigned to the educator for remuneration unless approved by the local board of education/governing board or authorized designee; and
(4) Coaching, instructing, promoting athletic camps, summer leagues, etc. that involves students in an educator's school system and from whom the educator receives remuneration unless approved by the local board of education/governing board or authorized designee. These types of activities must be in compliance with all rules and regulations of the Georgia High School Association.

(g) *Standard 7: Confidential Information*: An educator shall comply with state and federal laws and state school board policies relating to the confidentiality of student and personnel records, standardized test material and other information. Unethical conduct includes but is not limited to:

(1) Sharing of confidential information concerning student academic and disciplinary records, health and medical information, family status and/or income, and assessment/testing results unless disclosure is required or permitted by law;
(2) Sharing of confidential information restricted by state or federal law;
(3) Violation of confidentiality agreements related to standardized testing including copying or teaching identified test items, publishing or distributing test items or answers, discussing test items, violating local school system or state directions for the use of tests or test items, etc.; and
(4) Violation of other confidentiality agreements required by state or local policy.

(h) *Standard 8: Abandonment of Contract*: An educator shall fulfill all of the terms and obligations detailed in the contract with the local board of education or education agency for the duration of the contract. Unethical conduct includes but is not limited to:

(1) Abandoning the contract for professional services without prior release from the contract by the employer, and
(2) Willfully refusing to perform the services required by a contract.

(i) *Standard 9: Required Reports*: An educator shall file reports of a breach of one or more of the standards in the Code of Ethics for Educators, child abuse (O.C.G.A. §19-7-5), or any other required report. Unethical conduct includes but is not limited to:

(1) Failure to report all requested information on documents required by the Commission when applying for or renewing any certificate with the Commission;
(2) Failure to make a required report of a violation of one or more standards of the Code of Ethics for educators of which they have personal knowledge as soon as possible but no later than ninety (90) days from the date the educator became aware of an alleged breach unless the law or local procedures require reporting sooner; and
(3) Failure to make a required report of any violation of state or federal law soon as possible but no later than ninety (90) days from the date the educator became aware of an alleged breach unless the law or local procedures require reporting sooner. These reports include but are not limited to: murder, voluntary manslaughter, aggravated assault, aggravated battery, kidnapping, any sexual offense, any sexual exploitation of a minor, any offense involving a controlled substance and any abuse of a child if an educator has reasonable cause to believe that a child has been abused.

(j) *Standard 10: Professional Conduct*: An educator shall demonstrate conduct that follows generally recognized professional standards and preserves the dignity and integrity of the teaching profession. Unethical conduct includes but is not limited to any conduct that impairs and/or diminishes the certificate holder's ability to function professionally in his or her employment position, or behavior or conduct that is detrimental to the health, welfare, discipline, or morals of students.

(k) *Standard 11: Testing*: An educator shall administer state-mandated assessments fairly and ethically. Unethical conduct includes but is not limited to:

    (1) Committing any act that breaches Test Security; and
    (2) Compromising the integrity of the assessment.

(4) ***Reporting***:
(a) Educators are required to report a breach of one or more of the Standards in the Code of Ethics for Educators as soon as possible but no later than ninety (90) days from the date the educator became aware of an alleged breach unless the law or local procedures require reporting sooner. Educators should be aware of legal requirements and local policies and procedures for reporting unethical conduct. Complaints filed with the Professional Standards Commission must be in writing and must be signed by the complainant (parent, educator, personnel director, superintendent, etc.).
(b) The Commission notifies local and state officials of all disciplinary actions. In addition, suspensions and revocations are reported to national officials, including the NASDTEC Clearinghouse.

(5) ***Disciplinary Action***:

(a) The Professional Standards Commission is authorized to suspend, revoke, or deny certificates, to issue a reprimand or warning, or to monitor the educator's conduct and performance after an investigation is held and notice and opportunity for a hearing are provided to the certificate holder. Any of the following grounds shall be considered cause for disciplinary action against the holder of a certificate:

    (1) Unethical conduct as outlined in The Code of Ethics for Educators, Standards 1-10 (PSC Rule 505-6-.01);
    (2) Disciplinary action against a certificate in another state on grounds consistent with those specified in the Code of Ethics for Educators, Standards 1-10 (PSC Rule 505-6-.01);
    (3) Order from a court of competent jurisdiction or a request from the Department of Human Resources that the certificate should be suspended or the application for certification should be denied for non-payment of child support (O.C.G.A. §19-6-28.1 and §19-11-9.3);
    (4) Notification from the Georgia Higher Education Assistance Corporation that the educator is in default and not in satisfactory repayment status on a student loan guaranteed by the Georgia Higher Education Assistance Corporation (O.C.G.A. §20-3-295);
    (5) Suspension or revocation of any professional license or certificate;
    (6) Violation of any other laws and rules applicable to the profession; and
    (7) Any other good and sufficient cause that renders an educator unfit for employment as an educator.

(b) An individual whose certificate has been revoked, denied, or suspended may not serve as a volunteer or be employed as an educator, paraprofessional, aide, substitute teacher or in any other position during the period of his or her revocation, suspension or denial for a violation of The Code of Ethics. The superintendent and the superintendent's designee for certification shall be responsible for assuring that an individual whose certificate has been revoked, denied, or suspended is not employed or serving in any capacity in their district. Both the superintendent and the superintendent's designee must hold Georgia PSC certification.

Georgia PSC: Moral Turpitude Definition

It has been stated that the term "moral turpitude" is so clear that there is no duty on the trial judge to define it in the absence of a request. The term has been defined in Georgia as follows:

> Turpitude in its ordinary sense involves the idea of inherent baseness or vileness, shameful wickedness, depravity . . . In its legal sense it includes everything contrary to justice, honesty, modesty or good morals . . . The word "moral," which so often precedes the word turpitude, does not seem to add anything to the meaning of the term, other than that emphasis which often results from a tautological expression. All crimes embraced within the Roman's conception of the *crimen falsi* involve turpitude; but it is not safe to declare that such crimes are the only ones involving turpitude." In *Ramsey v. State*, the court said that a crime involving moral turpitude is one which is *malum in se* rather than *malum prohibitum*. In Georgia, the test for whether a felony is one involving moral turpitude is "does the [crime], disregarding its felony punishment, meet the test as being contrary to justice, honesty, modesty, good morals or man's duty to man?

It has been held that the following offenses are crimes involving moral turpitude:

* Fraud or false pretenses in obtaining something of value
* Larceny or a misdemeanor theft by taking
* Larceny after trust
* Murder
* Soliciting for prostitutes
* Voluntary manslaughter
* Sale of narcotics or other illegal drugs
* Pattern of failure to file federal tax returns in years in which taxes are due
* Criminal Issuance of a bad check
* Making a false report of a crime

The following have been held to be offenses which are not crimes involving moral turpitude:

* Public drunkenness
* Driving under the influence
* Carrying a concealed weapon
* Unlawful sale of liquor

* Fighting
* Simple Battery
* Simple Assault
* Misdemeanor criminal trespass
* Child abandonment
* Misdemeanor offense of escape
* Misdemeanor offense of obstructing a law enforcement officer
* The federal misdemeanor offense of Conspiracy in Restraint of Interstate Trade and Commerce
* Possession of less than one ounce of marijuana

[From *Handbook of Criminal Evidence* by Davis, 2000 edition.]

Georgia PSC Disciplinary Actions:

Warning: A Warning admonishes the educator for his or her behavior but does not invalidate the educator's certificate. The warning cautions the educator that future unethical behavior could lead to a more severe action.

Reprimand: A Reprimand admonishes the educator for his or her behavior but does not invalidate the educator's certificate. The reprimand cautions the educator that future unethical behavior could lead to a more severe action.

Suspension: Suspension is the temporary invalidation of any certificate, license, or permit held by the educator for a period specified by the Commission. An individual whose certificate has been suspended may not serve as a volunteer or be employed as an educator, paraprofessional, aide, or substitute teacher or in any other position during the period of his or her suspension. The educator's certificate is automatically reinstated at the end of the suspension, provided it did not expire during the suspension period. If the certificate expires during the suspension period, the educator must meet the current renewal requirements at the end of the suspension.

Denial: Denial is the refusal to grant a certificate to an applicant for disciplinary reasons. An individual who has been denied a certificate may not serve as a volunteer or be employed as an educator, paraprofessional, aide, or substitute teacher or in any other position during the period of his or her denial. An applicant whose certificate has been denied may petition for the right to reapply for certification no sooner than two years from the date of denial. A written petition must be submitted to the Commission with evidence that the reasons for the initial denial are no longer a factor in the performance of the educator. Should the Commission deny the right to reapply, the educator may repetition for the right to reapply no sooner than one year from the date of denial.

Revocation: Revocation is the invalidation of any certificate, license, or permit held by the educator. An individual whose certificate has been revoked may not serve as a volunteer or be employed as an educator, paraprofessional, aide, or substitute teacher or in any other position during the period of his or her revocation. An educator whose certificate has been revoked may petition the Commission for the right to reapply for certification no sooner than three years from the date of revocation. A written petition must be submitted to the Commission with evidence that the reasons for the initial revocation are no longer a factor in the performance of the educator. Should the Commission deny the right to reapply, the educator may repetition for the right to reapply no sooner than one year from the date of denial.

Chapter 10: Tort Law and other Liability Issues

Tort law is civil law recognizing duties to refrain from wrongful or negligent acts, and an injured party's legal right to just compensation for damages. The law of torts and contracts are similar, but the tort law "contract" is an implied social contract to act reasonably in interactions with others. If you have a legal duty to others, then there is also the implied social contractual obligation of acting reasonably in fulfilling that duty. Potential tort law causes of action include torts resulting from negligence; malpractice; defamation; assault and battery; false imprisonment; invasion of privacy; and intentional infliction of emotional distress. Liability may also be incurred through assessments of civil or criminal fines, statutory damages, property losses, etc.

This chapter focuses on school safety and security as the areas of potential damages that are both the most important to address to protect people and property, and among the most preventable areas of serious liability. Failures in these areas can result in devastating losses. Nonetheless, warnings of potential dangers are too often ignored, and commonsense precautions too often neglected. This chapter is intended to call attention to potential dangers before tragedy strikes. Negligence in these areas may not only lead to significant tort liability, but far more importantly, result in unnecessary damages, injuries, and loss of life.

School Safety and Security

The core lesson of tort law is that you must do what a reasonable person would do under the circumstances. By recognizing potential safety and security dangers in advance, and taking reasonable, commonsense precautions, you can promote safety, avoid foreseeable risks, and prevent unnecessary losses. Addressing potential problems before they become emergencies or disasters is the key to good school safety and security management and liability prevention.

> **Recognize Potential Dangers and Take Reasonable Precautions to Mitigate Risks**

Concerning school safety and security, an ounce of prevention is worth many pounds of cure. If it is not already in operation, school officials should consider establishing a School Safety and Security Task Force made up of, for example: School administrators, teachers (including teachers with expertise in higher risk areas, e.g., athletics; labs; vocational education; etc.), law enforcement and safety personnel, a school nurse or other medical personnel, transportation personnel, buildings and grounds personnel, student and community representatives as appropriate, and the school attorney. The general charge of the Task Force is to anticipate and proactively address emerging dangers and oversee ongoing safety and security efforts. Although prevention efforts do require the investment of time and resources, prevention is far superior to unnecessary damages, injuries, deaths, and liability.

It is hoped that the overviews and examples in this section will encourage readers to think further about safety and security concerns in their schools; review applicable state laws and local policies; and discuss with colleagues, safety personnel, students, and community members how everyone can work together to improve safety and security in their schools.

The school safety and security measures suggested below are illustrative only, and it is essential that you consider not only these general examples, but also any unique concerns in your area and circumstances. Be certain you comply with applicable laws and policies, and seek professional advice when needed. These materials should, however, be helpful in getting you started towards a safer and more secure school for everyone.

Further information on school safety and security can be obtained through your state and federal department of education websites and through other public and private sector resources. A search of these and other related websites should produce many useful resources. The issues addressed below include personnel safety and security; child supervision; choking hazards; harassment, assaults, and abductions; safety intervention and self-defense; safe facilities; safe grounds, parking areas and transportation; safe play areas; accident and injury prevention; gang violence prevention; environmental safety; and emergency planning and response.

Personnel Safety and Security

Because resources are always limited, school officials must be good stewards of school resources and take care not to expose the school to unnecessary liability. Regardless of costs or concerns about liability, however, the safety of personnel, and especially children, must always remain the top priority for school officials. All safety and security efforts must be planned in accordance with safety as the non-negotiable priority. With wise planning, however, safety and security efforts can prevent harm and liability, protecting both people and limited resources.

Adequate Child Supervision

School officials have a duty to reasonably protect the health and safety of children left in their care. Adequate child supervision is a legal duty and a community expectation. It is *per se* negligence to leave children unsupervised. A responsible adult must be in charge at all times, supervising children from the moment school officials take physical custody until physical custody is transferred back to the parent.

If children are not adequately supervised and an assault or injury occurs because of inadequate supervision, school officials may be held liable for negligent supervision and dismissed for neglect of duties. Adequate supervision includes protecting children from foreseeable dangers and reasonably rendering aid when necessary. Although there is a far greater duty to supervise and protect children in their care, school officials have a general duty to guard all persons on school property from foreseeable dangers. Among these foreseeable dangers are:

Choking hazards: Choking hazards are serious but often overlooked dangers until tragedy strikes. School administrators, classroom teachers, students, parents, school nurses, and cafeteria personnel must work together to reduce risks associated with choking in schools. Younger children are at higher risk of choking, but choking is a serious danger for all persons. Younger children may choke on a toy or other small object. But food is the most common cause of choking for everyone. Allergic reactions resulting in anaphylactic shock can also cause choking when the airway becomes blocked from severe allergy-related inflammation. A blocked airway caused by any means is a critical emergency with only minutes to respond before permanent injury or death occurs.

Take action:

• Avoid serving younger children round, firm, or sticky foods such as grapes, hotdogs, meat or cheese chunks, gumballs, caramels, etc., or serve these foods cut in safer-sized pieces appropriately portioned for younger children to safely eat.
• Prohibit running and other strenuous physical activities while eating as exerted breathing while eating greatly increases the risks of choking for all persons.
• Do not allow any risky antics, pranks, or games that increase the risk of choking.
• Require parents and students to notify school officials of student allergies.
• Instruct students in how to take age-appropriate actions to protect themselves from choking hazards and allergens, and what to do in an emergency.
• School personnel should be trained in administering first-aid to a choking victim, including when appropriate, techniques for very small children and children with special needs.
• All school personnel should be trained in recognizing the symptoms of a serious allergic reaction, and in administering first-aid and the school's emergency plan for anaphylactic shock victims.
• Consistent with applicable laws, epinephrine should be stored in strategic locations and readily available for emergency use when needed.

Harassment, Assaults, and Abductions

Despite media hyping of incidents of school violence, schools remain relatively safe places for children. In fact few places provide greater physical safety for children than the classroom. It is always possible, for example, that an armed intruder could invade and attack a school. But this is certainly not the most common risk facing most children in schools. The sections below address awareness and prevention measures for harassment, assaults, and abductions as these are preventable risks to the health and well-being of children.

Harassment

The most common risk to the health and well-being of most children in schools likely comes from the daily psychological violence of bullying and harassment from peers and sometimes teachers who may allow or even participate in the abuse. Bullying and harassment can cause severe suffering for its victims leading to psychological and emotional damage; stress related physical illnesses; impaired school performance; increased absenteeism; increased risk of suicide; and revenge motivated violence.

Perpetrators of bullying and harassment can be either students or teachers, and victims may be either students or teachers. If not addressed, bullying and harassment can cause serious harm to its victims or trigger retaliation through spontaneous physical violence. More rarely and alarmingly, relentless bullying and harassment may provoke planned attacks on schools involving weapons and the potential for significant casualties.

Many acts of violence could be prevented by addressing interpersonal conflicts and improving the social culture of the school, supplanting destructive bullying and harassment with mutual respect and a collective focus on achievement. It is also important to note that the same types of school climate and culture changes that make schools safer places for everyone are also likely to improve teaching, learning, and student achievement: Safe schools are also good schools. As incidents of harassment and violence decline, the well-being and achievement of students will increase.

> **Safe Schools are also Good Schools: When Children Feel Safe, Secure, and Respected they can focus their Full Attention on Learning**

Assaults

Guard against threats of assaults from external persons by securing the building and establishing safe routes to school for students who walk to school. Safe routes should be planned considering both avoiding potential dangers and getting the children to school efficiently. The first priority must be planning a route that avoids any serious known dangers. But if the designated route is too indirect, some children will likely travel the more direct route anyway because it is easier and faster. They will be both isolated and at risk. Also, the longer children are on the street, the longer they are exposed to general dangers. The planned route must be safe, but it must also be realistic and efficient.

As needed, law enforcement agents, school officials, and community volunteers can be posted along the safe route to assure that children are supervised and safe. It may also be useful to designate safe houses along the route with trusted persons children know they can go to for help and safety in an emergency. Also explain to students that there is safety in numbers, that whenever possible they should travel together with other children, and that everyone must make sure no one gets left behind in a dangerous situation.

Guard against threats of assaults by internal persons by removing known dangerous individuals from the school. Criminal acts should be dealt with as crimes and perpetrators removed from the school or incarcerated. If the dangerous behavior is a manifestation of a disability, a student that is not able to confirm his or her conduct and who presents a serious danger to others must be placed in a more restrictive environment until the student can safely return to a less restrictive setting.

Provide adequate supervision of all personnel and students at all times. Encourage everyone to stay together in dangerous areas and situations. Instruct them in what to do in the event of a safety emergency. And as necessary, instruct personnel and students in how to protect themselves from assaults.

Abductions

To guard against risks of abductions, children should only be released to the custody of parent authorized and school approved and confirmed safe, sober, adult pick-up persons. When there is any doubt, always confirm the identity and valid authorization of the adult seeking to take the child from the school before releasing the child. The time necessary for a little extra caution by school staff and a brief delay for pick-up persons is a small price to pay to protect children from potential abductions (*see also* under Safe Grounds, *infra*).

Take action:

- Secure the exterior and interior areas of the building with a thorough security audit and necessary remediation including establishing a general plan adequate for the level of security necessary in the area; securing all routes of entry (*e.g.*, doors; windows; rooftop entryways; etc.); adequate lighting; removal of brush and other physical and visual obstructions; a security system; video surveillance; posting school resource officers and other school personnel in strategic locations, etc.
- Identify "safe routes" and "safe houses/persons" along the safe routes for students walking to school in high risk areas.
- Consistent with state law establish a system requiring all visitors to report to a central location for security clearance prior to entering the school. School personnel should be instructed to politely question any unknown persons they find in the school or any persons outside of designated event areas.
- Any suspicious person should be reported to school administrators or law enforcement officers to either confirm that the person has a legitimate cause to be present and poses no danger, or to remove the person from school property or into police custody.
- To deter child abductions, do not rely only on the child identifying the adult (e.g., "that's my Daddy"), as unauthorized non-custodial parents are among the most likely persons to abduct a child.
- Even if an unknown person is wearing a uniform or showing official credentials, confirm the person's identity and valid legal authority with a call to an official phone number of the authorizing institution (e.g.., the Police Department; Child Protective Services; etc.). For a planned child abduction uniforms and false credentials can be purchased or fabricated, and an accomplice's phone number can be given for a fraudulent confirmation.
- Take extra precautions on field trips beyond the secured boundaries of the school. Students must be adequately supervised at all times and strictly prohibited from talking with strangers or leaving the group. Adequate numbers of teachers and parent/chaperones must be present to safely supervise children. Parent/chaperones must be trusted persons who have been cleared through a criminal background check consistent with state law and school policy.
- Encourage everyone to take responsibility for school safety and security. Promote a culture of responsibility in which it is not acceptable to ignore abuse and violence, and everyone understands it is their duty to report abuse and call for help when violence occurs. This will only work, however, if the reporters of abuse and violence see that school officials will take prompt, consistent, and effective action when needed and that the reporters are protected from retaliation.

Many safety programs are now available for schools, and some are better than others. The programs with the greatest likelihood of success are those that help school officials to clearly identify the core causes of violence and address those causes in a systematic, comprehensive way. A single video or lecture is unlikely to have any long-term impact. Unless a program can help to improve the culture and climate of the school and community, making violence socially unacceptable, it is unlikely to succeed in reducing violence longer-term. For all programs, and especially for-profit programs, *caveat emptor* (let the buyer beware). There are increasingly many good free or low-cost programs available for reducing violence. Programs, however, are like diets: They don't work unless they change long-term behaviors, replacing harmful daily behaviors with healthier daily behaviors for long-term progress.

In general adopt a practical, persistent, preventive approach to addressing abuse and violence. If a few students are disproportionately responsible for conflict and violence in the school, for example, lawfully remove these students to more restrictive and appropriate educational settings. Do this first to protect safety and order in the school. But also so that these students can focus on learning better social and academic skills, the skills they need for a better future. Determine what factors (e.g., social; economic, cultural; environmental; etc.) are stimulating violence and abuse and work to move everyone toward healthier behaviors. Provide everyone with education in respecting diversity and healthy conflict resolution skills to build a culture of mutual respect and non-violence in the school. When necessary, however, provide instruction in safety intervention and self-defense to minimize risks of injury to all persons.

Safety Intervention and Self-Defense

The goal of safety intervention and self-defense is to keep others and yourself safe, not to "win" battles that could have reasonably been avoided. As the ancient philosopher and strategist Sun Tzu said, the greatest victory comes from the battle that was never fought. You want to achieve your goal of keeping everyone in the school safe without violence and the resulting risks to safety. The first rule of safety intervention and self-defense, therefore, is to always avoid unnecessary conflicts.

> *Anticipate and Plan Ahead to Avoid Unnecessary*
> *Conflicts and to Protect Safety if a Conflict Occurs*

High risk areas, people, and situations should be avoided whenever possible. Remember also that an area that may be safe during the day or during school hours may not be safe at night or when other people are not present. When high risk areas, people, and situations cannot be avoided, try to choose the most favorable time and circumstances possible to deal with potential threats, and be as prepared as possible to safely deal with foreseeable dangers. When faced with a potential threat of violence:

> 1) *Leave the area*: Trust your instincts. If a situation doesn't seem right, just leave. If needed, try to lead others who may be in danger out of the area with you. No explanation to potential attackers is required. Don't provoke aggressors. Keep calm, keep moving, and keep interaction and eye contact with potential aggressors to a minimum. Before attacking, assailants often attempt to "shark bump" potential victims with seemingly benign requests (e.g., "can I borrow a cigarette?") or more aggressive verbal provocations to single out the victim and gauge vulnerability. Engaging potential assailants in unnecessary interactions may increase the risk of becoming the target of an attack.
>
> What if you can't just leave an area with no explanation, such as your office during a meeting turned ugly? If you encounter a threat of violence and under the circumstances you can't just get up and leave with no explanation, attempt to politely excuse yourself (e.g., "please excuse me; I will be right back" but you are not really coming back of

course). Proceed to a safe location and send a school resource officer to your office to safely escort the person out of the building or into police custody as appropriate. What if your exit is blocked and the assailant will not let you leave?

2) *Try to de-escalate the conflict*: If you cannot leave the next best option may be to try to de-escalate the anger/conflict. Who was right in an argument is not the priority at this point. Do not further provoke a potentially violent person. Try to delay any violent confrontation while calling for backup (e.g., covertly text message the school resource officer for help; have a pre-arranged emergency verbal code to use to signal the office secretary to surreptitiously call for emergency help (e.g., "Mrs. Smith, I need some coffee please" (her name is not really Mrs. Smith and you don't really need any coffee); try to get the angry potential attacker to sit down, wait for the "coffee", calmly dialogue or at least monologue his or her list of demands while you wait for security personnel to arrive). Before a crisis occurs think through possible strategies that would work best in your circumstances and have an emergency plan ready for addressing potential violence.

3) *If you are attacked*: Try to get away and to get others to safety. If you cannot get away, defend yourself and others until help arrives. If you must defend yourself:

- Continue to call for help. If you cannot stop the attacker by yourself, you need others to help you as soon as possible.
- Never go willingly into an isolated area with a potential attacker or abductor. If necessary it is better to resist and fight the person where you are and where help from others is still possible.
- Try to stay on your feet or get back on your feet. When you are on the ground your options for escape and self-defense become much more limited.
- Always try to avoid violence, and to end the violence as soon as you safely can. But do what is necessary to defend yourself and others, including using available objects as barriers, shields, or weapons to stop the attacker.
- If you are facing a mortal threat and cannot escape, fight back as hard as you can when protecting your life and the lives of others requires violent resistance.
- When using self-defense, however, be certain it is only self-defense. Do not allow yourself to become emotionally out of control and become the aggressor, even in response to an attack. You want to have the violent person arrested. You do not want to be arrested also. When in doubt, however, do what is necessary to defend yourself and others from a violent aggressor, using force that is reasonable necessary to defend yourself and other innocent persons.
- Do not pursue a fleeing attacker. Secure the premises so the attacker cannot return to harm others, and call 911 for emergency medical personnel if needed and for police to pursue the attacker. Then focus on providing first-aid and security for any victims while awaiting the arrival of emergency personnel.
- Understand that having a well thought out and practiced plan for dealing with violent persons in advance of an emergency situation may make the difference between safety and tragedy.

Safe Facilities

To enhance safety and avoid liability buildings and grounds should be regularly inspected, identifying and correcting security risks and safety hazards. Periodic checks for school security risks should include inspections of all possible routes of entrance including doors, windows, and roofs, examining whether unauthorized persons could gain access through these areas. Inspectors should attempt to see these areas through the eyes of a potential intruder who may break windows, force weak locks, remove grates or covers, or break weak walls to gain entry.

Among the questions inspectors should ask is what level of security is necessary in this circumstance; are security fences, lighting, cameras, or alarm systems needed; what affordable building or landscaping modifications could enhance security; how can the most security sensitive areas within the school be protected even if an intruder enters the building; how can students and personnel be protected from an intruder; are room numbers clearly marked and is an accurate map available for emergency personnel; do systems to keep intruders from getting in interfere with the ability of persons to get out in the event of an emergency; and are security measures compatible with daily uses of the school? Inconvenient systems will be unused or circumvented (e.g., not turning on the security system; propping open doors, etc.).

Mobile classrooms and other outbuildings must be included in inspections and planning. Assure that persons in these units are also safe, and that they have an emergency means of communicating with security personnel in the main building if needed. Be certain to plan for students and personnel with special needs as well.

Buildings and grounds should also be inspected to identify and correct safety hazards such as tripping hazards (e.g., objects in walkways, weather heaved or broken side-walks, exposed drain pipes, cords, cables, rodent holes, tree roots, etc.); fire and electrical safety; sharp or protruding objects; heavy objects that could fall; defective chairs, desks, and other equipment; and dangerous animals (e.g., feral dogs, rabid animals, poisonous snakes, spiders, hornets, fire ants, etc.). Athletic areas should be inspected to assure safety for students and to reduce the risk of injury to players and spectators from flying baseballs, unsafe seating areas, etc.

To guard against theft, vandalism, and inappropriate or unlawful uses, unsupervised areas of the school should be secured during school events open to outside visitors. Through postings and/or verbal notices, visitors should be instructed to remain in authorized event areas only. For larger events a school resource officer or other law enforcement officer should be present. Additional law enforcement officers are needed for events with larger crowds or with hard to manage crowds (e.g., events more likely to attract intoxicated persons). For smaller, lower risk events, faculty and staff supervising the event should have an established emergency procedure for contacting law enforcement officers and school officials.

Take action:

- Conduct periodic, thorough security and safety inspections of all buildings and grounds supplemented with daily inspections of areas as needed.
- Logically and clearly number all rooms and areas. Provide security personnel with copies of the most current maps of buildings and grounds. Have a current copy available in the building, in the central office, and an electronic copy available remotely.
- Using a current map of the building and school grounds, divide areas (inside and outside the building as necessary) into zones properly sized for adequate supervision by

an individual; assign an individual to monitor each zone; and hold the individual responsible for supervising/patrolling that zone as needed during high risk times (e.g., during athletic events; dances; recess; class changes; etc.).
• Trim or remove any brush that could be used as cover by an attacker or others engaged in misconduct on school property.
• Confirm that fences are in good repair and have not been compromised with breaks or areas dug out under the fence (to deter intruders, feral dogs, etc.).
• Check illumination systems at night. Be certain the coverage of lighting is adequate. Reposition lights as needed and replace non-working lights.
• Test security systems as recommended by the monitoring company.
• Make sure that video monitoring systems are functioning properly; that security cameras have not been moved, covered, or damaged to create blind spots; that the recording system is working; and that live video of high risk areas is properly monitored.

Safe Grounds, Parking Areas, and Transportation

Although students spend relatively short periods of time outside of the school building in comparison to time in the classroom, nonetheless, most injuries on school property occur outside of the school. The majority of injuries to younger students happen on the playground, and older students are most often injured on athletic fields. Safety issues for playgrounds and athletic fields are addressed in more detail in the subsequent sections. This section addresses safety and security issues on school grounds generally, including parking areas, and transportation safety.

Serious and even fatal injuries can occur anywhere. Many serious or fatal injuries, however, are associated with the areas where traffic passes, enters, exits, and travels through school grounds. A busy road adjacent to the school creates an ever present risk for children crossing that road and vehicles entering or exiting school grounds. If traffic is traveling at a higher speed the risk is greatly increased. Designated "school zones" commonly have reduced speed limits. But the lower speed limits only reduce risks of accidents and injuries when drivers actually slow down and pay greater attention to children and vehicles entering and exiting the school grounds.

Schools located near high traffic areas also have special security risks. The more people that view the school area, the more likely someone will see the school and children as potential targets. School officials may want to consider fencing or landscaping barriers between the school and busy roads to limit the view of the school from high traffic areas and to reduce distracting noises, exhaust fumes, etc., from the road.

Schools near interstates may also be at greater risks for abductions. The interstate brings countless numbers of strangers into the area. An abductor could quickly spot the school, abduct a child, make an escape on the interstate, and otherwise have no known link to the community making these individuals and their victims very difficult to locate once they have left the area. In response to this danger the U.S. Congress passed Public Law 108-21 (2003) including the "Amber Alert" national communication network.

An Amber Alert is designed to enlist the help of the entire extended community in locating an abductor and the victim as soon as possible, so that law enforcement agents can rescue the child. The alert is broadcast through mass media, electronic traffic alert signs, cell phone networks, etc. The system recognizes that delay can be deadly, but also that unwarranted over-use of the system diminishes its efficacy. To balance these concerns the criteria for issuing an Amber Alert are:

• There is reasonable belief by law enforcement that an abduction has occurred.
• The law enforcement agency believes that the child is in imminent danger of serious bodily injury or death.
• There is enough descriptive information about the victim and the abduction for law enforcement to issue an AMBER Alert to assist in the recovery of the child.
• The abduction is of a child aged 17 years or younger.
• The child's name and other critical data elements, including the Child Abduction flag, have been entered into the National Crime Information Center (NCIC) system. *See* www.amberalert.gov

If a child has been abducted, time is of the essence. An alert must be issued as soon as possible to maximize the chances of safely retrieving the child. Call law enforcement officials immediately. Share as much information about the child (e.g., age; description; clothing worn; distinguishing features; etc., and forward a recent photo); the abductor (physical description; clothing worn; distinguishing features; and forward any recorded security video, etc.); and the vehicle (make; model; year; color; license number; distinguishing features; recorded video; etc.). School personnel must know what to do before there is an emergency. Surprise and shock must not prevent them from attempting to stop the abduction, getting as much information as possible if they cannot stop the abduction, and knowing who to contact immediately to issue a proper alert without delay when minutes and even seconds may matter.

School bus stops are also areas that may attract potential abductors. Parents should be instructed to supervise their children until the child is safely on the bus. Children should be instructed to stay in a group with other children whenever possible; not to talk to strangers (e.g., take candy, gifts, help "look for a lost puppy" etc.); never to accept a ride from a stranger; to go with the other children to a safe house or safe person if a suspicious stranger appears; to tell the bus driver, teachers, principals, parents, police, etc., about any suspicious behavior; and if someone tries to grab them they should scream for help and fight to get away so that anyone in hearing or sight range can clearly see what is happening and help or call for help.

Parking areas create special dangers for serious or fatal injuries. All students are at risk. But younger students are harder to see in parking areas and they are less likely to pay attention to traffic. Further, because of their fragile bodies and small size relative to vehicles, being hit by a vehicle is far more likely to result in serious injuries or death for a smaller child. But older students also pose unique risks in traffic areas and parking lots. Older students tend to take greater risks as pedestrians crossing busy roads. And as new drivers they have very little experience and limited comprehension of the finality of serious injury and death, leading them to take greater risks as drivers. For all of these reasons, potential dangers in parking lots and traffic lanes near schools must be taken very seriously, appropriate precautions must be taken, and adequate supervision must be provided.

For children riding school buses, school buses are generally a very safe mode of transportation. Children are far safer traveling in a school bus than in other vehicles. The greatest danger to children from school buses is being run over by the bus when attempting to board or depart. Drivers illegally passing stopped buses also create a serious danger for children. The youngest and smallest children are at the greatest risk. Bus drivers and other drivers are less likely to see small children, and small children are more likely to act unpredictably and not be aware of the danger from the bus or an oncoming vehicle.

School bus drivers have a very difficult job. They are first and foremost responsible for safely driving the bus, which requires them to keep their eyes on the road at all times, and to be aware of the movement of traffic around them as well. If this was not a sufficient burden, bus drivers are responsible for the safety and discipline of students while they are riding on the bus. Anything school officials, parents, drivers, and students can do to improve student conduct on the bus also improves student safety on the bus.

Take action:

- Informed by both an aerial view map and a ground level personal tour of the site, consider (in consultation with other professionals as needed) what structural and landscaping changes can be made to school grounds, parking areas, and traffic lanes to improve safety and security on and around school property.
- Work together with local government planners and law enforcement agents to reduce the volume of traffic and the speed of vehicles in the school zone.
- Provide training to all school personnel in how to prevent and respond to abductions.
- Instruct parents and children in how to promote safety and security at bus stops.
- Strictly enforce safety and speed rules in the school parking lot area.
- Have adequate staff on duty to supervise the school parking lot area.
- Design the parking lot area to maximize the safe flow of traffic and pedestrians.
- Clearly mark all parking lot lanes, walking lanes, and bus drop-off/pick-up areas.
- Clearly mark the areas children are required to stand in and wait until the bus has come to a complete stop, the door has been opened, and they are signaled to board.
- Be aware that a crowd of children surging forward toward an oncoming bus can push a child in front, off the curb and into danger. If necessary, assign seats to avoid any temptation for children to rush forward to get a favored seat when the bus is coming.
- Regularly remind bus drivers that they must be 100% certain where the child leaving a bus is located before putting the bus in motion, and to be certain the child's clothing, backpack, etc., is not caught on the door or any other part of the bus.
- Instruct children to never hang an arm, head, etc., out of a bus window because of possible impact with tree branches, passing vehicles, etc.
- Warn children and parents that fighting, yelling, or anything that distracts the bus driver creates a serious danger for everyone on the bus. Warn everyone that in order to protect the safety of all riders conduct violations on the bus will be swiftly and severely punished. Encourage constructive peer pressure to improve student behavior on the bus.
- Install video cameras on the bus to monitor student behavior. Make certain all students know they are being video recorded to deter misconduct. If students engage in serious misconduct punishment must be swift and certain to maintain the deterrent effect.
- Consistent with state and local laws, install video cameras monitoring traffic around the bus to deter and punish drivers who pass a bus when children are boarding or departing the bus, or otherwise risk the safety of children.
- Consider having a second adult on the bus to help with discipline, safety, and security (e.g., escorting children across a busy street or into a safe building in high crime areas). If there are severe discipline, safety, or security issues, assign a security guard to ride until the problem is resolved.
- Train bus drivers in essential behavior management and discipline skills.

- Train bus drivers in emergency procedures, and make sure they know who to call in the event of an emergency.
- Never assume that children will watch for vehicles. Drivers must watch for children. Drivers must be regularly reminded to do so through posted signs, periodic reminders, and warnings from parking lot supervisors.

> ***Because Children by definition Lack Experience and Maturity***
> ***Adults Must Diligently Watch Over and Protect Children***

Safe Play Areas

Play areas and playground equipment merit special attention as frequent and sometimes severe injuries occur in these areas. The U.S. Consumer Product Safety Commission found that more than 200,000 U.S. children receive emergency room treatment each year as a result of playground injuries. A third of these injuries are classified as severe, and at least 15 children die each year due to playground injuries, mostly caused by falls to hard surfaces, strangulation by entanglement, or head-entrapment.

Playground safety is an important area of concern with rapidly evolving standards. The general rule of tort law is that one must do what a reasonable person would do under the circumstances. As the circumstances change, so does what is reasonable under those circumstances. In decades past a major factor in the design of playground equipment was durability. This resulted in playground areas dominated by steel structures embedded in concrete. In retrospect these ultra-durable playgrounds presented unnecessary safety risks for children. They would fail current safety requirements, creating potential tort liability.

Child safety and tort law concerns drove dramatic advancements in playground safety standards. To protect safety and avoid liability play areas and equipment must comply with current safety standards. Outdated and unsafe equipment should be removed and the play area should be regularly inspected to assure proper maintenance of equipment and to guard against preventable safety hazards. In reviewing the play area for safety, it may be helpful to inspect the area not only from the height, view, and mindset of an adult, but also to examine the area from the height and perspective of a child at play, identifying otherwise hidden dangers and likely triggers for child behaviors that could result in injuries.

While out-dated and un-repaired equipment may pose special risks, injuries are not confined to a few aging playgrounds. Safety problems are shockingly widespread. Most playground injuries and deaths could be prevented with safer equipment and play area designs, regular safety inspections, and proper adult supervision of children. Playground safety standards published by the U.S. Consumer Product Safety Commission in its *Handbook for Public Playground Safety* are available free online.

Take action:

- Be certain there is adequate supervision of children in play areas as inadequate supervision is a major contributing factor to child injuries and liability.
- Make certain that supervising teachers understand that while the children are given free-time during play periods, this is not free-time for teachers. Teachers are on duty and special vigilance is necessary to prevent child injuries.

- Make a list of clear, simple, but effective safety rules for children to follow during playtime. Make sure the children are taught the rules; that they understand the rules are necessary for their safety; and make sure the rules are consistently enforced.
- Do not tolerate harassment. Harassment causes serious harm to its victims and may provoke violence. Bullying; sexual harassment; racial, ethnic, or religious harassment, etc., have no place in a healthy play environment and cannot be tolerated by teachers.
- Students intent on dangerous misconduct will likely seek unobserved areas. Be certain there are no blind spots in the play area and supervisors are positioned to observe all areas adequately. Patrols of the grounds should be regular but not overly predictable.
- Conduct a safety and security inspection of your play area. Check online for current standards for play area safety and do a field inspection of the play area to assure that:

> _ Play equipment meets current safety standards.
> _ Ground surfaces have adequate depths and widths of impact safety materials.
> _ Play equipment and ground safety materials are non-toxic.
> _ Swings are made of soft materials and appropriately located.
> _ Play equipment is safely spaced.
> _ Elevated areas have adequate guard rails to prevent falling.
> _ Hardware is properly tightened and not protruding.
> _ There are no sharp edges, splinters, broken glass, etc., in the area.
> _ There are no dangerous dogs, wild animals, snakes, spiders, etc., in the area.
> _ There are no tripping, strangling, trapping, or pinching hazards.
> _ Only authorized persons have access to the play area.
> _ Children are adequately supervised.

For a free copy of the U.S. Consumer Product Safety Commission's *Handbook for Public Playground Safety*, see: http://www.cpsc.gov/cpscpub/pubs/325.pdf

Accident and Injury Prevention

Accidents and injuries involving older students are most likely to occur in athletic instruction, training, and competition, calling for special precautions in these activities. To help prevent accidents and injuries school officials must assure that physical education teachers, coaches, and other athletic instructors are qualified to safely supervise activities; safety equipment is appropriate and checked regularly for wear or defects; activities are safe and appropriate for the ages and abilities of students; proper safety instruction is documented; medical safety for each student's participation in strenuous athletic training is documented; and students are adequately supervised at all times.

Safety equipment and activities must comply with current standards of practice accepted in the sport for children the ages, sizes, and abilities of those participating. It cannot be assumed that activities appropriate for high school students are necessarily safe for younger children also. Before engaging in physical activities students must be instructed in all necessary safety rules related to the sport (e.g., precautions in using a baseball bat; hitting a gulf ball, diving; etc.). Coaches and students should regularly review safety rules and practice emergency safety procedures so they know exactly what to do in the event of a serious injury or emergency.

It is important to include all interested students in school athletics if the students are able to safely participate, including students with special needs whenever possible. Remember, however, that individual students have different levels of physical health and fitness. Coaches and instructors should not push students beyond their individual safe physical limits, especially under hot and humid weather conditions. Unreasonably dangerous activities should be prohibited for everyone (e.g., javelin throwing; activities that risk serious neck injuries; etc.).

Coaches and other instructors should be trained in first-aid. Necessary first-aid equipment should be stored and available near the area it will most likely be needed. For everyone's protection treat all body fluids as potentially infectious at all times. Wear gloves to protect yourself and others. For each individual treated, use new and clean disposable gloves, bandages, wipes, and towels. Properly dispose of all potentially infectious waste and thoroughly clean all contaminated areas with an appropriate disinfectant solution.

Locker rooms, weight rooms, and shower areas must be adequately supervised. Access to these areas should be restricted unless authorized and under adult supervision. Students should be instructed that running, roughhousing, and other activities that risk slipping and falling or other injuries are strictly prohibited. Further, students should be instructed that they have an affirmative duty to immediately report any abuse, hazing, misconduct, injuries, or breaches of safety protocols to the supervising coach or instructor.

Science labs, vocational training classes, and other instruction involving chemicals, tools, and hands-on work also have higher rates of accidents and injuries than traditional paper and pencil classroom instruction. The above precautions generally apply in these higher risk settings also. Be certain that instructors are qualified to safely supervise the activities; equipment is appropriate and regularly checked for safety, wear, or defects; assigned activities are safe and appropriate for the ages and abilities of students; instruction in safety procedures is documented; and students are adequately supervised to assure safe participation in instructional activities.

Take action:

• Be certain that persons teaching in higher risk settings (e.g., activities involving contact sports; chemicals; power tools; etc.), are properly trained and certified.
• Require all teachers to provide adequate supervision, consistently observe applicable safety protocols, and regularly inspect equipment and work areas for safety.
• Assure that students are instructed in safety practices and what to do in the event of an emergency before beginning any potentially hazardous educational activities.
• Consider using safety contracts that require older students to affirm that they have been taught the necessary rules of safety, understand the rules (summarized in the contract), and that they will comply with applicable safety protocols.
• Stress to all teachers that while there may be greater dangers in some learning environments, safety hazards exist in every classroom (e.g., cords and other tripping hazards; broken glass or other sharp objects or edges; intentional acts of violence; etc.) and that all teachers must regularly inspect their classroom for safety and security risks and provide adequate supervision of students at all times.

Gang Violence Prevention

Gang related activity in schools creates a serious danger to the health and safety of everyone in the school. Gang members are responsible for their own criminal acts. But school officials have a duty to take reasonable precautions to protect against known dangers, including gang violence in schools. To protect the academic integrity of the school, and the health and safety of everyone in it, school officials must act aggressively to prevent gang violence in the school.

Children often turn to gangs in a misguided effort to find the caring and support they do not believe they are getting from their family, school, and community. Further, they are seeking power and status from membership in the gang. Gang membership may seem to fill many of their unmet needs and desires. Children are too young, however, to see the bigger picture: Eventually gang membership will do grave harm them and everyone around them.

Adults must explain to children that gang membership may seem to meet their immediate needs, but it does so in very unhealthy and unsustainable ways. Any short-term benefits of gang membership are never worth the price. Gang membership brings emotional, physical, and sexual abuse; exploitation; crime; substance abuse; and other grave dangers into children's lives. What they really get from gang membership is abuse, a ruined future, and a fast track towards jail and an early death. Behind the lies of the gang as a "family" gang leaders are enslaving younger children for their own selfish purposes and treating these children as disposable.

Factors associated with gang membership are poor school performance and experiences; poor family relationships and experiences; alcohol and drug use; criminal activities; and association with friends who are gang members. Move any of these factors in a healthier direction for the child and you can help to protect the child from gang involvement.

Teachers, counselors, and principals need to build relationships of trust with students. Students must know that the adults in their school genuinely care about them and want to help them find a positive future. Teachers should be firm in discipline and have high expectations for students. But when educators devalue, demean, and disrespect children they are driving the students away from school and into gangs. It is natural for children, like all humans, to only want to work with and respect persons who treat them with respect. Further, students will only tell educators about gang activity, violence, weapons, etc., if they know they can trust the educators to take action to solve the problem and to protect them from retaliation.

> *Students Respect Educators Who Respect Them*

Gang activity may come to the attention of school officials directly through reports by students, teachers, parents, or police, or indirectly through evidence of graffiti, gang symbols, or changes in student behavior. Gangs use violence and fear to control members and intimidate others in the community. Criminal activities (e.g., drug dealing; theft; extortion; etc.), are used to fund the gang and support senior members. By stopping the violence you can end the fear. And by stopping the crime you can starve the gang and its leaders.

Work with law enforcement agencies to achieve these objectives, and parents and community leaders to create positive alternatives. To stop the flow of new recruits into the destructive gang lifestyle, the community must offer healthy alternatives for all children, including efforts to strengthen families; religious affiliations; recreation; pride in community culture; education; and employment opportunities. Students have no need for gang membership when the have strong support from their family, school, and community and a clear vision for a better future.

Take action:

- Work with parents and community members to prove to students that you do have a caring community ready to support them now and help them find a better future.
- Help students to understand that through education and hard work they can acquire genuine and lasting self-esteem and economic power.
- Connect students with positive role models and mentors to help them on the path to positive personal growth and achievement.
- Educate students and parents about the dangers of gangs including powerful antidotal evidence showing what happens to gang members, and statistical evidence concerning the numbers of children injured, incarcerated, and killed because of gang activity.
- Get dangerous gang leaders out of the school, including working with police to arrest, convict, and incarcerate those guilty of gang related crimes.
- Strictly prohibit the display of gang symbols and activities in the school through the school dress code and the student code of conduct.
- Work with parents to keep their children off the streets at night and out of areas frequented by gang members.
- Work with parents, students, community members, and law enforcement agents to develop a comprehensive plan to protect your community from gang violence.
- Save as many children as you can from the dangers of gangs. But remember, even if you were only able to save one child that too is a great victory. Every child matters.

Environmental Safety

Students and school personnel spend much of their waking hours at the school. For good or ill the school environment has a significant impact on their health and safety. For this reason school officials must do all they can reasonably do to protect students and personnel from known dangers related to environmental toxins, infectious diseases, etc. School officials must comply with federal and state laws concerning hazardous materials (e.g., asbestos, lead, mercury, etc.), storage and use of chemicals, mold control, and any other significant environmental, biological, or other known hazards.

The primary law governing work place safety is the Occupational Safety and Health Act (OSH Act), 29 U.S.C. § 651 (2011). This federal Act is administered by the U.S. Occupational Safety and Health Administration (OSHA). Section 654 (a) (1) of the OSH Act established a general duty for employers to protect employees from known hazards, stating: "Each employer shall furnish to each of his employees employment and a place of employment which are free from recognized hazards."

In some states, state laws supplement OSHA safety standards, creating additional safety protections for workers. In all states employees have a "right to know" concerning recognized hazards in the workplace, so that they may take reasonable precautions to protect themselves and others from known dangers such as the presence of potentially harmful levels of chemicals, radiation, bio-hazards, etc.

Modern life would be impossible without chemicals. But even very useful chemicals may create unnecessary health and safety risks when improperly or excessively applied. Children are especially susceptible to environmental toxins, including cleaning chemicals and pesticides.

Cleaning chemicals can release harmful vapors that may cause irritation to eyes, noses, and throats; trigger asthma attacks and allergic reactions; and cause long-term health problems resulting from prolonged and repeated exposures. Whenever possible, chemicals should be applied when children are not present, and custodial staff must assure the use of proper ventilation and appropriate safety gear (i.e., respirators; goggles; gloves; etc.).

Many pesticides use neurotoxins to kill pests. While these chemicals may be effective in killing pests, over time repeated exposures may also do serious harm to humans, increasing risks of neurological disorders, cancer, and other serious health problems. Concerning the dangers of pesticides in schools, the U.S. Environmental Protection Agency (EPA) recommends the use of Integrated Pest Management (IPM) in schools. State laws may require the use of IMP in schools.

In using IPM, school officials working with the custodial staff first attempt to use non-toxic means of controlling pests, including sanitation, traps, and other non-toxic methods. If these non-toxic methods prove ineffective, they next use the least-toxic means of controlling pests. If the use of more toxic chemicals is ever necessary these are only used sparingly and at the times most remote from when students and personnel will be present in order to limit human exposure to toxins as much as possible.

School custodial staff should be trained in the safe use of necessary pesticides and herbicides; only use these products when necessary and consistent with federal and state laws; and always wear appropriate protective gear during application. Where toxic chemicals have been applied warning signs must be posted in the area consistent with state laws.

Most infectious diseases can be prevented through regular attention to basic hygiene. Hand washing is an essential and inexpensive first line of defense. To protect themselves and others from preventable infections, children should be instructed in proper methods of hand washing and taught that hand washing is essential before eating, after bathroom use, and after contact with any body fluid (e.g., mucous, saliva, blood, etc.).

Regular hand washing by all students and personnel should be encouraged by making hand washing facilities available in classrooms, cafeterias, and work areas when possible. If this is not possible hand sanitizer should be available. Students should be cautioned not to drink or eat from shared containers, share personal hygiene items, or engage in any activities that result in an exchange of blood or other body fluids.

Cafeteria and custodial staff can help keep everyone healthy through careful attention to hygiene in food preparation and storage, and by regularly and thoroughly cleaning commonly used surfaces (e.g., tabletops, desktops, computer keyboards, hand rails, door handles, water fountains, sinks, and bathrooms). Athletic surfaces (e.g., weight training benches; wrestling, gymnastics, and yoga mats; etc.), must be regularly cleaned and sanitized, and all open wounds must be properly treated and dressed before students engage in contact sports or contact with commonly used athletic surfaces.

Universal biological safety precautions must always be used, treating all body fluids as potentially infectious. Disposable protective gloves should be worn, and bio-hazardous materials (e.g., used needles, body fluids, contaminated bandages, etc.) must be safely disposed of in accordance with federal and state laws. Consistent with § 504 and the ADA, persons who pose a significant risk of transmitting a serious communicable disease should be supported with reasonable accommodations in continuing their studies or work from home or a medical facility until they can safely return to the school.

Take action:

- Begin to replace chemical-based cleaning supplies, etc., with less toxic or natural alternatives.
- Work with custodial personnel to find ways to reduce their exposure, and everyone else's, to any toxic chemicals that are still used on the buildings or grounds.
- Use Integrated Pest Management (IPM) techniques to address pest problems.
- Educate all students and personnel about the necessity to use good hygiene, including regular hand washing.
- Make it easy for everyone to practice good hygiene by making hand washing facilities and hand sanitizer available when and where these are needed.
- Be certain that all commonly used surfaces are regularly cleaned and sanitized by custodial personnel.
- Assure that good hygiene and food safety are practiced in the school cafeteria.
- Offer healthy foods in the school cafeteria to support good health and strong immunity.
- Properly dispose of all used needles, body fluids, contaminated bandages, and other bio-hazardous materials.
- Conduct an environmental review of your school. To help in improving the health of the school environment, the EPA has created a "One-Stop Location for Information and Links to School Environmental Health Issues" which can be found at: http://cfpub.epa.gov/schools/index.cfm

Emergency Planning and Response

Consistent with federal and state laws and local ordinances, school officials must have an emergency management plan ready to respond to the dangers most likely in their areas including fires; storms; earthquakes; floods; chemical and bio-hazards; and violent attacks. The U.S. Department of Education's Readiness and Emergency Management for Schools (REMS) Technical Assistance (TA) Center describes four phases of emergency management:

Prevention-Mitigation: Identifying all potential hazards and vulnerabilities and reducing the potential damage they can cause;
Preparedness: Collaborating with community partners to develop plans and protocols to prepare for the possibility that the identified hazards, vulnerabilities or emergencies will occur;
Response: Working closely with first responders and community partners to effectively contain and resolve an emergency in, or around, a school or campus; and
Recovery: Teaming with community partners to assist students and staff in the healing process, and restore a healthy and safe learning environment following an emergency event.

Additional information is available through the U.S. Department of Education website, and further assistance can be obtained through state and local safety officials.

After the Columbine tragedy special concern has been given to preventing and responding to risks from persons within the school, i.e., potentially dangerous students or personnel. Because some identified behavioral concerns may be manifestations of mental illnesses or other disabilities, it is essential that school officials strike an appropriate balance between respect for the rights of individuals under the IDEA, § 504, and the ADA, and protecting the safety of the community. In cases where the individual clearly poses a safety threat to the community, however, public safety must always be the first priority.

The problem, however, is that it is often not clear whether identified behavioral concerns are relatively benign symptoms of mental illnesses; other disabilities; social maladjustment; or a red flag signaling an impending danger. Further, individuals may have pieces of information that do not indicate any imminent danger in isolation, but would indicate a serious danger if all the pieces of the puzzle were seen and understood together.

To address these problems some schools have established a Behavioral Intervention Team (BIT) made up of persons with relevant multi-disciplinary expertise (e.g., a counselor; psychologist; special educator; social worker; health care professional; school lawyer; safety and law enforcement professional; etc.). The mission of the BIT is to:

1) Fairly and systematically review reports of behavioral concerns;
2) Help the individual whenever possible by proactively addressing identified needs; and
3) Protect the individual and others in the institution by preventing an imminent danger whenever possible.

The BIT can help school officials to make an informed decision concerning whether services are needed or intervention is warranted. Based on the findings of the BIT school officials may determine the individual poses no current threat; merits continued monitoring; needs educational or health services; needs a referral or mandate for counseling; should be reassigned; or should be removed from the school through the disciplinary process or a report to law enforcement officials.

Take action:

• Clearly establish emergency chains of command and command centers before a crisis so that everyone knows who and where to turn to for leadership in an emergency.
• Provide current maps of buildings and grounds to local emergency personnel. Have an electronic copy available for fast off-sight access if needed. Be certain that all rooms and areas are clearly and logically numbered (on-site and on the map), and that all strategic locations (e.g., helicopter landing sites; triage centers; emergency supplies; dangerous or flammable materials; utility shut-offs; etc.) are clearly identified on the maps.
• Establish strategically located triage and treatment centers for emergency care and adequately stock these areas with necessary emergency supplies.
• Identify safe helicopter landing areas in strategic locations (e.g., near school buildings; athletic fields; etc.). Keep the areas ready and free of parked vehicles, tree branches, and other obstructions.
• Locate and do an on-site visit of all utility shut-off areas (e.g., electricity, water, gas, etc.). Be certain these areas are accessible for emergency use and that the sites are recorded on maps of the buildings and grounds.
• Confirm that you have adequate and fully charged fire extinguishers ready for emergency use throughout the building. Confirm that personnel know how to access and safely use the fire extinguishers.

- Develop a list of personnel with first-aid certification and experience. Support all personnel in learning additional emergency response skills as needed.
- Develop a safe and fast means of getting children away from areas of danger, and for accounting for all children to assure that no one is left behind. Be certain to plan for children and personnel with special needs (e.g., mobility; vision; hearing impairments; etc.) in emergency planning.
- Develop systems for on-sight emergency communications to students and personnel (e.g., battery powered bullhorns, etc.), and off-sight communications to parents (e.g., e-mail; text messages; phone messages; mass media; etc.). Remember that bad information can be worse than no information, and also that people quickly stop listening to too much information or noise.
- Adopt protocols assuring that emergency safety communications always receive first priority; that all emergency messages are communicated as quickly as possible; but the messages are confirmed as accurate, concise, clear, helpful and consistent in communicating the needed information.
- Identify appropriate locations and develop procedures for parents to pick-up children out of the way of emergency personnel, vehicles, and operations, and safely away from a potentially dangerous disaster or crime-scene.
- Work with local emergency personnel to conduct regular emergency drills to identify areas of needed improvement and to assure a rapid and effective emergency response.
- Establish or improve your Behavioral Intervention Team (BIT).
- Proactively address potential problems before they become emergencies.
- Regularly review, update, and improve your school's emergency management plan. Additional resources and online training courses from the Department of Education's Readiness and Emergency Management for Schools (REMS) Technical Assistance (TA) Center can be found at: http://rems.ed.gov
- Get everyone involved. Make safety and security discussions, preparations, and drills a regularly part of meetings with personnel, students, and the community.
- Brainstorm constructive ideas with colleagues and local safety personnel to assure that your school is well prepared for any emerging or foreseeable dangers.
- Document your ongoing reasonable safety and security efforts to help assure that in the event of a disaster, litigation is not one of your concerns.

It is hoped that the overviews and examples in this chapter will encourage you to think further about safety and security concerns in your school; review applicable state laws and local policies; and discuss with colleagues and community members how everyone can work together to improve safety and security in your school. Avoiding unnecessary liability is a high priority for school officials. But protecting everyone's safety must always be the first priority.

State laws, local ordinances, and local school policies may address many of the above issues. The State Department of Education, State Professional Organizations, and State School Boards Associations are often good sources for information on state specific laws. The National School Boards Association (NSBA), www.nsba.org is a useful source of information on school law and policy generally, and the NSBA provides links to State School Boards Associations with information on state specific laws and policies. The local Sheriff, Fire Chief, and other local officials may be helpful sources of information concerning compliance with local ordinances and protocols.

Selected Georgia Laws

Georgia Constitution

Paragraph IX: Sovereign immunity

(a) The General Assembly may waive the state's sovereign immunity from suit by enacting a State Tort Claims Act, in which the General Assembly may provide by law for procedures for the making, handling, and disposition of actions or claims against the state and its departments, agencies, officers, and employees, upon such terms and subject to such conditions and limitations as the General Assembly may provide.

(b) The General Assembly may also provide by law for the processing and disposition of claims against the state which do not exceed such maximum amount as provided therein.

(c) The state's defense of sovereign immunity is hereby waived as to any action ex contractu for the breach of any written contract now existing or hereafter entered into by the state or its departments and agencies.

(d) Except as specifically provided by the General Assembly in a State Tort Claims Act, all officers and employees of the state or its departments and agencies may be subject to suit and may be liable for injuries and damages caused by the negligent performance of, or negligent failure to perform, their ministerial functions and may be liable for injuries and damages if they act with actual malice or with actual intent to cause injury in the performance of their official functions. Except as provided in this subparagraph, officers and employees of the state or its departments and agencies shall not be subject to suit or liability, and no judgment shall be entered against them, for the performance or nonperformance of their official functions. The provisions of this subparagraph shall not be waived.

(e) Except as specifically provided in this Paragraph, sovereign immunity extends to the state and all of its departments and agencies. The sovereign immunity of the state and its departments and agencies can only be waived by an Act of the General Assembly which specifically provides that sovereign immunity is thereby waived and the extent of such waiver.

(f) No waiver of sovereign immunity under this Paragraph shall be construed as a waiver of any immunity provided to the state or its departments, agencies, officers, or employees by the United States Constitution.

Georgia Statutes

§ 20-2-992: Immunity or Privilege Not Waived

Nothing in this article shall be construed as waiving any immunity or privilege now or hereafter enjoyed by the State Board of Education, by the board of control of any cooperative educational service agency, by any local board of education, by any member of any such board, or by any employee of the state board, school superintendent, principal, teacher, administrator, or other employee or as waiving any immunity or privilege of any state or other public body, board, agency, or political subdivision.

§ 20-2-1000: Civil Liability for Discipline of Students

(a) As used in this Code section, the term "educator" means any principal, school administrator, teacher, guidance counselor, paraprofessional, school bus driver, volunteer assisting teachers in the classroom, tribunal members, or certificated professional personnel.

(b) No educator shall be liable for any civil damages for, or arising out of, any act or omission concerning, relating to, or resulting from the discipline of any student or the reporting of any student for misconduct, except for acts or omissions of willful or wanton misconduct.

(c) If a judgment or finding is rendered in favor of a defendant educator in any action, complaint, disciplinary proceeding, or other administrative proceeding brought by a student, a parent or guardian of a student, or any other person on behalf of a student and arising out of or resulting from the discipline of such student or if the complaint is found to be non-meritorious, frivolous, or without just cause, all reasonable court costs, reasonable attorneys' fees, and reasonable expenses incurred by the defendant educator in defending such action or complaint shall be assessed by the court, agency, or other tribunal against the plaintiff and shall be paid by the plaintiff. Any educator shall have a right to bring an action or a counterclaim against the plaintiff in any such action or proceeding for any damages suffered by the educator as a result of the actions of the student or the filing of any frivolous or non-meritorious action, complaint, or report. Nothing in this subsection shall be construed to apply to any educator filing a complaint as required by the rules, regulations, or code of ethics of the Professional Standards Commission; any child abuse reporting statute; any applicable local board of education rule, regulation, or policy; or any State Board of Education rule, regulation, or policy.

(d) If any civil action is brought against any educator or any report or complaint is made or filed against any educator with the county or local board of education, the Department of Education, the Professional Standards Commission, or any other regulatory agency or tribunal by a student, a parent or guardian of a student, or any other person on behalf of a student and arising out of or relating to the discipline of such student, it shall be the duty of the county or local board of education employing such educator to provide counsel for the educator, if requested by the educator, unless such board of education determines, after an independent investigation of the report or complaint, that the act or omission of the educator constituted willful or wanton misconduct or constituted gross misconduct in violation of the express written policies of the board of education. Neither testimony given in such independent investigation nor the results of any such independent investigation by the board of education shall be admissible in any other proceeding. The provision of counsel to such educator shall be for an educational purpose and any funds available to the board of education may be expended for such purpose. Any attorneys' fees recovered pursuant to subsection (c) of this Code section attributable to the services furnished by any counsel provided to an educator by his or her employer shall be paid to the employer.

§ 20-2-1001: Good Faith Immunity from Criminal Liability re: Student Discipline

(a) As used in this Code section, the term "educator" means any principal, school administrator, teacher, guidance counselor, paraprofessional, school bus driver, volunteer assisting teachers in the classroom, tribunal members, or certificated professional personnel.

(b) An educator shall be immune from criminal liability for any act or omission concerning, relating to, or resulting from the discipline of any student or the reporting of any student for misconduct, provided that the educator acted in good faith.

§ 20-2-1180: Remaining upon School Premises without Legitimate Cause

(a) It shall be unlawful for any person to remain upon the premises or within the school safety zone as defined in paragraph (1) of subsection (a) of Code Section 16-11-127.1 of any public or private school in this state or to remain upon such premises or within such school safety zone when that person does not have a legitimate cause or need to be present thereon. Each principal or designee of each public or private school in this state shall have the authority to exercise such control over the buildings and grounds upon which a school is located so as to prohibit any person who does not have a legitimate need or cause to be present thereon from loitering upon such premises. Each principal or designee of each public or private school in this state shall notify the appropriate law enforcement agency to prohibit any person who does not have a legitimate need or cause to be present therein from loitering within the school safety zone.

(b) Any person who:

> (1) Is present upon the premises or within the school safety zone of any public or private school in this state and willfully fails to remove himself or herself from such premises after the principal or designee of such school requests him or her to do so; or
>
> (2) Fails to check in at the designated location as required by subsection (c) of this Code section shall be guilty of a misdemeanor of a high and aggravated nature.

(c) Upon entering any school building between the official starting time and the official dismissal time, any person who is not a student at such school, an employee of the school or school system, a school board member, an approved volunteer following the established guidelines of the school, or a person who has been invited to or otherwise authorized to be at the school by a principal, teacher, counselor, or other authorized employee of the school shall check in at the designated location as stated on posted signs and provide a reason for his or her presence at the school.

(c.1) Subsections (b) and (c) of this Code section shall not apply to:

> (1) Law enforcement officers, firefighters, emergency medical technicians or paramedics, or any public safety or emergency management officials in the performance of an emergency call or to other persons making authorized deliveries to the school;

(2) Any person entering a school on election day, for purposes of voting, when the school serves as an official polling place; or

(3) Any person attending or participating in an academic or athletic event while remaining in the authorized area or a parent, grandparent, or guardian listed on a child's pick-up list who fails to sign-in while delivering school supplies, food, clothing, other legitimate business and who has not previously been sanctioned by school officials for disrupting a school.

(d) A school administrator or his or her designee may ask any visitor to explain his or her presence in the school building at any time when the school is in official session.

(e) If the school posts signs on entrances to the school requiring visitors to check in at the designated location, such signs shall be deemed prima-facie evidence that persons entering the school were on notice of the requirements of this Code section.

(f) Nothing in this Code section shall be construed to prohibit school administrators from prohibiting the admission of any person who has violated school policy or state law.

§ 20-2-774: Student use of Asthma Medications in School

(a) As used in this Code section, the term:

(1) "Medication" means a medicine prescribed by:

(A) A physician licensed under Chapter 34 of Title 43; or
(B) A physician assistant licensed under Chapter 34 of Title 43 who is authorized to prescribe medicine for the treatment of asthma in accordance with said chapter.

(2) "Self-administration of asthma medication" means a student's discretionary use of asthma medication prescribed for him or her.

(b) Each local board of education shall adopt a policy authorizing the self-administration of asthma medication by a student who has asthma, provided that any student who is authorized for self-administration of asthma medication under such policy may possess and use his or her asthma medication:

(1) While in school;
(2) At a school sponsored activity;
(3) While under the supervision of school personnel; or
(4) While in before-school or after-school care on school operated property.

(c) Each public school in this state shall permit the self-administration of asthma medication by a student who has asthma, subject to the local policy adopted pursuant to subsection (b) of this Code section; and the school district and its employees and agents shall incur no liability other than for willful or wanton misconduct for any injury to a student caused by his or her self-administration of asthma medication.

§ 20-2-775: Automated External Defibrillator Required

(a) As used in this Code section, the term "automated external defibrillator" means a defibrillator which:

(1) Is capable of cardiac rhythm analysis;
(2) Will charge and be capable of being activated to deliver a counter-shock after electrically detecting the presence of certain cardiac dysrhythmias; and
(3) Is capable of continuously recording cardiac dysrhythmia at the scene with a mechanism for transfer and storage or for printing for review subsequent to use.

(b) No later than July 1, 2008, each public high school in this state which has an interscholastic athletics program shall have at least one functional automated external defibrillator on site at such school at all times and easily accessible during any school related function, including athletic practices, athletic competitions, and other occasions where students and others will be present, for use during emergencies.

(c) Each high school possessing and maintaining an automated external defibrillator shall:

(1) Ensure that expected users of the automated external defibrillator receive American Heart Association or American Red Cross training in cardiopulmonary resuscitation and automated external defibrillator use or complete an equivalent nationally recognized course;
(2) Notify the appropriate emergency medical services system of the existence and location of the automated external defibrillator prior to said automated external defibrillator being placed in use;
(3) Ensure that the automated external defibrillator is maintained and tested according to the manufacturer's operational guidelines;
(4) Ensure that there is involvement of a licensed physician or other person authorized by the composite board in the site's automated external defibrillator program to ensure compliance with requirements for training, notification, and maintenance; and
(5) Ensure that designated personnel activate the emergency medical services system as soon as reasonably possible after any person renders emergency care or treatment to a person in cardiac arrest by using an automated external defibrillator and reports any clinical use of the automated external defibrillator to the licensed physician or other person authorized by the composite board who is supervising the program.

(d) Subject to appropriations by the General Assembly, the Department of Education shall provide funds to local school systems to assist in the purchase of automated external defibrillators pursuant to this Code section.

(e) The department and local school systems shall use diligent efforts to identify private sources of funding or donation of funding and equipment to meet the requirements of this Code section.

§ 20-2-776: Use of Auto-injectable Epinephrine Authorized

(a) As used in this Code section, the term "auto-injectable epinephrine" means a disposable drug delivery device that is easily transportable and contains a premeasured single dose of epinephrine used to treat life-threatening allergic reactions.
(b) Each local board of education shall adopt a policy authorizing a student to carry and self-administer prescription auto-injectable epinephrine. Such policy shall provide that in order to carry and self-administer prescription auto-injectable epinephrine, the student's parent or guardian shall provide:

> (1) A written statement from a physician licensed under Chapter 34 of Title 43 detailing the name of the medication, method, amount, and time schedules by which the medication is to be taken, and confirming that the student is able to self-administer auto-injectable epinephrine; and
>
> (2) A written statement by the parent or guardian consenting to the self-administration, providing a release for the school nurse or other designated school personnel to consult with the physician regarding any questions that may arise with regard to the medication, and releasing the school system and its employees and agents from civil liability if the self-administering student suffers an adverse reaction as a result of self-administering auto-injectable epinephrine pursuant to this Code section.

The written statements specified in this subsection shall be provided at least annually and more frequently if the medication, dosage, frequency of administration, or reason for administration changes.
(c) The policy adopted pursuant to subsection (b) of this Code section shall include provisions to protect the safety of all students from the misuse or abuse of auto-injectable epinephrine.
(d) Any student who is authorized for self-administration of epinephrine pursuant to this Code section may possess and use auto-injectable epinephrine:

> (1) While in school;
> (2) At a school sponsored activity;
> (3) While under the supervision of school personnel; or
> (4) While in before-school or after-school care on school operated property.

(e) A student may be subject to disciplinary action if he or she uses auto-injectable epinephrine in a manner other than as prescribed.
(f) A local school system and its employees and agents shall incur no liability other than for willful or wanton misconduct for any injury to a student caused by his or her use of auto-injectable epinephrine.
(g) Nothing in this Code section shall be construed to prohibit a school from receiving and storing prescription auto-injectable epinephrine onsite on behalf of a student who is not able to self-administer the medication because of age or any other reason if the parent or guardian provides:

(1) A written statement from a physician licensed under Chapter 34 of Title 43 detailing the name of the medication, method, amount, and time schedules by which the medication is to be taken; and

(2) A written statement by the parent or guardian providing a release for the school nurse or other designated school personnel to consult with the physician regarding any questions that may arise with regard to the medication, and releasing the school system and its employees and agents from civil liability.

The written statements specified in this subsection shall be provided at least annually and more frequently if the medication, dosage, frequency of administration, or reason for administration changes.

§ 20-2-776.1: Auto-injectable Epinephrine; Emergency Use Authorized

(a) As used in this Code section, the term "auto-injectable epinephrine" means a disposable drug delivery device that is easily transportable and contains a premeasured single dose of epinephrine used to treat life-threatening allergic reactions.

(b) Each local board of education shall adopt a policy authorizing school personnel to administer auto-injectable epinephrine, if available, to a student upon the occurrence of an actual or perceived anaphylactic adverse reaction by the student, whether or not such student has a prescription for epinephrine.

(c) Each local board of education shall provide information to school personnel on how to recognize the symptoms of anaphylactic shock and the correct method of administering the auto-injectable epinephrine.

(d) Any school personnel who in good faith administers or chooses not to administer epinephrine to a student pursuant to this Code section shall be immune from civil liability for any act or omission to act related to the administration of epinephrine, except that such immunity shall not apply to an act of willful or wanton misconduct.

Georgia Regulations

160-1-3-.03: Infectious Diseases

(1) Definitions.

(a) Centers for Disease Control and Prevention (CDC): a major operating component of the United States Department of Health and Human Services with responsibilities at the national level for monitoring health, detecting and investigating health problems.

(b) Family Educational Rights and Privacy Act (FERPA): Federal legislation applicable to all educational institutions receiving Federal Funds that protects the privacy of students' personally identifiable information.

(c) Infectious Disease: an illness due to an infectious agent, or its toxic products, which is transmitted directly or indirectly to a person from an infected person or animal.

(d) Personal Protective Equipment (PPE): any type of face mask, glove, or clothing that acts as a barrier between infectious materials and the skin, mouth, nose, or eyes.

(e) Local Education Agency (LEA): a local school system pursuant to local board of education control and management.

(f) Standard Precautions: a set of precautions designed to prevent the transmission of infectious diseases which include, but not limited to, hand washing procedures, use of protective gloves, and directives on covering the mouth and nose when coughing or sneezing.

(g) Tasks with Exposure Potential: tasks associated with the evaluation and treatment of students with actual or potential infections.

(2) Requirements.

(a) LEAs shall develop policies, regulations, and procedures related to the impact of infectious diseases on school system management and operations.

(b) LEAs shall annually provide employees with information, education, or training related to infectious diseases, including transmission, risk education, and standard precautions, based on CDC guidelines or recommendations.

(c) LEAs shall make personal protective equipment (PPE) readily available and appropriate to tasks with exposure potential.

(d) Where LEAs have reasonable suspicion to believe that an employee or student has an infectious disease, school authorities shall counsel that person immediately, or if the person is a minor, notify his or her parent or guardian of the need to obtain an appropriate medical evaluation.

(e) Operational decisions related to employees or students infected with communicable diseases shall be made in conjunction with the school nurse, state and/or local public health agency representatives, health care professionals, and school system administrators.

(f) Each LEA shall limit the disclosure of health-related information of its employees and students. FERPA prohibits the unauthorized disclosure of information from educational records except in certain limited circumstances, such as a health and safety emergency as described in 34 C.F.R. §§ 99.31(a) (10) and 99.36. Additionally, the disclosure of certain confidential health information may be a misdemeanor punishable under O.C.G.A. § 24-9-47.

Authority: O.C.G.A. § 20-2-240

160-4-8-.18: Diabetes Medical Management Plans

(1) Definitions.

(a) Diabetes medical management plan: a document developed by the student's physician or other health care professional that sets out the health services, including the student's target range for blood glucose levels, needed by the student at school and is signed by the student's parent or guardian.

(b) Health care professional: a doctor of medicine or osteopathy licensed by the Georgia Composite Medical Board pursuant to Article 2, Chapter 34, Title 43 of the Official Code of Georgia Annotated or a legally authorized designee acting pursuant to job description or nurse protocol agreement approved by the Georgia Composite Medical Board.

(c) Trained diabetes personnel: a school employee who volunteers to be trained in accordance with this rule. Such employee shall not be required to be a health care professional.

(2) Requirements.

(a) Each local board of education and state-chartered special school shall ensure that there are at least two school employees trained in accordance with the Georgia Department of Education's, Guidelines for the Care Needed for Students with Diabetes in each school that has a student with diabetes. This training shall be conducted by a school nurse or other health care professional with expertise in diabetes and shall take place prior to the commencement of each school year, or as needed when a student with diabetes enrolls at a school, or when a student is newly diagnosed with diabetes. Local boards of education shall ensure that the school nurse or other health care professional provides follow-up training and supervision as necessary for compliance with this rule.

(b) Each local school system and state chartered special school shall provide information in the recognition of diabetes related emergency situations to all employed or contracted bus drivers responsible for the transportation of a student with diabetes.

(c) Each school shall review and implement the diabetes medical management plan provided by the parent or guardian of a student with diabetes who seeks diabetes care while at school.

(d) In accordance with the request of a parent or guardian of a student with diabetes and the student's diabetes medical management plan, the school nurse or, in the absence of the school nurse, trained diabetes personnel shall perform functions including, but not limited to, responding to blood glucose levels that are outside of the student's target range; administering glucagon; administering insulin, or assisting a student in administering insulin through the insulin delivery system the student uses; providing oral diabetes medications; checking and recording blood glucose levels and ketone levels, or assisting a student with such checking and recording; and following instructions regarding meals, snacks, and physical activity. These activities shall not constitute the practice of nursing and shall be exempted from all applicable statutory and regulatory provisions that restrict what activities can be delegated to or performed by a person who is not a licensed health care professional.

(e) The school nurse or at least one trained diabetes personnel shall be on site at each school and available during regular school hours to provide care to each student with a diabetes medical management plan being implemented by the school. For purposes of field trips, the parent or guardian, or designee of such parent or guardian, of a student with diabetes may, at the discretion of the school, accompany such student on a field trip.

(f) A student's school choice under O.C.G.A. § 20-2-2130 or other applicable law shall in no way be restricted because the student has diabetes.

(g) Upon written request of a student's parent or guardian and if authorized by the student's diabetes medical management plan, a student with diabetes shall be permitted to perform blood glucose checks, administer insulin through the insulin delivery system the student uses, treat hypoglycemia and hyperglycemia, and otherwise attend to the monitoring and treatment of his or her diabetes in the classroom, in any area of the school or school grounds, and at any school related activity, and he or she shall be permitted to possess on his or her person at all times all necessary supplies and equipment to perform such monitoring and treatment functions.

(h) No physician, nurse, school employee, local school system, or state chartered special school shall be liable for civil damages or subject to disciplinary action under professional licensing regulations or school disciplinary policies as a result of the activities authorized or required by O.C.G.A. § 20-2-779 when such acts are committed as an ordinarily reasonably prudent physician, nurse, school employee, local school system, or state chartered special school would have acted under the same or similar circumstances.

Authority: O.C.G.A. §§ 20-2-240; 20-2-779

General Index

Abductions: *208-210*; 214; 216
Abuse; emotional: 34-35
Abuse; indicators: 34-35
Abuse; parents: 34-37
Abuse; physical: 35
Abuse; questioning: 36
Abuse; reporting: 32; 36; 38
Abuse; sexual: 35; 39
Abuse; verbal: 35
Accident prevention: 218
ADA: 134-136; 141; 163; 222; 224
Administrative searches: 75-76
Admissibility: *85*; 93-94; 171
Amber alert: 214-215
Appeals process: 92; *96*
Applications; job: 161-162; 164-165
Assaults: 88; 99; 100; 114-115; *208-209*
Authentication: 94
Bailment: 79
Background checks: *164-165*; 198; 210
Behavioral Intervention Team: 224
BFOQ: 163-164
Blaine Amendments: 54; 57
Burden of proof: 73; 94; 169; 171
Bus safety: 77; 99-100; 113; *215-216*
Case law; interpretation: 14
Child abuse: *32-42*; 49
Child supervision: 207
Child witnesses: 88
Choking: 207-208
Civil Rights Act: 125
Closing statements: 89
Competency, witness: 93
Cross examination: *90-91*; 93-95; 101; 120
Davis v. Monroe: 126
Direct evidence: 92-93
Direct examination: 89; 93-94
Disability: 125; *134-159*; 162
Dismissals; defenses: 169
Dismissals; employment: 167
Dog searches: 78

Due process: 84-85; 165-170
EEOC: 161-162
Electronic privacy: 77
Emergency planning: 223-225
Employee; search of: 78-79
Employee; speech: 66-67
Employment interviews: 162-164
Employment law: 160
Employment sanctions: 66
Equal opportunity: 161
Equal protection: 123
Equal protection test: 125
Environmental safety: 221
Establishment clause: 55
Evaluations: 165
Evidence: 84-95
Facilities; safety: 213
Federalism: 1
Factual relevancy: 93
Franklin v. Gwinnett: 126
Fraser (v. Bethel): 64-65
Free exercise test: 56
Free speech: 62
Fourteenth Amendment: 123
Fourth Amendment: 71
Gang violence: 220
Gebser v. Lago Vista: 126-127
Grounds; safety: 214
Harassment; bullying: 208
Harassment; sexual: 126-128
Hazelwood v. Kuhlmeier: 64-65
Hearings: 84-88; 94-96; 101-102; 120
Hearsay: 85; 91; *94*; 95
Hostile witnesses: 86; *90*; 91; 93; 95
IDEA: 135
IDEA; dangerous student: 139
IDEA discipline: 136-139
IDEA; inclusion: 141
IDEA; indicators: 143
IDEA; parents: 140
IDEA; services: 142

Impeachment of witnesses: 89; 90; 93
Indirect evidence: 93
Individual student speech: 64
Injury prevention: 218
Interpretation; case law: 14
Interpretation; legislation: 12
Interviewing witnesses: 85
Interviews; employment: 162-164
Investigations: 85
Integrated Pest Management: 122-123
Irrelevant evidence: 84
Job announcements: 161
Job applicants: 161
Leading questions: 88-91; 93; 95
Legal authorities; strength: 15
Legal relevancy: 84-85; 93; 183
Legislation; interpretation:
Local governance: 5; 7-8
Local school boards: *4-5*; 8; 97
Locker searches: 75
Manifestation determinations: 138
Marbury v. Madison: 12
Meetings: 5-10
Metal detectors: 75-76
Munchausen syndrome: 37
Negative rights: 54
Neglect; indicators: 34
Objections; guide: 95
O'Connor v. Ortega: 78-79
Ontario v. Quon: 79
Opening statement: 89
OSHA: 221
Parental care: 33
Parking areas; safety: 214-216
Performance evaluation: 165
Personnel safety: 207
Pickering test: 66-67
Play areas; safety: 217
Positive rights: 11
Prejudicial effect: *84-85*; 91; 93; 95
Probable cause: 72
Questioning; guide: 95
Questions to avoid: 91
Rational basis test: 124
Reasonable suspicion: 73
Recruitment; employment: 161

Redding test: 74
Reference checks: 164
Rehabilitation of witnesses: 90
Robert's Rules: 5
Rules of evidence: 92; 120
Safford v. Redding: 74
School boards; local: 4
School safety: 206
School sponsored speech: 64
Search and seizure: 71
Section 504: 135
Security: 77; 206; 207; 210
Security cameras: 77
Seizure: 79
Self-defense: 211-212
Separation of powers: *1-2*; 11-12
Sexual harassment: 126-128
Speech; employee: 66-67
Speech; student: 64-65
State constitutional law: 10
State laws; hierarchy: 11
State laws; sources: 4
State powers: 2
Statutes; interpretation: 12
Strict scrutiny: 125
Strip searches: 75-75
Student searches: 73
Student speech: 64
Student speech test: 65
Supervision; child: 207
Supervision; employee: 165
Supremacy clause: *2-3*; 10
Suspect classification: 124-125
Tangible evidence: 93
Tenth Amendment: 2
Tenure: *168-169*; 172; 175
Testimonial evidence: 93
Tinker v. Des Moines: 64-65
Title IX: 99; 115; *126-128*
Title IX litigation: 128
T.L.O. test: 73-74
Torts: 205
TPM restrictions: 68
Transportation; safety: 214-215
Witnesses; interviewing: 85

Georgia State Law Index

Abuse and neglect regulations: 38; 49
Appeals; student: 102; 120
Appeals; employee: 178
Arms; right to bear: 18
Assembly; right to: 18; 65
Assistive technology: 148
Asthma medication: 229
Attendance; mandatory: 45
Beliefs protected: 17-18; 57
Bible course: 58
Bill of Rights: 17
Blaine amendment: 57
Board; as court: 97
Board of Education: 22
Board of Regents: 21
Board powers; employment: 175
Bullying; mandated policy: 104
Capital outlay: 17; 24
Causes for dismissal: 170
Charter schools; IDEA: 150
Child abuse reporting: 38; 49
Child find; IDEA: 152
Chronic disciplinary problems: 103
Church and State Separation: 16; 17; 18; 57
Clubs; student: 65
Code of conduct; students: 95
Code of ethics; educators: 198
Collective bargaining; prohibited: 178
Complaints policy: 176
Compulsory attendance: 45
Contracts; employment: 174
Corporal punishment: 103
Counselors: 49; 51
Crimes; mandated reporting: 102; 114
Custody; change of: 43
Defibrillator; required: 230
Demotion: 172
Diabetes: 233
Disciplinary hearings confidential: 102
Disciplinary orders; honoring: 107
Disciplinary summaries required: 102

Discipline; regulations: 114
Discipline; immunity: 228
Discipline; liability: 227
Dismissals; employment: 170
Disrupting school; sanctions: 113
Due process: *17*; 19; 97
Due process; employees: 170
Education clause: 20
Education records: 43
Eligibility; IDEA: 158
English learners: 130
Enrollment eligibility: 43
Enumeration of rights: 20
Epinephrine: 231
Epinephrine; emergency: 232
Equal protection: 17; 129
ESOL: 130
Ethics; professional: 198
Evaluations; IDEA: 153; 156
Evidence; admissibility: 101; 171
Ex post facto laws: 18
Expulsion; defined: 102
Extended year services: 149
Fair dismissal act: 170
FAPE: 144
Fees: 129
Felony acts; students: 113
Freedom of conscience: 17; 18
Freedom of press: 65
Freedom of religion: 16; 17; 18; 57
Freedom of speech: 65
Free instruction; mandated: 129
Grade changes: 170; 178
Grounds for termination: 170
Guidance counselors: 51
Hearing; employee: 171
Hearing; student: 101
Home school: 46
Immunization required: 60
Immunization; exemptions: 60
Infectious disease: 232

Insulting personnel: 113
Jury trials: 18
Language assistance: 130
Libel: 18
Local school governance: 26
Local school systems: 22
Local taxation:
Lotteries: 16
Mandatory reporting; abuse: 38; 49
Moment of silence: 57
Moral turpitude: 203
Neglect; reporting: 38; 49
Nonrenewal: 172
Open meetings: 178
Open records: 182
Organization; student: 65
Origin of government: 16
Parental consent; IDEA: 154
Parent permission; clubs: 65
Physical education; IDEA: 150
Prayers at private schools: 58
Pre-kindergarten: 17
Private school: 46
Private school; prayers: 58
Police; reports to: 102
Power of boards: 22
PSC Code of Ethics: 198
PSC disciplinary actions: 202
Purpose of government: 16
Religious exemption; immunization: 60
Religious freedom: 16-18; 57
Remaining on school premises: 228
Reprimand; due process: 176
Reporting child abuse: 38; 49
Reporting crimes: 102; 114
Residential placement: 146
Restraint; student: 81
Right to legal action: 103
Right to petition: 65
Sales tax: 23
School attendance: 45
School board as court: 97
School councils: 27
School fees; prohibited: 129

School law tribunals: 120
School premises; order to leave: 228
School superintendent; local: 22; 30; 46-49; 120
School superintendent; state: 21
Search and seizure: 19; 81
Seclusion; student: 81
Separation of powers: 16
Sovereign immunity: 226
Special schools: 22
State board of education: 20
State superintendent: 21
Student clubs; organizations: 65
Student code of conduct: 99
Student discipline regulations: 114
Student; felony act: 113
Student hearings: 101; 102
Student support services: 49
Student violence against employee: 106
Structure of government:16
Suspension; defined: 102
Suspensions; employment: 170; 171
Taxation; local: 23
Tax rate: 23
Tenure; teacher: 172
Tenure; administrator: 174
Terminations; employment: 170
Transfer; employee: 175
Tribunals: 120
Tuition: 129
University System: 21
Unlawful change of custody: 43
Unsafe schools (USCO): 117
Upbraiding personnel; sanctions: 113
Violence against employees: 106
Visitors; mandated check-in: 228
Warrants: 19
Weapons: 108
Weapons; exemptions: 110
Weapons; expulsion required: 109
Weapons; federal definition: 108
Weapons; safety zones: 110
Weapons; state definition: 110

Made in the USA
Columbia, SC
05 June 2018